WRITING for Psychology

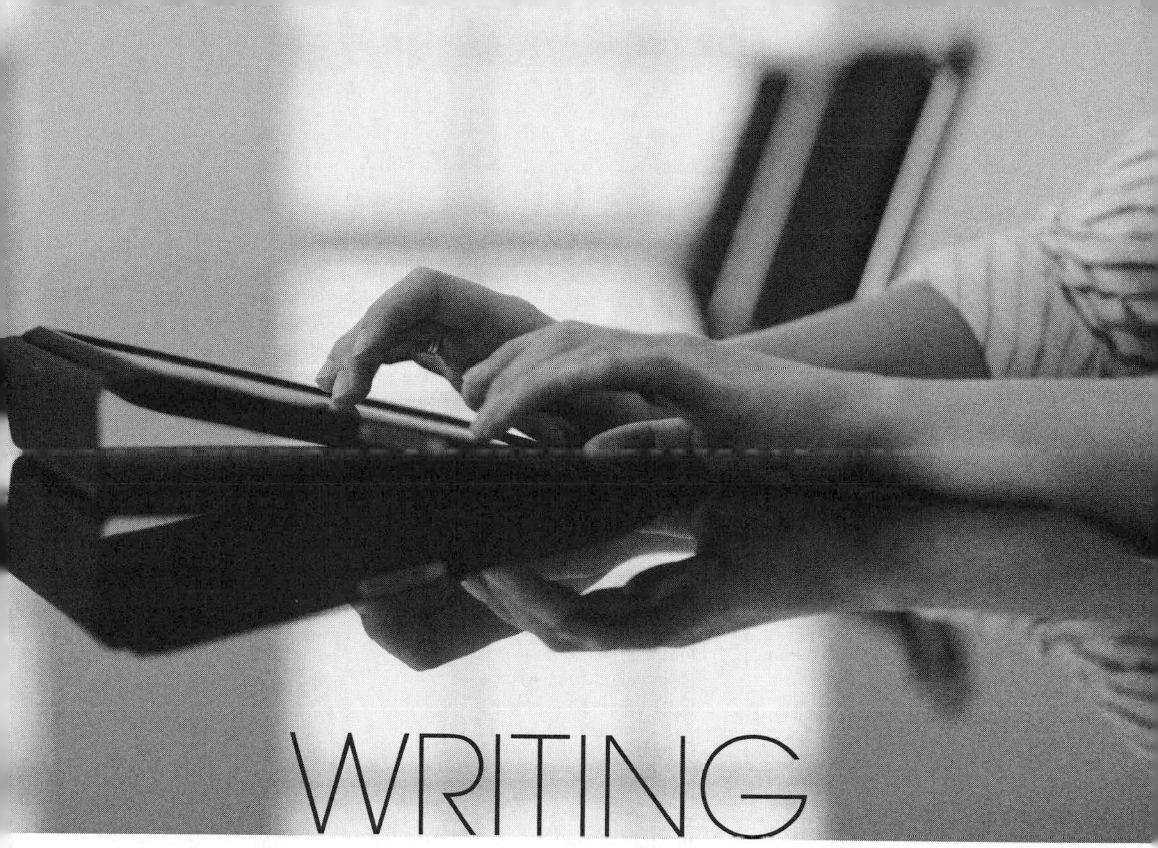

WRITING for Psychology

FOURTH EDITION

Mark L. Mitchell and **Janina M. Jolley**
Clarion University of Pennsylvania

Robert P. O'Shea
Southern Cross University

Australia • Brazil • Japan • Korea • Mexico • Singapore • Spain • United Kingdom • United States

Writing for Psychology, **Fourth Edition, International Edition**
Mark L. Mitchell, Janina M. Jolley, Robert P. O'Shea

Publisher-in-Chief: Linda Ganster

Publisher: Jon-David Hague

Acquiring Sponsoring Editor: Timothy Matray

Editorial Assistant: Nicole Richards

Media Editor: Mary Noel

Marketing Program Manager: Janay Pryor

Manufacturing Planner: Karen Hunt

Rights Acquisitions Specialist: Don Schlotman

Art and Cover Direction, Production Management, and Composition: PreMediaGlobal

Cover Image: Diego Cervo/ Shutterstock

International Edition:
ISBN-13: 978-1-133-30841-6
ISBN-10: 1-133-30841-4

Cengage Learning International Offices

Asia
www.cengageasia.com
tel: (65) 6410 1200

Australia/New Zealand
www.cengage.com.au
tel: (61) 3 9685 4111

Brazil
www.cengage.com.br
tel: (55) 11 3665 9900

India
www.cengage.co.in
tel: (91) 11 4364 1111

Latin America
www.cengage.com.mx
tel: (52) 55 1500 6000

UK/Europe/Middle East/Africa
www.cengage.co.uk
tel: (44) 0 1264 332 424

Represented in Canada by Nelson Education, Ltd.
www.nelson.com
tel: (416) 752 9100 / (800) 668 0671

Cengage Learning is a leading provider of customized learning solutions with office locations around the globe, including Singapore, the United Kingdom, Australia, Mexico, Brazil, and Japan. Locate your local office at: **www.cengage.com/global**

For product information and free companion resources: **www.cengage.com/international**

Visit your local office: **www.cengage.com/global**

Visit our corporate website: **www.cengage.com**

Printed in the United States of America
1 2 3 4 5 6 7 16 15 14 13 12

CONTENTS

CHAPTER 7

Preparing the Final Draft 225

TO THE STUDENT

Your professor has asked you to use this book to guide you in writing a paper. In response, you may be asking yourself three questions:

1. Why is my professor asking me to write a paper?
2. Why is it important to write a good paper?
3. How can this book help me?

In the next few sections, we will answer these questions.

Why Professors Assign Papers

Some day, employers may use brain scans to find out which applicants will become trusted, expert workers. Today, professors use papers to help you develop and display the skills that will help you become a trusted expert: learning independently, thinking critically, communicating clearly, representing both the evidence and other people's contributions honestly, and working conscientiously.

Producing an original paper shows that you are someone who can leave the classroom to find, evaluate, and produce knowledge. Producing a well-written paper shows that you can share your knowledge and sell your ideas. Producing an intellectually honest paper—one that not only gives proper credit to others for their ideas, words, and contributions but also includes evidence that goes against your position—shows that you can be fair, considerate, and honorable. Producing an "A" paper shows that you can

- complete tasks on time,
- follow directions,
- work independently, and
- produce an excellent product.

The skills that you will display in your paper will be refined as you write that paper. As you prepare to write your first draft, you will become a more independent learner and thinker because you have to do the following tasks:

- find relevant material in journals,
- read and understand complex material,
- evaluate what you read,
- organize both your notes and your thinking about what you read, and
- create new knowledge by pulling together information from several different sources and critically analyzing that information.

As you write and rewrite drafts of your paper, you refine two general skills: thinking clearly and writing clearly. Finally, as you proof and polish your paper so that you can present your professor with an error-free paper by the deadline, you develop time management, stress management, and detail management skills that will help you in almost any job.

Why You Should Write a Good Paper

Writing a good paper will help you impress teachers and employers with your integrity and independence, your professionalism and persistence, as well as your resourcefulness and reliability. Writing will also help you achieve the goals that make psychology appealing: describing, explaining, and controlling thoughts and behavior. As a writer, you are trying to describe, explain, and control your own thoughts. By writing well, not only will you discover your own thoughts (to quote Forster, 1927, p. 101, "How can I know what I think until I see what I say?"), but you will also learn to evaluate your own thinking. You will see where your thinking is logical, where it is biased, where it is based more on faith than on evidence, and where it is slightly disorganized—and you will use those insights to improve your thinking.

Successful writing also requires that you understand and control the mind of the reader. Indeed, King (2000) argues that writing is almost like telepathy—your vision is sent into a reader's mind. At a more practical level, you want to control the reader's heart, mind, and behavior. For example, you want the reader (your professor) to give you a good grade.

Finally, writing a good paper is its own reward. As Chesterfield (1739/1827) wrote, "Next to the doing of things that deserve to be written, there is nothing that gets a person more credit or pleasure than to write things that deserve to be read" (p. 99). Ideally, as you prepare to write your paper, you will be doing things—conducting research studies or having insights—"that deserve to be written," and, as you polish your paper, your work will "deserve to be read." Thus, our dream is that, after writing one of your papers, you will—at least momentarily—feel like Plato (trans. 1932) felt when he wrote, "What task in life could I have performed nobler than this … to bring the nature of things into the light for all to see?" (Epistles, 7.341.d).

How This Book Can Help You

This book is full of tips, checklists, and practical advice to improve your writing. You will gain so much insight into how professors look at papers that you will be able to grade—and correct—your paper before it reaches your professor.

- Chapter 1 helps you understand what teachers look for in papers so that you can avoid the most common errors that students make, regardless of what kind of paper you are writing.
- Chapter 2 helps you write better essays and term papers by telling you the secrets of writing such papers, showing you an example paper, and giving you a checklist that helps you evaluate and improve your own paper.

- Chapter 3 helps you write better research reports and proposals by giving you useful tips, an example research report, and a research report checklist.
- Chapter 4 helps you find the references you need and shows you how to make sense of them after you have found them. Then, it helps you avoid two common student mistakes: (a) not citing sources correctly and (b) not referencing sources correctly.
- Chapter 5 helps you understand what professors mean by "critical thinking." After reading Chapter 5, (a) you will be more likely to find flaws that others made in their research and in their arguments, and (b) you will be less likely to make those mistakes in your research and in your arguments.
- Chapter 6 contains a review of basic grammar as well as some tips on how to write well. You will probably consult this chapter when you are editing the next-to-final draft of your paper. You may also find the definitions of grammatical terms helpful in trying to decipher the American Psychological Association's (APA) *Publication Manual.*
- Chapter 7 will be useful as you prepare to print out the final draft of your paper. Follow the formatting tips in that chapter to ensure that your paper makes a good first impression.
- Appendix A lists the key differences between APA copy style (the format of an unpublished manuscript submitted to an editor for review) and APA final-form style (the format of a published article). If your professor asks you to use APA final-form style, Appendix A will be invaluable. By highlighting the formatting rules that published articles follow, it will help you use a published article as a model for your paper. If your professor asks you to use APA copy style, Appendix A will still be valuable. By highlighting the differences between published articles and unpublished manuscripts, it will help you know what you should not model from published articles. For example, you will know that although published articles are single-spaced, your unpublished manuscript should be double spaced.
- This book's website (http://www.writingforpsychology.com) contains many useful resources, including
  - screen shots that show you exactly how to set up your word processor to make it work for you,
  - templates that you can use so that your paper will be correctly formatted,
  - practice quizzes that you can take, and
  - sample papers that you can grade.

Formatting Practices We Use That You Should Not

As you can see from the table of contents, the section headings of this book contain both a number and a title (e.g., Chapter 1's third section is "1.3 Understanding APA Style"). When you have a specific question about how to write your paper, having these section numbers in the headings will help you quickly find the section of this book that has the answer to your question. However, in your papers, *do not use numbers to label your headings*.

We have also used formatting to help you easily spot examples. All examples are in a "typewriter" font (like this). When we are contrasting examples of correct and incorrect writing, we include these symbols for quick reference:

✔ a check mark next to good examples

✗ an "x" next to bad examples

However, in your papers, *use Times New Roman font*.

Finally, we use footnotes to draw your attention to particular points. However, when you write papers for psychology classes, *do not use footnotes*.

To the Professor

When you ask students to write an APA-style paper, many of them are clueless both about why you are forcing them to go through such an onerous ritual and about whether you will find their sacrifices (their papers) acceptable. In this book, we help students understand and meet your expectations by (a) explaining the purpose behind papers, (b) helping students understand how to write for an academic audience, (c) giving them strategies for accomplishing the many tasks involved in writing a good paper, (d) showing them how to avoid common mistakes, (e) giving them examples they can model, and (f) giving them checklists so that they can monitor their own performance.

Admittedly, if you had enough time, you could do what this book does. You could give your students lectures on APA style; assign the APA's *Publication Manual;* prepare handouts that explain the *Manual;* take students on tours of both the library and the writing center; and teach students about grammar, logic, and plagiarism. However, if you assign this book, you will not need to provide detailed instructions about writing in APA style; avoiding plagiarism; or finding, citing, and referencing sources. Instead, the only instructions you will need to give your students are a general description of the project, a due date, and a word limit.

Acknowledgments

The first edition of this book was an adaptation of the fourth edition of Robert O'Shea's *Writing for Psychology* (2002). Therefore, we owe a great debt to the individuals whose constructive comments shaped that successful book: Kypros Kypri, Lea McGregor Dawson, Lorelle Burton, Sue Galvin, Jamin Halberstadt, Cindy Hall, Neil McNaughton, Jeff Miller, David O'Hare, Ann Reynolds, Rob Thompson, Diana Rothstein, and 13 anonymous reviewers.

The second edition of this book was an improvement over the first edition, thanks mostly to award-winning journalist K. Lee Howard's editing skills, psychology professor Ruth Ault's advice on teaching APA style, and English professor Darlynn Fink's advice on teaching writing. In addition, psychology professor Jeanne Slattery's comments about how to teach writing to psychology majors improved Chapter 1, philosophy professor Todd Lavin's comments about how to teach critical thinking improved Chapter 5, and history professor Robert Frakes's comments about how to prevent student writing errors improved Chapter 6.

This edition of *Writing for Psychology: A Guide for Students* owes a tremendous debt to two people we consider coauthors of this book: psychology professor Ruth Ault and English professor Darlynn Fink. We thank them not only for their editing skills but also for their insights about how to teach writing. In addition, we owe a substantial debt to psychology professor Thomas Vilberg for his extensive comments on Chapter 3, to philosophy professor Jamie Phillips for his invaluable comments on Chapters 1 and 5, and to reference librarian Mary Buchanan for her comments on Chapter 4.

We would also like to thank the following reviewers for their constructive comments: Marie Balaban, Eastern Oregon University; Shannon Edmiston, Clarion University; Michael Hulsizer, Webster University; Hal Miller, Brigham Young University; Moises Salinas, Central Connecticut State University; Vann B. Scott Jr., Armstrong Atlantic State University; Linda Mezydlo Subich, University of Akron; and Daniel Webster, Georgia Southern University. In addition, we would like to thank the entire team at Cengage, particularly Timothy Matray, Acquiring Sponsoring Editor; Lauren K. Moody, Assistant Editor; and Dewanshu Ranjan, Project Manager at PreMediaGlobal.

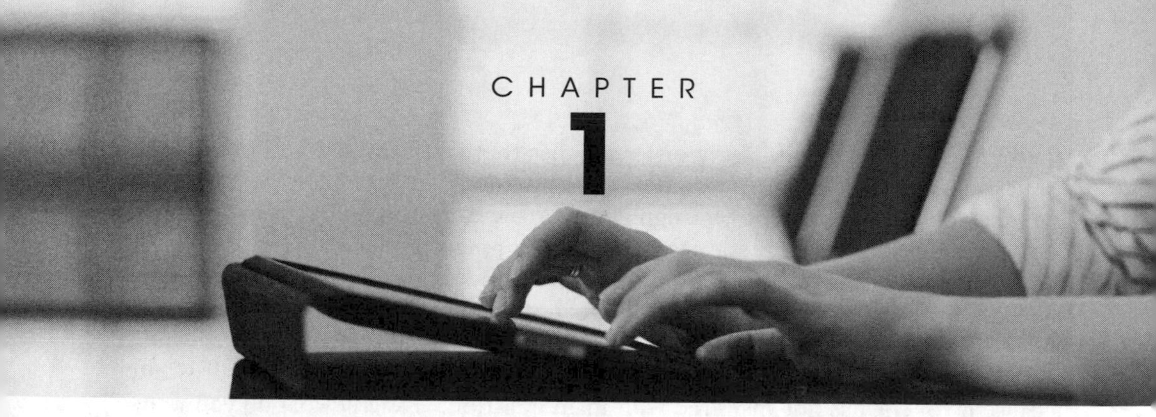

What Every Student Should Know About Writing Psychology Papers

To write successfully, you need to write for your audience. Unfortunately, most students do not understand how writing for a psychology professor is different from writing an e-mail to a friend or writing an essay for an English teacher. Therefore, in this chapter, we will help you understand your professor's expectations about how you should plan, write, revise, and present your paper so that you can write a paper that has the intellectual weight, formal tone, editorial sound, and professional look that your professor—and you—will like.

1.1 Understanding the Written and Unwritten Directions

Most professors will expect you to write your paper using American Psychological Association (APA) copy style, the style used for submitting a manuscript to a journal. Therefore, this book focuses on helping you write in that style. However, you still need to pay attention to your professor's formatting instructions because your professor may impose formatting requirements that are more extensive than APA's. For example, your professor may require a special cover sheet or require that your paper be between 10 and 12 pages long.

Although it is important to know your professor's formatting requirements, it is essential that you know what type of assignment you have and what goals your professor has for the assignment. You should know whether you are writing a paper about a study that you either conducted or plan to conduct (if so, consult Chapter 3) or whether you are writing an essay or term paper that will be based on other people's studies (if so, consult Chapter 2).

Once you know what type of assignment you have, try to find out your professor's goals for the paper. For example, if your professor's main goal for a term paper is that you analyze strengths and weaknesses of research studies, you should write a different paper than you would if your professor's goal is that you find and summarize recent research on your topic.

Once you understand your professor's main goals, you may still be frustrated because he or she has not answered your main question: "Exactly what do you want?" Three obstacles prevent your professor from answering that question in as much detail as you might like.

First, if your professor told you exactly how to write the paper, the professor would be writing the paper for you. Thus, just as your professor would not tell you exactly how to take a multiple-choice test ("Answer 'a' for question 1, 'c' for question 2"), your professor is not going to tell you exactly how to write the paper.

Second, if your professor gave you detailed instructions on how to write the paper, those instructions would be hundreds of pages long. Consequently, your professor must use shorthand. For example, "appropriately referenced" is shorthand for the rules you will find in Chapter 4; "making a logical argument and informed criticisms" is shorthand for following the rules you will find in Chapter 5; "grammatical and well written" is shorthand for following numerous grammatical rules, the most important of which are explained in Chapter 6; and "conforming to APA format" is shorthand for following the rules we describe in Chapter 7.

Third, if, as is usually the case, many of your professor's goals for the paper are the same goals that almost all professors have, your professor may think those goals "go without saying." One reason that almost all professors have similar expectations is that almost all professors share certain underlying values that affect what professors expect from a paper. Unless you understand those values, you cannot write a paper that your professor—or other psychology professors—will like. Therefore, we will devote the next section to helping you understand how academic values should guide you throughout the writing process.

1.2 Understanding Academic Values

Researchers across all academic disciplines value objective understanding and genuine knowledge. Consequently, academics value virtues that lead to achieving such understanding and knowledge (e.g., basing opinions on facts, being open to new evidence) and reject those human tendencies that work against such understanding and knowledge (e.g., forcing evidence to fit preconceived opinions, being closed-minded).

Behaving consistently with traditional academic values is not something only academics do. It is something most professionals do. Indeed, one reason psychologists, physicians, accountants, judges, and other professionals go to college is to make it more likely that they will behave consistently with academic values such as being honest and seeking knowledge. You and the rest of society hope that experts will carefully come to conclusions based on thoughtful, fair, and honest evaluations of the evidence, and then clearly state those conclusions.

To help you visualize how academic values are the values professionals should hold, imagine that a crime scene investigator (CSI) is testifying in court. You hope that the CSI is behaving consistently with academic values by being fair, being honest, and presenting a conclusion that makes sense based on a careful examination of the best evidence available. You would not want to hear that the CSI had used a discredited procedure, hidden some evidence, or not considered an alternative explanation for the evidence. Similarly, when your professor looks at your paper, the professor would not want to see that you failed to be fair, failed to consider key evidence, or failed to consider alternative explanations. Instead, as you will see in the next sections, your professor will expect your paper to show that you have the following academic values:

- the curiosity to find out what others have said, done, and thought;
- the humility and wisdom to learn from what others have said, done, and thought;
- the honesty to give others credit when you use what you have learned from them, such as when you quote, paraphrase, or summarize what others have said;
- the originality to come to a conclusion that is not merely a summary of what others have said, but rather is based—at least in part—on your own thinking;
- the rationality to support your conclusion with logic and evidence;
- the integrity to present evidence that does not fit with your conclusion; and
- the objectivity to acknowledge alternative explanations for the evidence that you present in support of your conclusion.

1.2.1 Be Informed: Read to Write

Professors value knowledge, learning, and tracing the history of an idea. Most professors want you to demonstrate these values by expressing well-supported and well-informed opinions. They want you to build on what others have found and done. Therefore, before writing your paper, find, study, and understand what is already known about your topic. (In section 4.1, we will show you some strategies for using the library and the Internet to get resources that both you and your professor will find worthy. In section 4.2, we will discuss strategies to help you digest the information you obtain.)

1.2.2 Make a Claim: Have a Point, Get to That Point, and Stick to That Point

To show that you have found what is already known about your topic, you would cite key sources (usually, by stating the source's author's last name and the year the source was published) and quote, paraphrase, or summarize material from that source. If you merely ***quote*** other people's words, your acknowledgment that you are quoting others (by citing the source's author, year it was published, and page number and indicating—usually by quotation marks—which words are from that source) shows that you have found background material, but not that you understand that material. If you ***paraphrase***—restate other people's ideas in your own words—from a source, your paraphrase shows that you understand the individual sentences that you paraphrased, but does not show that you understand the passage as a whole. If you ***summarize*** material from a source, your summary shows that you understand the main point of what you found, but not that you can use what you found. Therefore, to show that you are not merely regurgitating (quoting), restating (paraphrasing), or condensing (summarizing) the information you have found, use that information to support a claim. Ideally, that claim will be an original idea based on your thinking about what you have read.

If you are writing a term paper, your claim will be a thesis statement (see 2.1). You must support your thesis statement by interpreting, analyzing, and synthesizing the information you have uncovered. (For more on writing a term paper, see Chapter 2.)

If you are writing a research paper, your claim will be your hypothesis. You will use the works of others to argue that (a) the hypothesis being tested is reasonable and interesting, (b) the procedure used was a good way to test the hypothesis, and (c) the results have important implications. (For more on writing a research paper, see Chapter 3.)

1.2.3 Defend Your Claim with Logic and Evidence

Not only must you make a claim, but you must also support it. However, you should not support it by asserting how strongly you feel that it is true—deluded people can feel quite strongly that they are being controlled by radio waves. Nor should you use techniques common to talk-radio hosts: ridiculing those who support other claims, appealing to emotions, and arguing that popular opinion must be right. Instead, support your claim with logic and evidence.

To see how well you supported your claim with logic, read your paper while taking the position of someone who disagrees with your conclusion. Start by questioning whether your conclusions logically follow from your assertions. Specifically, assume that your evidence is factually sound and then ask two questions.

First, ask, "Do the reasons and arguments I give clearly lead to my conclusion?" Asking that question may help you identify places where your reasons seem to contradict each other, where you included reasons that seem irrelevant to your conclusion, where you failed to spell out all of the steps in your reasoning, or where you leapt to a conclusion—and may prevent your professor from writing "does not follow" on your paper.

Second, ask, "Could someone use my arguments to support a different conclusion?" Asking that question may help you realize that your argument is not as strong as you originally thought—and may prevent your professor from writing "not necessarily" or "that is just one interpretation" on your paper.

Once you establish that your conclusions logically follow from your assertions (if you need help finding or fixing problems with your paper's logic, see Chapter 5), question whether your assertions are true and supported by evidence. If you find that you have made unsupported statements that a skeptic could question, cite evidence to back up those claims by using at least one of the following two approaches.

The first, and most common, way to mount an empirical defense is to cite evidence from a study someone else conducted. For example, if you assert that children with high self-esteem are more resistant to peer pressure than children with low self-esteem, support would be that someone has tested children's resistance to conformity and found children with high self-esteem to be more resistant to conformity pressure than children with low self-esteem. Your citation will usually include a description—in your own words—of the study or its findings, along with the last name(s) of the person(s) who conducted it and the year it was published. Thus, you might cite such a study this way:

> Miller (1988) found that, relative to children with low self-esteem, children with high self-esteem are more likely to resist pressure from peers to use drugs and alcohol.

A full reference to each citation should appear in the reference list at the end of your paper (see 4.10). For example, you would reference the Miller (1988) study this way:

> Miller, R. L. (1988). Positive self-esteem and alcohol/drug related attitudes among school children. *Journal of Alcohol and Drug Education, 33,* 26–31.

(To learn more about citing material in the body of your paper and referencing it in the reference list, see Chapter 4.)

The second way to mount an empirical defense is to present evidence from a study you conducted. We will discuss how to report such evidence in Chapter 3.

Although you should present evidence to support your main point, you should make the case for both sides because (a) your professor will expect you to present both sides and (b) fairness and honesty demand that you present both sides. To avoid being unfair, identify weaknesses in studies that appear to support your main point and discuss studies that seem to contradict your main point.

1.2.4 Be Honest

Whereas being unfair may hurt your grade, being dishonest may end your college career. The two types of dishonesty that are most likely to lead to a range of penalties including being kicked out of school are (a) falsifying data and (b) plagiarism.

Falsifying data is either altering or inventing data. Most of your professors are deeply committed to using data to find truth. Therefore, most of your professors would be outraged at anyone who falsified data. In short, do not falsify data: For most class projects, both the chances and the costs of getting caught are high.

Plagiarism involves presenting someone's words or ideas as your own. The words or ideas that you must be most careful about crediting are those that come from classmates, roommates, professors, and published authors.

Although isolating yourself from classmates would prevent you from plagiarizing from them, such isolation is often undesirable or impossible. On group projects, your professor may require you to work with other students. Even on individual assignments, your professor may encourage you to work with other students to share readings and to review each other's work. However, unless your professor clearly says otherwise, when you turn in a paper with your name on it, you are pledging that you wrote that paper and that the content and ideas—except for the ones that you have specifically credited to others—are your own. To reiterate, your instructor will expect any assignment that you turn in to be independent of, and different from, every other student's paper. If the words or ideas of even a sentence of your assignment are identical to another student's work, you—or that other student—may be accused of plagiarism.

Not seeing other classmates' papers does not completely shield you from plagiarizing from someone at your school because plagiarism is not limited to lifting passages or ideas from a classmate's paper. Plagiarism can result from not giving people credit for something they said to you. For example, if a professor, study partner, classmate, or roommate gave you an idea that you used in your paper, you should give that person credit (to see how, see 4.3.3). If you do not give the person credit, you are guilty of plagiarism.

Even if you could avoid all contact with people at your school, you would still need to read works from other authors. If you did not credit these authors for the ideas or the words that you borrowed from them, you would be guilty of plagiarism. To illustrate, suppose you read the following paragraph on page 91 of the 1974 *APA Publication Manual.*

> Psychologists have developed various approaches to therapeutic change, most involving one-to-one relationships between practitioner and client. However, for many people these therapies are unavailable, undesirable, or too expensive. So these people have often turned to popularized self-help techniques. (Mikulas, 1974, p. 91)

If you were to use the preceding paragraph in your paper, you would have to make it clear that you were quoting it.[1] Otherwise, you would be guilty of plagiarism. As a general rule, if you take three or more consecutive words from another author, you should place those words in quotation marks, cite the author, and list the page(s) of the quoted words. Thus, if you turned in the following passage, you would be guilty of plagiarism.

> ✗ Mikulas (1974) has stated that various approaches to therapeutic change have been developed.

You would be guilty of plagiarism because you would be using Mikulas's words without admitting that you were doing it. The five-word phrase "various approaches to therapeutic change" should have been surrounded by quotation marks, and the page number from which those five words were taken should have been cited. If you steal

[1]As with all quotations, you need to cite the author, year, and page number. If this quotation had been shorter than 40 words, you would have surrounded the quotation with quotation marks. However, because the quotation is longer than 40 words, you should use the block quote format that APA prescribes for long quotes (see 4.8.2).

words, expect to be caught. Even if your professor does not have specialized software such as TurnItIn™ that automatically looks for any matches between your paper and passages in published works, websites, and other student papers, your professor can enter suspicious passages into a search engine such as Google™.

Thus far, we have presented cases of stealing words. To see a case of stealing ideas without stealing words, imagine we wrote the following.

(✗) Most people find these therapies too expensive, undesirable, or unavailable and so have turned to self-help techniques.

Although we are not using Mikulas's words, we would still be guilty of plagiarism because we are using his ideas without giving him credit for those ideas. To avoid plagiarizing Mikulas's ideas, we should have made it clear that he—rather than we—originated them. If we did not want to quote Mikulas, an acceptable version of the whole text would be:

(✓) Mikulas (1974) noted that many people dislike current psychotherapies in which a single client is seen by a single counselor. He gives their unavailability, expense, and lack of appeal as reasons. Mikulas suggests that many prospective clients have instead tried self-help techniques.

In the previous paragraph, we avoided plagiarism by using two techniques that you should use. First, to avoid plagiarizing words, we used our own words. Second, to avoid plagiarism of ideas, we referred to our source in every sentence that used ideas from that source (Mikulas's name is in the first and third sentence, and "he" is used in the second).

1.2.5 Use Your Own Words

To make sure you do not plagiarize, you might be tempted to put most of your assignment in quotation marks. Resist that temptation. Your professor is interested in your thoughts about a topic, not in your ability to string others' words together with linking sentences. Therefore, your professor will probably not let you get away with having more than 50 words of quotation for every 1,000 words (four pages) of your own.

One reason professors dislike quotation marks is that when you quote, professors do not know whether you understand what you have quoted. Therefore, try to summarize or, at the very least, paraphrase—restate in your own words—what the author wrote. If your first try at restating what the author wrote does not work, try again.

Paraphrase rather than quote except in three cases. First, quote if you are using a famous quotation. Second, quote if you fear that your paraphrase, because you disagree with the author's position, unfairly represents the position expressed in the original passage. Third, quote if you fear that your paraphrase is so close to the original passage's wording (e.g., you kept the same words and merely changed the order of those words) or phrasing (e.g., you merely replaced a couple of words with synonyms) that you are taking not only the author's ideas but also the author's way of expressing those ideas. In such a case, to give proper credit for taking the author's wording and thus to avoid plagiarism, you need to use the author's words—and quotation marks.

1.3 Understanding APA Style

As you have seen, your professor expects you to write a paper that does the following:

- draws on the work of others but proposes an original idea,
- cites the work of others but describes their work in your own words, and
- uses logic and evidence to build a case for an idea but addresses contradictory evidence.

Although you may think that meeting those demands would be enough to get a good grade, it is not. Your professor will also require that your paper meet some style and formatting guidelines. A few of these guidelines may be specific to a certain assignment (e.g., a particular word limit). Most, however, will be the same no matter what psychology class you are taking. These style and formatting requirements are described in the *Publication Manual of the American Psychological Association* (2010). In the next section, we will provide an overview of APA's requirements. (APA style requirements will be discussed in more depth in Chapter 6; APA formatting requirements will be discussed in Chapter 7.)

1.3.1 Ideals

APA style requires that grammar, spelling, and punctuation be perfect. Consequently, your professor will probably penalize you for each grammatical error, each spelling error, and each punctuation error. However, avoiding these errors in mechanics does not mean that you have met APA's standards for good writing. According to APA, good writing[2]

> must be precise in its words, free of ambiguity, orderly in its presentation of ideas, economical in expression, smooth in its flow, and considerate of its readers. A successful writer invites readers to read, encourages them to continue, and makes their task agreeable by leading them from thought to thought in a manner that evolves from clear thinking and logical development. (American Psychological Association, 1974, p. 25)

If you think that meeting APA's requirements is easier said than done, you are right. Although Chapter 6 provides useful writing tips, writing well is a skill that must be attained like any other—through practice.

---

[2]The passage quoted from the *Manual* is longer than 40 words and, therefore, instead of being surrounded by quotation marks, is an indented block of text. Two clues tell you this is a quotation. First, it is blocked. Second, in addition to containing the information other citations would contain (the last name of the source's author(s) and year the source was published), it contains what you find only in a citation for quotation: the quotation's page number.

Apart from practice, the next best way to improve your writing is to read good writing. The more you read articles in psychological journals, the more you will be exposed to the works of authors who have met APA's writing standards. We do not mean that all published works are of high quality. Unfortunately, some are poorly written, hard to follow, and boring. Others are a pleasure to read: Imitate those.

1.3.2 Appropriately Personal Prose: The Objective "I"

One thing you will learn by studying good writers is that you can write in a professional, formal style without writing in a completely impersonal style. For example, although APA style essentially bans the use of the word "you," it does allow you to use the personal pronoun "I." Note, however, that being allowed to use "I" is not a license to write in an extremely personal way. The focus of a paper should be on the ideas and findings of the paper, not on the author. Consequently, skilled writers never use the phrases "I feel," "I think," or "I believe." Many of them never use the word "I." All of them will check sentences in which they used the word "I" to see whether the sentence would be better without the "I." They will take the "I" out of the sentence if they believe that it is focusing the reader's attention on the writer rather than on the paper's content.

To remove the "I" from a sentence such as "I read the list to participants," an author could write, "The list was read to participants." That is, rather than use the stronger *active voice*, in which the subject of the sentence actively does something (e.g., "I hypothesized . . ."), writers sometimes use the weaker *passive voice*, in which the subject passively has something done to it (e.g., "It was hypothesized . . ."). In unskilled hands, the passive voice can sound clumsy and wordy (e.g., "It was hypothesized by me . . ."). Even in skilled hands, the passive voice should be used sparingly.

Fortunately, writers can often replace "I" without using the passive voice. Rather than write, "The list was read to the participants," they may write, "The participants listened to the list." Rather than write, "It was hypothesized," they may write, "The hypothesis was."

However, as we mentioned earlier, writers do not always have to replace the word "I." Skilled writers can use the words "I" or "we" when that is what they mean. In other words, skilled writers do not violate the rules of either reality or grammar to avoid personal pronouns.

In reality, researchers make hypotheses, conduct studies, and come to conclusions. Skilled writers respect that reality and the laws of grammar. Therefore, skilled writers may use verbs to describe researchers' actions and make the researcher performing the action the subject of the sentence. Occasionally, such skilled writers may also add an adverb (e.g., "thoroughly") to an action verb to describe how the researcher performed the action (e.g., "I *thoroughly* debriefed the participants.").

Some less skilled writers, on the other hand, attempt to disown their own thoughts and end up violating the laws of grammar. For example, some authors misuse the adverb "hopefully" when they mean "I hope." Consequently, rather than writing,

"Future researchers should use a more representative sample"[3] or "I hope researchers will use a more representative sample," they write, "Hopefully, future researchers will use a more representative sample." The problem is that students are using an adverb ("hopefully"), intended only to modify a verb (e.g., "she stared hopefully at the candy"), to be both a subject ("I") and a verb ("hope").

In the past, writers were encouraged to disown their own thoughts—even if that meant violating the laws of nature. For example, authors routinely credited their thoughts to nonliving entities, such as experiments (e.g., "this experiment will test the hypothesis") and papers (e.g., "this paper will argue" or "this paper will examine"). Currently, however, APA's position is that writers should not ***anthropomorphize***: give human qualities to nonhumans. In addition, the editors of the current *APA Publication Manual* warn against two strategies that were once used to avoid writing "I": (a) replacing "I" with "the author," "the researcher," or some other role that you have and (b) replacing "I" with "we."

To avoid both anthropomorphism and using "I," some authors used to attribute their actions to a role. For example, they wrote, "It will be argued by the present author that" rather than "I will argue that." The price they paid for avoiding "I" was that they wrote wordier and clumsier sentences. Similarly, instead of writing, "I told the participant," some authors wrote, "The experimenter told the participant," leaving the reader to guess whether the author paid someone else to be the experimenter or whether the author was also the experimenter.

Another, even more awkward technique for avoiding "I" was to replace "I" with "we." For example, if the writer of a single-author paper, instead of writing, "I hypothesized," wrote, "We hypothesized," readers may suspect that the author is either a plagiarist or a member of a royal family.

In short, you should not use "I" frivolously. However, if using "I" is the only way to meet the APA ideal of saying what you mean as clearly and simply as possible, use "I."

1.3.3 Simple Language: Do Not Confuse the Reader

The APA ideal of saying what you mean as clearly and simply as possible applies not only to using simple, active sentences but also to using simple vocabulary. To use vocabulary that complies with the APA ideal, you should obey two rules.

First, do not use fancy words or fancy phrases just to impress your professor. If you do, you will be disappointed. Rather than being impressed with your writing, your professor will probably see your writing as pretentious, wordy, or unclear.

Second, do not banish technical terms from your paper. At the very least, your professor will expect you to use and define your topic's key terms. Your professor will probably also expect you to show that you understand the field's key terms well enough (a) to use those terms to express your ideas more precisely and concisely than if you had used everyday language and (b) to make distinctions between related concepts. Thus, if you wrote a paper on behavior modification and never used the term "reinforcement," your professor would be disappointed. In such an assignment, your professor would

[3] We thank the anonymous reviewer who pointed out that students would be better off writing, "Future researchers should use a more representative sample."

expect you to use key terms in a way that showed that you understood key distinctions between related concepts, such as the distinction between negative reinforcement and punishment. In such an assignment, your professor would probably also hope that you would use key terms, such as "schedules of reinforcement," in a way that showed that your understanding of the effects of reinforcement was more sophisticated than "giving rewards increases behavior." In short, if you want to sound knowledgeable rather than pretentious and if you want to be clear rather than vague, use terminology from psychology—but not jargon from other fields (Silvia, 2007; Whyte, 2005).

1.3.4 Respectful Language: Do Not Offend

To write in APA style, you must use words that are not only clear and precise but also respectful and inclusive. Avoid language that might suggest that another group is less competent, less important, less moral, or less likely to occupy a certain role (e.g., professor) than your own. If you must differentiate among individuals on bases such as gender, race, disability, or age, be accurate, specific, cautious, and respectful. To see what you should do, study the following examples of disrespectful language (italicized) and solutions:

✗ *Subjects* were 10 men and 10 *girls*.

✔ Participants ["subjects" is considered disrespectful because it does not acknowledge that individuals voluntarily participated in the study] were 10 men and 10 women [if you use "men" to describe male participants, then use the equivalent, parallel term "women" when describing female participants].

✗ *He* [the participant] was required to use *his* right index finger to press the response button.

✔ Participants used their [using the plural is often a good way to avoid the problem of using the generic "he," a term that is sexist if there were both men and women participants because it excludes women] right index fingers to press the response button.

✔ Participants used the [when using a pronoun would be sexist or awkward, see if you can eliminate the pronoun] right index finger to press the response button.

✗ These results have important implications for the development of *man*.

✔ These results have important implications for human development. ["Human" includes both women and men.]

Although you should use gender-inclusive language, you still have a duty to write clearly and smoothly. Thus, you would be penalized for using such clumsy—but nonsexist—phrases as *(s)he* and *he/she*. Furthermore, inclusiveness should not come at the expense of accuracy. Thus, if all the participants were boys, you could write the following paragraph:

✔ Participants were 10 boys. . . . *He* was required to use his right index finger to press the response button. . . . These results have important implications for male development.

Now, look at an example of disrespectful language involving race (italicized) and a solution:

✗ Participants were 100 Whites and 100 *Non-Whites*.

✓ Participants were 100 European Americans, 60 African Americans, and 40 Asian Americans. [The American Psychological Association (2010, p. 75) states that parallel construction should be used when describing racial and ethnic identity. Thus, if you describe European Americans as "Whites," you should describe African Americans as "Blacks." We prefer using European American over "White" because it is (a) more specific and (b) avoids the confusion of whether the group includes Hispanic or Latino Americans.]

Next, examine a case of disrespectful language involving individuals with disabilities (italicized) and a solution:

✗ Participants were 100 *normals* and 100 *schizophrenics*. [Labeling the group as schizophrenics depersonalizes them. They are individuals who have a condition, but they are not the condition. Avoid labels that focus on an individual's limitations or problems.]

✓ Participants were 100 people with no previously diagnosed psychiatric illness and 100 people diagnosed with schizophrenia.

Finally, consider an example of disrespectful language involving age (italicized) and a solution:

✗ Participants were 100 adults and 100 *elderly*. [Labeling a group by a quality, "elderly," depersonalizes them and is ageist. "Older adults" is the preferred term.]

✓ Participants were divided into two groups based on age: a middle-aged group (ages 45–60) and an older-age group (ages 70–85).

1.4 Writing and Revising

1.4.1 Plan to Finish Early

Now that you understand what your professor wants, you need to produce it. Perhaps the greatest obstacle to meeting your professor's expectations is procrastination. Procrastination may prevent you from turning in the paper on time—and, because most professors strictly enforce due dates, being late can mean flunking the assignment.

You might believe that "pressure of other commitments" is an excuse for turning a paper in late. It is not. Most students would do a better job if they were given more time. Therefore, it is unethical for professors to give you more time than other students without penalizing you (Keith-Spiegel, Wittig, Perkins, Balogh, & Whitely, 1993).

You might believe that "I had some unexpected problems" is an acceptable excuse. It is not because your professor expects you to know that Murphy's Laws apply to any major project:

- Anything that goes wrong will have the worst possible outcome.
- Anything that can possibly go wrong will.
- It will go wrong at the worst possible time.

Therefore, do not expect to be exempt from the deadline just because you had some unusual problem at the last minute. Your professor expects you to have everything done at least 48 hours before the due date because, when applied to writing assignments, Murphy's Laws mean that 48 hours before the due date, you can expect the following:

- Any vital piece of equipment (computer, printer, bicycle) will break down irreparably.
- Any people vital to the assignment (reference librarian, person commenting on your drafts, computer repair person, professor, head of department, head of the United Nations) will disappear.
- Anything about you vital to the assignment will cease functioning (your hand will become paralyzed, your memory will go blank, your motivation will evaporate).
- All material vital to the assignment (your notes, your computer files, the Internet) will disappear.

Even if you meet the deadline, procrastination can hurt you. Waiting until the last minute can lead to sloppiness. Consider yourself lucky if your sloppiness leads to errors—spelling errors, grammatical errors, punctuation errors, and formatting errors—that hurt only your grade. Sloppiness can lead to plagiarism—which can lead to expulsion.

Often, students do not realize how much their procrastination has hurt them. They do not know what they missed from the sources they failed to find, read, or contemplate. They are too tired and too rushed to evaluate their paper before they give it to the professor. They do not study the professor's comments on their paper when they get it back, and they do not know how much better they would have done had they spent more time revising, editing, and proofreading.

To avoid the many problems that procrastination can cause, start work on any major paper as soon as you can. At the very least, give yourself a deadline that is three days before the actual deadline. Ideally, draw up a schedule (e.g., days 1 to 3 for reading, days 4 to 6 for producing a first draft, days 7 to 10 for showing the assignment to others, days 11 to 14 for producing the final draft, and days 15 to 18 for emergencies)—and stick to your schedule.

1.4.2 Think, Search, Read, and Get Organized

Sticking to your schedule will not be easy. Even before you start to write, you may start to procrastinate. The problem is that getting started means doing five tasks that you may be uncomfortable doing:

1. choosing a topic;
2. developing a question or thesis statement that will guide you in searching, reading, summarizing, and evaluating articles;

3. finding relevant articles (for tips on using the library and computers to find relevant literature, see 4.1);
4. reading and critiquing those articles (see 4.2); and
5. taking, retaining, and organizing your notes on those articles.

Once you have accomplished these five tasks, you are almost ready to write the first draft. However, before you do so, organize your thoughts.

One way to organize your thoughts is to use an outline. You may find it useful to outline your paper on the computer. Fortunately, almost all word-processing programs have tools that can help you outline your paper. For more tips on outlining, see Box 1.1.

BOX 1.1 Outlining: Why and How

Like organizing a closet, outlining helps you know what you have, what you should throw out, what you need, and what you should put where. Like a to-do list, an outline helps you make sure you cover all the important points in the best possible order.

As you do research for your paper, your outline lets you know what notes to take and where to fit the ideas from those notes into your paper. As you start to write, your outline provides you with a jump-start. Rather than starting from nothing (the dreaded blinking cursor on a blank screen), your outline provides you with the key ideas, the major headings, and at least the start of many of your paragraphs' topic sentences. (For tips on using Microsoft Word to turn your outline—your paper's skeleton—into your paper's body, see this book's website.) As you continue to write your first draft, your outline—because it lists, orders, and groups your ideas from first to last and from more important to less important—can act as a guide that prevents you from leaving out important points, unintentionally going back and repeating important points, and wandering off topic (Meyer & Meyer, 1993).

You might think that you do not need an outline to write a rough draft. However, as Meyer and Meyer (1993) note, about the only way you can go wrong in writing a rough draft is if you have written the wrong stuff—and if you follow an outline, you will not have written the wrong stuff.

As you revise your paper, re-outlining the paper allows you to reduce the paper to its bare bones. Looking at this X-ray of your paper will expose flaws—missing parts or flawed structure—that you did not see before.

Despite the benefits of outlining, students invent reasons for not outlining. Below, we debunk four common excuses.

1. *Outlining is too constricting.* Outlines, like to-do lists, are not rigid. You can add, delete, and rearrange items in your outline as easily as you can make changes to your to-do list.
2. *Using roman numerals will not make my paper better.* When you write an outline for your own purposes, you do not have to use roman numerals.

BOX **1.1** (*Continued*)

3. *Rules like if you have an "A," you must have a "B," and that if you have a "1," you must have a "2," are arbitrary.* Although these rules may seem silly at first, the underlying logic is clear: If you are not splitting a whole into at least two parts, you are not splitting it at all.
4. *I do not need to outline my paper to organize my thoughts.* Just as you do not need a to-do list if you only have two things to do, you do not need an outline—a "to-write list"—if you have a short writing assignment. Thus, if your paper or a section of your paper is less than a page long, you might not need an outline. However, just as writing down a short to-do list would not take much time and might help you act more efficiently, jotting down an outline for a short assignment should only take you a few seconds and might help you write more efficiently (Hart, 2006). Furthermore, just as almost everyone who has many tasks to get done should have a to-do list, almost everyone should outline (a) the body of a term paper, (b) the introduction and discussion sections of a research paper, and (c) any long paper. As Hahn (2005, p. 79) states, "Never underestimate the power of a well-organized outline: An abbreviated list of what ideas should be presented when is a handy visual tool when you start writing ten-or twenty-page papers."

Many students who make excuses for not outlining doubt their ability to make an organized and useful outline. So that you will not be tempted to make excuses, we will show you that making an outline is easy.

To get started, just list the points you want to make. Next, try to put the related points together. Then, put the points in order. You should now be well on your way to having an outline—but even if you do not create an outline, you at least know what points to make and in what order (Meyer & Meyer, 1993).

Although you can easily make a list of points, you may have trouble converting your list of points into an outline because you have trouble grouping your related points. If you have trouble grouping your points, try at least one of the following four tips.

1. Ask whether a point is an example of, evidence for, or a reason for a larger point (Hahn, 2005). If it is, move that example, evidence, or reason under and to the right of the point it is supporting.
2. Write each point on a note card, make piles of cards that have related points, and then make titles that describe each pile (Kuehn, 1989). The titles will be major headings for your outline (e.g., I, II, III), and the cards would represent points under that heading (e.g., IA, IB).
3. Make a table. For example, if you were comparing two theories, the headings of the two columns (for Theory A and Theory B) would be major headings (e.g., I and II) and the headings for your rows (history, support, weaknesses) could represent the next level headings (A, B, C, etc.).
4. If you still cannot make an outline, write your first draft without an outline. After your first draft is complete, outline that draft. Next, refine your outline to make it more organized, and then use it to help you write your second draft.

Another way to organize your thoughts is to make a diagram of your ideas.[4] (Your English teacher might call such diagramming "clustering," "concept-mapping," or "mapping.") You can use concept-mapping software such as Inspiration[5] to help you visualize how your ideas fit together.

Yet another way to organize your thoughts is to make a table. For example, you could make a two-column table in which the left column lists evidence for a certain idea and the right column lists evidence against that idea.

Finally, you could just jot down a list of points you want to include in your rough draft. Once you have listed your key points, rearrange your list until those points are in a logical order (Meyer & Meyer, 1993).

1.4.3 Write Your First Draft

After you have organized your thoughts, start writing. Resist the biggest stumbling block in sticking to your schedule: talking yourself out of writing your first draft. Realize that almost any reason you give yourself for not writing is an excuse. If you are waiting for inspiration, realize that almost all good writers let a schedule—not a muse—dictate when they write. If you are waiting for your thoughts on the topic to be clearer and more coherent, realize that writing will often help your thoughts become clearer. As Howard and Barton (1986) put it, writing is "thinking on paper" (p. 1).

In your first draft, just get your ideas on paper. Do not worry about wording. As the saying goes, "Don't get it right; get it written."

One way to get it written is to set a deadline for starting and finishing the rough draft (Goldsberry, 2005). Once you start writing, make yourself type at least a page an hour. To keep that pace, do not answer the phone, text message, check e-mail, or go on the web. Instead, set your word processor to full-screen mode (for help on how to set your word processor to full-screen mode, see the Chapter 1 section of this book's website) and type. If you find you are missing some information or need to check something, do not leave full-screen mode. Instead, if what you need is not in your notes, type two asterisks, specify what you need to look up, type two more asterisks, then continue writing. Avoid the temptation to stop writing in order to search the Internet because stopping will probably cause you to lose time, focus, and momentum. In short, except for following your outline and referring to your notes, write your first draft like many people text—that is, rapidly produce many words without worrying about spelling or grammar.

If you are having trouble getting started because you have not done the background research or have not outlined your paper, go back and do those tasks. If you are having trouble getting started because you feel stressed, take a few deep breaths, and consider two facts. First, not writing the rough draft means you have the pressure of the first

---

[4]For more information on how to diagram ideas, see our website (http://www.writingforpsychology.com).

[5]Information on how to order Inspiration, as well as additional information on concept-mapping, is available from our website (http://www.writingforpsychology.com).

draft weighing on you; writing the rough draft removes that stress. Second, you do not need to worry about the first draft being bad because (a) you are the only one who will see it and (b) it is supposed to be rough. As a starting point rather than an ending point for your paper, the rough draft's value is in helping you (a) understand your own thinking on the topic and (b) remember the points you want to make (Howard & Barton, 1986).

If you still cannot get started on your rough draft, engage in *free-writing*. To free-write, just write—or type—continuously (no pausing or editing allowed) for 3 minutes. Try to get down as many words as you can in those 3 minutes.

1.4.4 Revise Your First Draft: Reorganize, Rethink, Reread, and Rewrite

As we have stated, your first draft is a rough draft. It is only the first of many steps in the writing process. In a way, writing is like going on a geological dig to produce a mineral exhibit for a museum. When you start writing, you are digging around in your mind, hoping to find something useful. Much of what you dig out is stuff that you cannot use. Some of it is, like dirt, clearly worthless. Some of it seems valuable but, on further examination, is really fool's gold. Some of it is valuable, but it is not suitable for the particular collection you have been asked to create. As you dig, you will find that some veins are dead ends and should be abandoned; other veins, although promising, need to be dug into more deeply before they yield valuable material.

Once you find the right material, you still have work to do. You must lay out the individual pieces, categorize them, and figure out how to organize them into a suitable collection. As you try different arrangements, you may realize that (a) you must cut some pieces from the collection because they are redundant, distracting, or do not fit and (b) you must acquire additional pieces to fill in the gaps in your collection.

Once you have a collection of pieces that you are excited about, you still need to do some work before viewers will share your excitement. You will have to clean up, cut, and polish each individual piece. You will need to put the pieces in the right order. You will have to add labels and text to help viewers appreciate what each piece is and how the pieces fit together. Finally, you will have to display the collection in a professional format so that viewers can fully appreciate the collection's beauty.

If the whole writing project is like the mineral collection project we just described, the rough draft corresponds to the early phase of the project: the "digging around" phase. That is, by using writing to talk to yourself, you have dug up some of your thoughts. When reading over the draft, you can extend this conversation with yourself (Howard & Barton, 1986)—and thus dig deeper—by saying things such as, "Yes, and it is also true that . . ." and "What I really mean to say here is . . ."

Once you have unearthed your thoughts, the next step is to organize them. To organize your thoughts, ask two questions of each paragraph. First, "What do I want this paragraph to do?" Second, "If I want the paragraph to accomplish that goal, is the paragraph in the right place?" As a result of asking these two questions, you may eliminate some paragraphs and move others.

Once you have moved and deleted material, you should outline your revised paper again. Even a glance at the outline may help you see the following:

- You are not pleased with the order in which the ideas are presented.
- You have included some ideas that do not relate to your main point.
- You have either not included or not emphasized some ideas you think are important.
- You have made some assertions that you have not supported with either logic or evidence.
- You have discussed one topic much more thoroughly than you have discussed an equally important topic.
- You have failed to make connections between related ideas.

As you struggle to correct the problems in your thinking that were apparent by looking at the outline, you will refine your thinking.

- You will put your ideas in a more logical order.
- You will ignore ideas and evidence that are irrelevant to your main point.
- You will distinguish between more important ideas and less important ideas.
- You will develop support for unsupported assertions.
- You will see connections among concepts that you had not previously recognized.

Like re-outlining, rereading will help you refine your thinking—if you ask questions as you read (Howard & Barton, 1986). At the very least, ask the following two questions: "Does this make sense?" and "Do I have adequate support for this idea?" (Howard & Barton, 1986).

Like re-outlining and rereading, rewriting helps you refine your thinking. With each rewrite, you will find that you have more arguments, more support for those arguments, and that your paper is becoming more organized, more insightful, and more original. Thus, as you rewrite, you will probably find (a) that passages you quoted in your rough draft now make enough sense to you that you can put them into your own words and (b) that the short, scattered outline of your rough draft is becoming longer and more organized because you have eliminated irrelevant material, rearranged relevant material, and added new material. In a sense, with each revision, you establish a better route to your conclusion by avoiding dead-end paths, replacing detours with more direct paths, and paving the paths to your conclusion.

1.4.5 Help the Reader Navigate Through Your Paper

Once you are satisfied that your own thinking on the topic is clear, you can devote your next few drafts to making your thinking clear to your audience. Although the audience of your paper may number in the thousands, we will call your audience "the reader" for two reasons. First, it is more useful to anticipate how a particular individual, such as a friend, another psychology major, or your professor, will react to reading your work than it is to picture an anonymous audience reading your work. Second, your audience may be a single reader: your professor.

A first step to making your thinking clear to the reader is to make the organization of your paper clear to the reader. You can do this by (a) adding short subheadings (often taken from your outline's main headings), (b) adding topic sentences (often taken from your outline's subheadings) to each paragraph, and (c) adding transitions between paragraphs (some of these transitions may be entire paragraphs that preview what the next few paragraphs are going to do). After you have tried to make the organization of your paper clear to the reader, you are ready for the real test: See if a friend can re-create your outline from reading your paper.

Once you are sure that a reader could follow the outline of your paper, it is time to help the reader understand the individual paragraphs. Thus, in the next few drafts, you may work on refining your topic sentences. If the topic sentence is the paragraph's first sentence, ask, "Does the topic sentence provide a preview of the paragraph?" If the topic sentence is the paragraph's last sentence, ask, "Does the topic sentence provide a summary of the paragraph?"

Once you have good topic sentences, you have done much of the work of organizing your paragraphs. However, there are still four things you should do to improve the organization within each paragraph. First, you should split long paragraphs into two: No paragraph should be longer than a page. Second, if a sentence is not tied to the topic sentence, you should remove it from that paragraph. Third, if a sentence restates what another sentence in the same paragraph says, delete one of those sentences. Fourth, if it is not clear how a sentence relates to the next one, consider using transition words (such as "consequently," "therefore," "however," and "although") to connect the sentences inside a paragraph with each other.

Once you have taken steps to prevent readers from getting lost between sentences, you should take at least three steps to prevent readers from getting lost within your sentences. First, see if you can eliminate, reword, or move remarks that are not relevant to the point you want to make. Often, material that is set off from the rest of the sentence by parentheses, a pair of commas, or a dash is material you can eliminate. Second, shorten sentences that are longer than 40 words. Usually, you can split these longer sentences into two shorter sentences. Third, go back and look at pronouns such as "it," "they," "those," "these," and "this" that you are using to refer back to another word or idea. If your pronouns do not clearly point back to their nouns, see 6.3.5.

Although you want to make each paragraph and sentence clear to the reader, there are at least two reasons you may fail to revise an unclear section. First, you suffer from the "curse of knowledge": You know what you are trying to say, so you may not recognize when a section is confusing. Second, you may be too attached to what you have written to delete unnecessary material.

You can overcome both of these self-imposed obstacles to revising an unclear section by using the following four tactics. First, put the draft aside for a few days. By the time you reread it, you may forget what you meant to write so that you can focus on what you actually wrote. By that time, you may also be less attached to passages that you should cut. Second, pretend that someone else has written the draft and that your task is to improve it. Third, read your paper aloud—or have the computer read it aloud to you (for detailed instructions on getting your computer to read your paper to you, see this book's website). Fourth, have a friend read your paper and make comments. If you show your friend how to use the computer's voice annotation feature,[6] you can click on sections in the paper to hear your friend's comments ("I'm confused about this point because . . .").

1.4.6 Address Readers' Objections

Some of your friend's comments may deal with objections to your argument. Even if your friend does not introduce objections, realize that other readers might. You want to address possible objections so that your reader does not say, "But the writer did not consider . . ."

In addressing potential objections, be firm but fair. If you can successfully fend off an objection, explain why the objection is not serious. If the objection is serious, admit it and qualify your conclusions to incorporate the objection.

1.4.7 Polish Your Writing

Now that you have polished your ideas, you can start polishing your writing. One way to do this is to vary the length of your sentences. For example, if almost all of your sentences are short (fewer than 10 words), combine some of your sentences: Not only will your writing be more interesting, but you will also be better able to show how your ideas are connected. To appreciate how overusing short sentences can lead to writing that is disconnected, repetitious, and boring, imagine reading a 2,000-word paper composed of sentences like the following: "See Spot. See Spot run. See Jane. See Jane run." You would not know whether Spot caused Jane to run, and, after reading several hundred words written in such a tiresome, repetitious, and choppy style, you would not care about Spot, Jane, or their relationship.

Although we will discuss more tips on improving your writing in section 6.4, we will give you one tip now: Strengthen your writing by weeding out unnecessary words. Your computer's grammar checker can help you purge unnecessary words because it points out wordy phrases and sentences. For example, your grammar checker might highlight the following:

- a clumsy phrase ("at this point in time") that you could replace with a single word ("now");
- a wordy, passive sentence ("It was written by me.") that you could replace with a shorter active sentence ("I wrote it."); and
- an unusually long sentence that you could split into two.

---

[6]For instructions on how to use MS Word's voice annotation feature, go to our website (http://www.writingforpsychology.com).

1.4.8 Check Language, Grammar, Spelling, Usage, and Punctuation

Your grammar checker, in addition to helping you cut "dead words" that make your writing less lively, can be a valuable tool for catching inappropriate language that might otherwise slip into your paper. By alerting you to the contractions, clichés, and slang terms that it finds in your paper, it can help you rid your paper of inappropriately informal language. By alerting you to words in your paper that are either non-inclusive ("chairman") or offensive, it can help you rid your paper of biased language.

You cannot, however, rely on a grammar checker to catch all instances of offensive language for at least two reasons. First, terms that were not offensive when the grammar-checking program was first released may now be considered offensive. Second, what is offensive may depend on context rather than on a specific word or phrase.

As you are using your grammar checker to check for inappropriate language, you will, of course, also be using it to check your paper's grammar. However, do not delegate the entire job of grammar checking to software. If you do, you will run into two problems. First, the grammar checker will fail to tell you that some ungrammatical passages are ungrammatical. Second, the grammar checker will tell you that some grammatical passages are ungrammatical. Therefore, to check the grammar of your work, you need to have a clear understanding of grammar (to get that understanding, read Chapter 6).

Although you may not be able to rid your paper of all grammatical errors, you should at least focus on the ones that are most likely to irritate your professor. Those errors probably include the following:

- subject-verb disagreement (the subject of a sentence is plural, but the verb used is appropriate only for singular noun ["They is," "Data is"]—or vice versa ["It are," "Datum are"]);
- pronoun-noun disagreement (the noun is plural, but the pronoun referring to it is singular ["The male experimenter received their training"]—or vice versa ["The male experimenters received his training"]);
- disagreements between verbs (one verb in the sentence is in one tense, but the other is in a different tense ["The results supported dissonance theory but do not support self-perception theory."]);
- "paragraphs" that are only one sentence long;
- "sentences" that are really sentence fragments (they are incomplete sentences because they do not contain a complete thought ["To deal effectively."]); and
- any other grammatical error that your professor mentions.

Although your professor may not expect your paper to be completely free of grammatical errors, your professor probably will expect your paper to be completely free of spelling errors. As is the case with grammatical errors, software can help you, but it will not do all the work for you. Although your spell-checking software will catch some errors, it will make mistakes. Spell-checking software will report many correctly spelled words as errors (e.g., names and psychological terms) and will not report cases in which you typed "there" for "their," "to" for "two," "then" for "than," "except" for "accept," "preformed" for "performed," "pervious" for "previous," "defiantly" for "definitely," "conscience" for "conscious," "casual" for "causal," or any other case in which you have "the wrong word spelled right" (Barkas, 1985, p. 75).

Using the wrong word is not always the result of a finger slipping on the keyboard. Sometimes, you may think you know what a word means, but you do not. By taking advantage of our table of commonly misused words (see Table 6.3, our "problem pairs" table, on pages 209–212) and your computer's dictionary, you can avoid common but costly mistakes such as using "affect" when you mean "effect." If you learn that you have consistently misused a word, term, or phrase, use your word processor's "find and replace" feature to replace all instances of that wrong word with the correct word.

You have checked your paper for inappropriate language, grammar, spelling, and usage. Now, print out your paper and read it aloud to (a) recheck it for inappropriate language, grammar, spelling, and usage and (b) check punctuation.

If you are like most students, you will tend to have the most punctuation problems with the comma. Remember that if you start a sentence with a dependent clause (e.g., "If the hypothesis is correct," "Although support for the hypothesis is weak," "After participants filled out the questionnaire," or "When researchers have tested the hypothesis"), you need to insert a comma at the end of that clause. You also need to put a comma before an "and" when it joins two complete sentences (e.g., "The participant ran, and the researcher hid."). However, you do not need to put a comma before every "and." For example, you should not use a comma when "and" is connecting two adjectives (e.g., "strong and consistent"), two nouns (e.g., letters and numbers), or connecting two verbs belonging to the same subject (e.g., "The participant ran and hid."). Remember that you should put commas inside, rather than outside, of quotation marks. If you need to learn or review how to use commas, see 6.2.2. (If you need a more complete review of punctuation, read 6.2.)

1.4.9 Final Formatting

After you have proofread your paper for writing errors, you are almost ready to proofread it for formatting errors. However, because preventing errors is easier than catching errors, check your word-processing software's settings to be sure that the following options have been selected: indent paragraphs five spaces, leave one space after punctuation marks, leave two spaces between sentences, double-space, use 12-point Times New Roman, and leave 1-inch margins (to see how to change your computer's settings or how to download a good template, see the Chapter 7 section of this book's website). After you have your word-processing software or template set up to prevent most formatting errors, print out a copy of your document and proof it using our formatting checklist (see 7.4.1).

1.4.10 Five Final Checks

You are almost finished. Still, potential disasters lurk, so take five steps to avoid them. First, make sure that you have not plagiarized by checking your paper against your original sources, against the checklist at the end of this chapter (1.6), and, if possible, against plagiarism-detection software, such as TurnItIn™. Second, make sure your citations follow APA format and that they match your reference list. (If you are not sure what a citation is, see 1.3; to learn more about APA format for citations, see 4.4 and 4.5.) Third, make sure that your reference list is in APA format (see 4.10). Fourth, make sure that your title page is in APA format (see 7.4.6). Fifth, make sure that your paper conforms to any additional requirements (e.g., word and page limits) that your professor has imposed.

1.5 Submitting the Finished Product

You have properly formatted your paper. As a result, it looks good on your computer screen. If you are submitting a paper copy to your professor, you should (a) put plain, clean, white, sturdy (20-pound) bond paper into a printer that produces dark, clear, clean print; (b) staple it together using one or two staples in the top left corner; and (c) **hand it in on time**.

1.6 Avoiding Common Problems: A Checklist

- ☐ I found important sources; read those sources carefully; wrote a rough draft; and then revised, edited, and proofread subsequent drafts.
- ☐ I did not plagiarize.
  - — When I borrowed someone's ideas without quoting them, it was clear that I was using that person's ideas.
  - — When I borrowed a person's words, it was clear that I was quoting that person.
  - — I double-checked my sources to make sure that I had neither inadvertently quoted someone nor paraphrased someone too closely.
- ☐ I made an original, fair, and evidence-based argument.
  - — I supported my argument with logic and with evidence from high-quality sources (to learn how to acquire information from high-quality sources, see 4.1).
  - — I reported evidence that ran counter to my argument.
  - — I quoted fewer than 50 words for every 1,000 (four pages) of my own.
  - — If I was unsure about my criticisms of the literature or the quality of the reasons for my position, I consulted Chapter 5.

- ☐ My argument was easy to follow because my paper was well-organized.
  - __ I wrote several drafts of my paper.
  - __ I outlined each draft and used that outline to improve the organization of subsequent drafts.
  - __ I revised any paragraphs longer than a page.
  - __ I made sure that every paragraph had a topic sentence that summarized my goal for that paragraph.
- ☐ I checked to make sure my paper did not contain offensive language (see 1.3.4) or grammatical errors (see Chapter 6).
  - __ I checked my paper against all examples, instructions, and warnings my professor gave the class.
  - __ I made sure my paper used professional rather than informal language. Thus, I did not use any contractions or exclamation marks and I did not use the word "you."
  - __ I read my paper aloud and made corrections based on my reading. For example, I do not have any missing words, and I have not written "then" when I meant "than."
  - __ I did not use "that" to refer to people; I used "who" instead.
  - __ I did not use "since" to mean "because," and I did not use "while" to mean "although."
  - __ I used computerized proofing tools, such as a spell checker and a grammar checker.
  - __ If I was unsure about the grammar or writing style of my paper, I consulted Chapter 6. If I was still unsure, I went to my school's writing center.
- ☐ I checked to make sure that my sources were correctly cited in the body of my paper.
  - __ Every reference in my reference list is cited in the body of my paper.
  - __ When I cited a source, I mentioned only the authors' last names and the year the source was published. I did not mention the authors' first names, university affiliations, degrees, or professional titles.
  - __ When I cited, I did not mention the title of the source—unless the source had no accredited author.
  - __ When I was unsure about how to cite a source in text, I consulted Chapter 4 or the *APA Publication Manual.*
- ☐ I properly formatted quotations (see 4.8).
- ☐ I made sure my reference list was properly formatted (see 4.10 and 4.11.4).

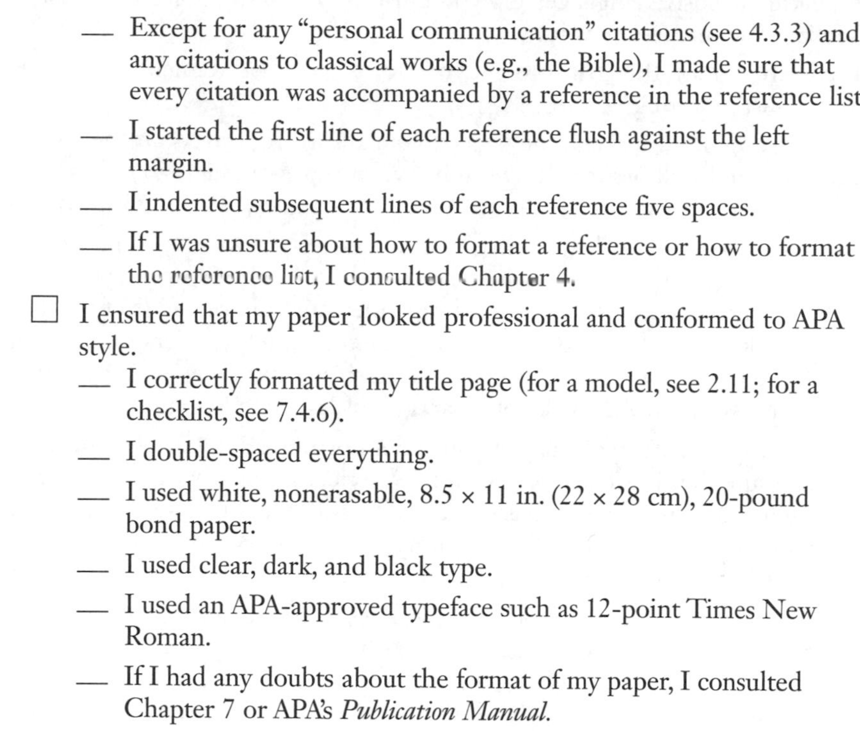

— Except for any "personal communication" citations (see 4.3.3) and any citations to classical works (e.g., the Bible), I made sure that every citation was accompanied by a reference in the reference list.

— I started the first line of each reference flush against the left margin.

— I indented subsequent lines of each reference five spaces.

— If I was unsure about how to format a reference or how to format the reference list, I consulted Chapter 4.

☐ I ensured that my paper looked professional and conformed to APA style.

— I correctly formatted my title page (for a model, see 2.11; for a checklist, see 7.4.6).

— I double-spaced everything.

— I used white, nonerasable, 8.5 × 11 in. (22 × 28 cm), 20-pound bond paper.

— I used clear, dark, and black type.

— I used an APA-approved typeface such as 12-point Times New Roman.

— If I had any doubts about the format of my paper, I consulted Chapter 7 or APA's *Publication Manual.*

1.7 Summary

1. Writing well means knowing your audience. The audience for a scholarly paper will be members of the academic community. This audience shares certain values. For example, the academic community condemns plagiarism, falsification of data, and other dishonest acts.
2. Plagiarism involves using other people's words or ideas without giving them credit.
3. The academic community values making a fair, logical argument based on careful consideration of the evidence.
4. To make your paper consistent with APA style, you must do more than follow APA rules on how to format your paper. For example, to make your paper consistent with APA style, you must use simple, clear language; you must use

respectful, inclusive language; and you must use the active voice much more than you use the passive voice.

5. In your first draft, the goal is to get your ideas on paper. Remember, your first draft is just a starting point.
6. In your second draft, revise the paper to make sure your ideas are well supported and well organized. Outlining your paper can help you revise it. You may need to write many drafts: As the saying goes, "Writing is rewriting."
7. After you have revised the paper so that it makes sense to you, you need to start editing it so that it will make sense to other people. Rework your paper (a) to address objections that a skeptical reader might have and (b) to make it easier for the reader to follow your argument. To help readers follow your thinking, you may want to add subheadings, strengthen topic sentences, cut out unnecessary words, divide long paragraphs, and divide long sentences.
8. After you have edited your paper, you should proofread it. Check your paper to make sure that it is consistent with APA style, as well as with any other requirements your professor has specified. In addition, make sure that it does not contain grammatical, spelling, or usage errors. As Wegner (2007) put it, you want "people to see your paper, not your errors."
9. Procrastination is one of the biggest obstacles to producing a good paper. Procrastination may prevent you from (a) obtaining valuable sources from interlibrary loan; (b) carefully evaluating your sources; (c) properly citing and referencing your sources; (d) revising, editing, and proofreading your paper; and (e) turning in your paper on time.

CHAPTER

2

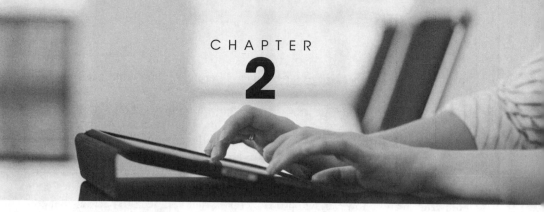

Writing Essays and Term Papers

To succeed in your desired career, you will probably need to be able to write high-quality memos, reports, letters, and position papers. Your professors help you develop the skills to write professional papers by assigning you term papers and essays. In this chapter, you will learn the core skills needed to write such papers: summarizing and evaluating information, stating your conclusion as a thesis, and defending that thesis in an objective manner. Although our focus will be on how to write an APA-style term paper, most of what we will say applies to any paper that requires you to make an organized, logical, evidence-based case for a position. (However, if you want to write a paper based on a study you conducted [e.g., a lab report] or plan to conduct [e.g., a research proposal], see Chapter 3.)

2.1 From Topic to Thesis Statement

Although the purpose of all term papers—and of most essays—is to answer a question, your professor will probably not give you the question (e.g., "Does aggression increase with age?"). Instead, your professor will probably give you only a general topic (e.g., "Your term paper should deal with an issue related to aggression."). Usually, you will have to narrow down that topic to a subtopic that can be treated within the limits of a term paper. For example, if your initial topic was aggression, you could not possibly learn everything about aggression in a few weeks, much less fit that information into a 15-page term paper. Therefore, you would need to choose a narrower topic.

One way to narrow your topic is look up "aggression" in the *Psychological Thesaurus* (in the library, use your library's catalog system to find the *Thesaurus*; online, access the *Thesaurus*—sometimes called *"Term Finder"*—from either *Psyc*INFO or *Psyc*Articles) to discover narrower terms for "aggression."[1] As a result of consulting the *Thesaurus*, you may decide that you want to look at a specific type of aggression, such as instrumental aggression: aggression used to achieve a goal, such as hitting another child to get a toy. Even a casual literature search, however, will probably reveal that you need to narrow your topic further. To do so, look at how another variable influences or is influenced by instrumental aggression. Thus, you might do a literature search on the effects of television violence on instrumental aggression. Based on your search, you may decide to limit your topic further by looking at whether a specific type of televised violence (e.g., cartoon) affects a specific type of aggression (e.g., instrumental) in a specific group (e.g., boys). If your topic was still too broad, you could add yet another variable to narrow your topic further.

As you add variables, you not only narrow your topic, but you also start thinking about how those variables are related. Thus, even before you start reading, you may come up with a *working thesis:* a statement—usually about a relationship among variables—that you think your paper will show to be true.

Note that your working thesis should not be an oversimplification (e.g., all aggression is due to television violence). Nor should it be an overgeneralization (televised violence makes everyone more aggressive). Instead, your working thesis statement should specify under what conditions a certain relationship will hold. For example, if your topic is aggression, your working thesis statement might be "Viewing cartoon violence on television leads to aggression in boys." Your working thesis statement, regardless of whether it is right, will help you find relevant articles and take relevant notes.

After you have read several articles (if you are having trouble finding enough articles, consult 4.1.1 and 4.1.2), you may realize that your working thesis is wrong. If so, modify it into a thesis statement that is consistent with the evidence. Depending on what you find out, your thesis statement might be one of the following:

- Viewing cartoon violence on television increases hostile aggression in boys.
- Viewing cartoon violence on television leads to aggression in introverted boys.
- Viewing cartoon violence on television leads to tolerance of aggression in boys.

You would choose one of these thesis statements, or one that we did not list, after extensive reading on the topic convinced you of its truth. To introduce your thesis, precede it with words such as "In this paper, I will argue that . . ."

Although you should believe that your thesis is true, your thesis should be one that some reasonable people might disagree with—before they read your paper. Thus, your thesis statement should not fall into any of the following types of unarguable assertions: (a) a well-documented fact ("some responses can be classically conditioned"), (b) an extremely vague statement ("environment affects behavior"),

---

[1]In the *Thesaurus* entry for your term, the narrower term will be to be the right of a capital "N" ("N" stands for "narrow"). If you do not have access to the *Thesaurus*, this chapter's section of our website has some tools that will help you find useful search terms.

Table 2.1
Examples of Unacceptable Thesis Statements

Assertion	Problem
Approximately 10% of humans are left-handed.	It is a statement of fact.
Performance on speeded tasks declines in old age.	It is a statement of fact.
Some human perceptions are not affected by prior expectations or knowledge but are instead solely the result of combining the raw data coming from the senses.	It is a statement of fact and vague.
I think drugs should be legalized.	It is a statement of opinion. A reader cannot reasonably argue, "No, you do not believe that."
IQ tests measure IQ.	It is a tautology.

(c) a statement of personal opinion ("I feel that shock treatment is morally wrong"), or (d) a *tautology:* a statement that must be true because the statement involves defining a term with itself (e.g., "effective behavioral treatments are effective").

To illustrate the problem of using a tautology—a statement that is true by definition—as your thesis, suppose your thesis was the following tautology: "Stereotypes are hateful, inaccurate views of a group held only by extremely prejudiced people. If we stop people from being extremely prejudiced, we will eliminate stereotypes." The reader may disagree with your definitions but, given your definitions, the reader must accept your conclusion. Similarly, if your instructor posed a topic in which the key issue was one of definition (e.g., "Are recovered memories accurate?"), accepting a particular dictionary definition (e.g., "recovered memories are accurate memories that were originally forgotten") would (a) make the thesis that recovered memories are accurate unarguable and (b) miss the point of the assignment: that some memories may not be accurate.

In summary, although you want your thesis to be true, do not state a thesis that is unarguably true. In Table 2.1, you can see examples of assertions that are not good thesis statements because they fail the test of allowing a reasonable person to disagree with them. To avoid having an unarguable thesis, ask yourself what evidence would disprove your thesis. If no pattern of results could disprove your thesis, you need a new thesis.

2.2 Parts of a Term Paper and Their Headings

Once you have a thesis statement, use it to guide you in writing three important parts of the main text of your paper: Introduction, Body, and Conclusion. Treat the first section of the main text (the Introduction) like a prosecutor's opening statement: Present your thesis statement and preview how you plan to defend it. Treat the second section (the Body) like a prosecutor making the state's case: Present evidence and theories in favor of your thesis statement and show how evidence and theories that seem to conflict with your thesis statement are actually consistent with it. Treat the third section of your main text (the Conclusion) like a prosecutor's closing statement: Review the case for your thesis statement and then conclude by stating that your thesis statement is probably correct.

Although the main text is the most important section of your paper, it is not the only section of your paper. Term papers typically have four sections: title page, Abstract, main text (body), and References. As you can see from Figure 2.1, you should start each of these four sections on a separate page and label that page with a centered heading that—except for the main text (which uses the paper's title as its heading)—corresponds to the section's name. Thus, the heading for the title page is the paper's full title, the heading for the Abstract page is "Abstract," the heading for the main text is the paper's title, and the heading for the references page is "References."

Often, those four centered headings will be the only headings you use. However, if you wish, you may add headings to the main text section to help readers see its structure. A simple step would be to use the boldfaced, centered heading "**Conclusion**" to mark the beginning of your Conclusion. A more involved—and useful—step would be to use headings in the Body section to help the reader follow the outline of your argument. An easy place to get such headings (which should start on the left margin and be boldfaced) is from your paper's outline. To see an example of how headings can be transferred from an outline to a paper, compare the sample paper's outline (Box 2–1) to the sample paper's headings (2.10).

FIGURE **2.1** Illustration of the Components of a Term Paper

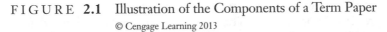

2.3 Formatting the Title Page, Wording the Title, and Writing the Author Note

2.3.1 Formatting the Title Page

As you can see from Figure 2.1, the first page of your paper should be the title page. The title page contains four components: the header, your paper's title, your name, and your school's name. In addition, the title page may also contain the "Author Note."

The title page's header has two parts. The first part starts at the top, left corner of the page and consists of the phrase "Running head:" followed by the ***running head***: a two- to six-word description of your paper's topic.

Be sure your running head follows these rules:

- It is in all capital letters (e.g., "OVERJUSTIFICATION EFFECT").
- It is fewer than 51 characters—and spaces count as characters.
- It includes either the names of the two main variables you discussed (typically joined by the word "AND") or the name of your topic. Ideally, it is either a shortened form of the title (e.g., if the title is "The Evidence Suggests That the Overjustification Effect Is Not Robust," the running head could be "OVERJUSTIFICATION EFFECT") or, if the title is short enough, the title itself.

To finish the page header, just put the page number ("1") near the top, right corner of the page. Thus, if your title was "Intellectual Declines in Old Age: Fact or Artifact," the top of your title page might look like this:[2]

Running head: INTELLECTUAL DECLINES IN OLD AGE 1

You will center the title page's next three components: your paper's title, your name, and your institution's name. You will start each component on a new line and capitalize the first letter of each major word: a word that either has more than three letters or is an adjective, adverb, noun, pronoun, or verb. For example, you would capitalize the verb "Is" and the pronoun "He," but you would not capitalize the articles "a," "an," and "the"; the prepositions "of," "in," and "on"; and the conjunctions "and," "but," and "or."

Begin by putting the title about a third of the way down the page. On the next line, put your name—including your middle initial.[3] On the following line, put your school's name. Thus, the top of your title page might look like this:

---

[2]To type your page header, first go to your word processor's "View" menu and choose "Header and Footer." You will then see the "Header" box. Starting at the left side of the "Header" box, type "Running head:" followed by—in all capital letters—the running head (e.g., "INTELLECTUAL DECLINES IN OLD AGE"). Next, space over to the right. Once you are one space away from the right edge of the box, insert "1" (for page 1). Then, click on the "Page Set Up" button (the icon for the button looks like two pages that are side-by-side) to open the "Page Set Up" window. Then, check the "Different first page" box. Click "OK" to close the "Page Set Up" window. Finally, to return to your title page, go to your word processor's "View" menu and choose "Normal." For more help with using headers, see this book's website (http://www.writingforpsychology.com).

[3]If you go by your middle name, put your first initial, middle name, and last name.

Running head: INTELLECTUAL DECLINES IN OLD AGE 1

Intellectual Declines in Old Age: Fact or Artifact?

Ann A. Student

Alpha University

To verify that you have formatted your title page correctly, do two things. First, compare your title page to the sample paper's title page (2.10). Second, compare your title page to our title page checklist (7.4.6).

2.3.2 Wording the Title

Although the format of your title page is the first thing your reader will see, the title is the first thing your reader will read. Write it last to ensure that it reflects the main point of your paper. In addition to keeping the title focused on your paper, keep the title short: It must capture your paper's essence in fewer than 15 words. Thus, if you were writing a term paper about the influence of psychoanalysis on modern counseling practice, a catchy, brief, and informative title might be "Modern Counseling: Freudian Theory With a New Face."

2.3.3 Writing the Author Note

If your professor wants an Author Note, the bottom of your title page will look like this:

Author Note

Ann A. Student, Department of Psychology, Alpha University.

I thank M. Y. Tutor for guiding my thinking on this topic and I. M. Good for commenting on previous drafts.

Correspondence[4] concerning this article should be addressed to A. A. Student, Department of Psychology, Alpha University, Alpha, CA 97804. E-mail: aastudent@alpha.edu

[4]Indent each of these paragraphs.

As you can see, the Author Note has four parts: (a) the centered heading "Author Note" (this heading starts one double-spaced line below your school's name); (b) the indented "paragraph" consisting of your name, your department's name, and your school's name; (c) the acknowledgments paragraph; and (d) the line starting "Correspondence concerning this article should be addressed to" that is followed by your name, your mailing address, and your e-mail address.

The most important section of your Author Note will be the acknowledgments paragraph. In that paragraph, be sure to disclose (a) who, if anyone, helped you with your paper and (b) what part of your paper, if any, was used in another class.

2.4 Abstract

2.4.1 Writing the Abstract

If your professor requires an Abstract, you must write a one-paragraph summary of your paper. In this paragraph, devote a sentence each to (a) the general topic area, (b) the evidence that supports your thesis, and (c) your conclusion (that your thesis statement is probably true). Do all this in fewer than 151 words.

Wait to write this one-paragraph summary until after you have written the rest of your paper because you will find it easier to write a summary once you have written what it is you are going to summarize. If you are having trouble writing this summary, outline your final draft and then use that outline to guide you in writing your Abstract.

Below your Abstract, indent five spaces and type "*Keywords:*" in italics. After the colon, put words and phrases that (a) might be used as search terms by someone who was trying to find an article on your topic and (b) are in the PsycINFO thesaurus.

2.4.2 Formatting the Abstract

The Abstract is formatted as follows:

- It is page 2 of your paper.
- Its page header consists of the running head—in all capital letters—and the page number.
- Its heading is the centered title "Abstract" typed in a normal (not italicized, not boldfaced, not underlined) font.
- It is one paragraph long.
- It is not indented.
- It is, except for any cases in which a number begins a sentence, free of spelled-out numbers (all numbers, except those that begin a sentence, are expressed using numerals).
- It is followed by a second "paragraph" that is indented five spaces and that starts with "*Keywords:*" and is followed by key words and phrases related to the article. Do not capitalize these key words or phrases. Separate the key words or phrases with commas. Do not put a period after the last key word or phrase.

For an example, see 2.10.

2.5 Introduction

Announce the beginning of the main text of your paper with a new page (page 3 if you have an Abstract, page 2 if you do not) that has, as its centered heading, the title of your paper. The first paragraph on this page should be the beginning of your Introduction.

Like the Abstract, the Introduction should be short. Like the Abstract, the Introduction should be self-contained: People reading your Introduction should understand it even if they have not read any other part of your paper. Despite the similarities between the Abstract and the Introduction, they have different goals: The goal of the Abstract is to summarize the entire paper; the goal of the Introduction is to foreshadow the rest of the paper.

2.5.1 Introduce Generally and Gently

Begin foreshadowing the rest of the paper by introducing your paper's general topic (see Figure 2.2). Your first two sentences should engage the reader. You hope that the reader will be saying, "That is interesting," "That is an important topic," or "I know something about that, and I would like to know more."

To highlight the importance of your issue, you might present either a statistic or an example that illustrates the issue's relevance or prevalence. Your example may also help the reader understand your topic area. If you think the example is not enough to help the reader understand your concept, you may also define your key terms. However, if those definitions will be lengthy or complicated, you may wait until later in the Introduction to introduce your terms (see 2.5.3).

After you make the reader receptive to your general topic, your next step is to make the reader receptive to your specific thesis. You hope the reader will be saying, "That sounds reasonable" or "I never thought about it like that, but that does make sense."

FIGURE 2.2 The Introduction Is Structured Like a Funnel

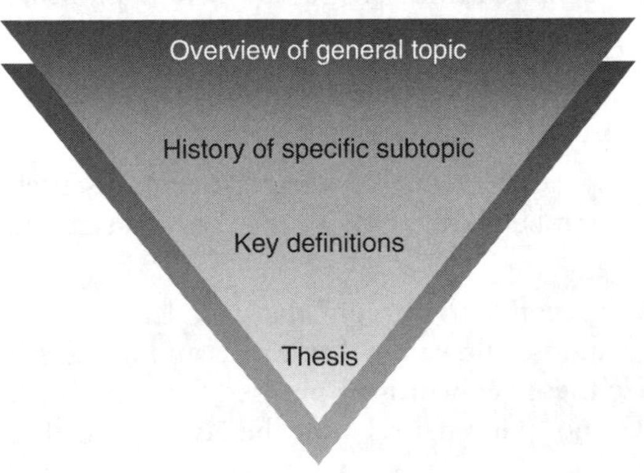

2.5.2 Introduce Key Issues

The way to make readers receptive to your argument is to review the problems with studies, the problems with theories, the conflicting findings, and the conflicting explanations that set up your thesis. A popular and efficient way of highlighting those controversies is to trace, concisely, the history of thought on the particular topic. Be sure to use citations to document this brief history.

Although you will have citations in the Introduction, do not use those citations to introduce specific findings. Instead, use citations only to introduce issues, themes, and alternative approaches to a particular topic. At this point in your Introduction, do not go into specific details about a particular study.

2.5.3 If Necessary, Introduce Key Definitions

No part of your paper should look like a glossary. Therefore, your goal is to provide detailed and clear definitions for only those terms that are central to understanding your thesis. When defining a term that both psychologists and ordinary people use, be sure to use the psychological definition. Otherwise, you will be in trouble, especially if you are using any of the following terms: "experiment," "personality," "random," "reliable," "reinforcement," "intelligence," or "motivation." Thus, if you use a dictionary to define a term, be sure that you are using a psychological dictionary, such as VanderBos's (2007) *APA Dictionary of Psychology*, rather than an ordinary English dictionary (e.g., *Merriam-Webster's online dictionary*).

Often, you can help your reader understand a term (and show your professor you know what it means), merely by going back to the first sentence in which you included the term and, right after the term, inserting a brief definition. Silvia (2007) suggests that the best way to insert such a definition is to separate the definition from the rest of the sentence by enclosing your definition between two *em dashes*—dashes that are as wide as the letter "m"—as we just did.

Provide a definition in a separate sentence or sentences only (a) if the definition of the term is an issue of debate, (b) if there are multiple accepted uses of the term, or (c) if your paper uses a specific definition of a more general term. In such cases, you should probably not merely define the term but also provide one or more examples that illustrate both the concept and its importance.

2.5.4 Introduce and State Your Thesis

Once you have defined key issues and key terms, introduce and present your thesis statement. If you have outlined your paper, you can probably introduce and present your thesis statement by outlining the plan of your paper (e.g., "I will review [this side of the question], then I will review [the other side of the question], to show that [my way of reconciling or combining these two sides—my thesis statement—is the best answer to the question, given the available evidence]."). In short, like a district attorney making an opening statement, you will lay out the case you plan to make.

Just as a district attorney must include the main conclusion (e.g., "the evidence will show that the defendant is guilty") in the opening statement, you must make sure to put your thesis statement in your Introduction. As a last resort, end your Introduction by writing, "In this paper, I will show that [my thesis statement] provides the best explanation of the available evidence." If you include such a sentence, you will not get any style points for how smoothly you introduced your thesis statement, but you will at least get points for putting your thesis statement in your Introduction.

2.5.5 Arouse the Reader's Curiosity

State your thesis, but be sure to state your thesis in a way that arouses the reader's curiosity. To stimulate the reader to think about your thesis, avoid the common mistake of stating your thesis as an established fact. For example, in a paper on the origins of handedness, do not state, "It has been established that handedness is caused by genetic factors (Annett, 2002)." If the reader believes you, the reader should not be interested in reading the rest of your paper. Not only are you saying that the answer to your paper's question is not a subject for debate, but you are also saying that the answer to your paper's question is in Annett (2002). If the reader wants to know more, rather than reading the rest of your paper, the reader should read the definitive source: Annett (2002).

If you had drafted such a thesis statement, you should rewrite it in a way that invites debate and makes the reader want to read your paper to learn your arguments. Thus, you might suggest that you are addressing a controversy—rather than a fact—by writing, "Annett (2002) has argued that handedness is caused by genetic factors; others, however, have suggested that the environment determines handedness (e.g., Collins, 2005)." Alternatively, you might write, "In this paper, I will argue that handedness is caused by genetic factors."

2.6 Body

The Introduction's structure (see Figure 2.2) funnels the reader to the paper's Body. Thus, just as an attorney's opening statement sets up the evidence the jury will hear, your Introduction sets up the Body.

In the Body (well-named because it usually contains at least 75% of your paper's words), fulfill the promises you made in the Introduction. Make the case for your thesis by discussing theories, data, procedures, and criticisms that are relevant to your thesis—and by making sure your reader understands the relevance of what you present. Remember that your main goal is to show how the evidence supports your thesis.

2.6.1 Make the Material Tell a Coherent Story: Have a Theme, Organize Your Notes, and Outline Your Paper

To show how the evidence supports your conclusion, you must do more than merely summarize one study after another. Instead of transcribing your notes into a disorganized and purposeless set of article summaries, you must organize the body of your paper around ideas—not around studies or authors. If you do not already have an organizing theme for your paper, use one of the following six:

1. *Provide a history of the topic*: Trace the development of ideas on the topic from the earliest thinking to the present.
2. *Evaluate solutions:* Pose a problem, set out possible solutions, and then evaluate the pros and cons of each solution.
3. *Evaluate opinions*: Present current opinions on a topic, then evaluate those opinions in light of scientific evidence and theory.
4. *Organize findings around theories*: Present findings that support one theory, then findings that support a second theory.
5. *Question the validity of a theory*: Introduce a theory, discuss evidence for the theory, discuss problems with the evidence for the theory (methodological flaws in the studies, alternative explanations for the evidence), discuss untested assumptions of the theory, discuss findings that refute the theory, and, finally, advocate either revising the theory or replacing it.
6. *Look for methodological differences*: If studies yield conflicting results, compare their procedures to see if methodological differences might account for the different results.

Once you decide on an approach to organizing your paper, organize your notes so that they are consistent with that approach. For example, suppose you have decided to look for methodological differences. Put your notes on studies with results that support your thesis in one stack and put your notes on studies that appear to refute your thesis in another stack. After you have your stacks, use them to construct a table. Your first draft of the table might be little more than two lists representing the two stacks: (a) a list of studies that obtained results consistent with your thesis and (b) a list of studies that obtained results that are not consistent with your thesis. Your second draft will usually be a more complex table, in which you evaluate the studies according to common criteria and list the similarities and differences among them (to see an example, see Exhibit 4.2 in Chapter 4). Your table may enable you to see that the studies supporting your thesis used similar procedures (e.g., studied university students, used the same measure, or used random assignment), whereas all the studies not supporting your thesis used different procedures (e.g., studied high school students, used a different measure, or did not use random assignment). Depending on what you found, you might modify your thesis. For example, you might write, "I argue that [something] is true for university students and that [something else] is true for high school students" or "The studies that support my thesis are more methodologically sound than those that do not support my thesis."

Even if you have an organizing theme (e.g., one of the six themes we listed previously) and an organized set of notes, you need an organized outline before you start to write your paper. Your outline will help you organize your paper in at least five ways. First, your outline will keep you focused on your main ideas. Second, your outline will help you see how your different ideas are connected so that your own thinking on the topic will become clearer. Third, your outline will help you see where—or whether—your notes fit into your paper. Fourth, your outline will help you try out different ways of ordering your points so that when you write your paper, your points are in the best order for making your argument. Fifth, your outline will show you where you will need transitions to connect the different parts of your paper. To see how to outline your paper, see Box 2.1. If you want additional help in organizing and outlining your paper, see Box 1.1 and visit the Chapter 2 section of this book's website.

BOX 2.1 How to Outline a Term Paper

Type the three major sections of your term paper: Introduction, Body, and Conclusions. Next, add subheadings under the relevant headings. In most cases, the start of your outline will look like this:

I. Introduction
   A. Overview of the issue
   B. Preview of the body
   C. Thesis statement
II. Body
   A. Relevant background information
   B. Thesis statement
   C. Evidence in support of the thesis
   D. Refuting or acknowledging evidence against the thesis
   E. Conclusions about the validity of the thesis
III. Conclusion
   A. Summary of body
   B. Current thesis statement (possibly reworded, revised, or qualified based on the evidence presented in the body) is probably correct.

If you start with the preceding outline, you will need to make it detailed enough to guide your writing by (a) modifying the general second-level headings so that they are specific to your paper (e.g., replace "II. B. Thesis statement" with your paper's thesis statement) and (b) adding third and even fourth levels to your outline so that your outline contains the specific points you need to make (e.g., under "D," you might add "D.1" and "D.2," and under "D.2," you might add "D.2.a" and "D.2.b").

To make your outline cover your entire paper, add headings to represent the other major sections of your paper (e.g., Title, Abstract, References). To see how your outline will change as you expand its breadth and depth, compare the general outline you just saw with our sample paper's outline:

I. Title: Intellectual Declines in Old Age: Fact or Artifact?
II. Abstract
   A. Difficult to know whether IQ declines with age because different types of studies obtain different results.
      1. Results from cross-sectional studies suggest IQ declines with age.
      2. Results from longitudinal studies suggest that IQ scores do not decline with age.

BOX 2.1 (*Continued*)

B. Difficult to know which results should be trusted because both types of studies have flaws.
C. Easier to trust studies that use the cross-sequential design—a design that uses both longitudinal and cross-sectional strategies and is superior to either alone.
D. Results from cross-sequential studies suggest that intelligence does not necessarily decline in old age.

III. Introduction: Intellectual Declines in Old Age: Fact or Artifact?
  A. Background
    1. Evidence from cross-sectional studies supports the assumption that intellectual function declines with age.
    2. Evidence from longitudinal studies suggests a less pronounced decline with age.
  B. I will argue that
    1. The designs' different methodological weaknesses are responsible for the different results.
    2. The cross-sequential design is superior to either design.
    3. Cross-sequential designs support the idea that intelligence does not decline substantially with age.

IV. Body
  A. **Cross-Sectional Research**
    1. How to use this design to study the relationship between aging and intellectual performance.
    2. Findings support a decline in IQ with age.
    3. Problem in interpreting the findings: Differences between age groups may be due to cohort effects rather than aging.
  B. **Longitudinal Research**
    1. How to use this design to study the relationship between aging and intellectual performance.
    2. Findings do not support a decline in IQ with age.
    3. Problems in interpreting the findings.
      a. Declines in intellectual function with age could be hidden if low scoring participants dropped out of the study.
      b. Changes in participants' scores over time may be due to environmental changes rather than aging.
  C. **Cross-Sequential Research**
    1. How to use this design to study the relationship between aging and intellectual performance.
    2. Design is superior to cross-sectional (because it rules out cohort effects) and longitudinal (because it rules out time of measurement effects).
    3. Findings do not support a substantial decline in intellectual performance with age.

(*continued*)

BOX 2.1 (*Continued*)

D. **Reinterpreting Past Research**
   1. **Problems with cross-sectional research.**
      a. Unduly influenced by low IQ scores of a few individuals suffering from chronic diseases.
      b. Unduly influenced by cohort effects because age groups differ greatly both in how they were educated and in how much experience they have with tests.
   2. **Problems in measuring intelligence.**
      a. Test items may not be appropriate for older adults.
      b. Younger adults may be more motivated to perform well on IQ tests.
   3. **Problems with speed tests.**
      a. May measure physical speed rather than mental speed.
      b. May measure mental speed (fluid intelligence) but not crystallized intelligence.

V. **Conclusion**
   A. Summary of evidence: Cross-sectional studies show older adults scoring lower than younger adults; cross-sequential studies do not show substantial differences between older and younger adults.
   B. Statement of thesis statement, with appropriate qualifications: Older adults score lower than younger adults on IQ tests but the differences are due not to aging, but rather to (a) cohort effects, (b) motivational effects, and (c) tests that measure fluid rather than crystallized intelligence.

VI. References

2.6.2 Be Both Concise and Precise

As you write from your outline, you will find that although your outline tells you which studies to discuss and when to discuss them, it does not tell you how to describe the studies you are discussing. The key is to be both concise and precise.

You should be concise because you should not describe every aspect of every study. When you include irrelevant details, you risk plagiarizing or needlessly quoting the source—and you risk distracting your reader from your point. Therefore, most of the time, you should highlight only what happened in the study, what was found, and what was concluded.

When describing a study that supports your point, you must be precise because you need to show the reader how that study supports your point—and sometimes you can do that only by producing relevant details. Without those relevant details, you can tell—but not show—the reader that the study supports your point. Telling ("Trust me: I am right") is not nearly as convincing as showing ("See for yourself that I am right").

Showing, rather than telling, is especially important when describing a study that, on the surface, appears to contradict your thesis. The results of such a study can usually be interpreted in many different ways, some of which will be consistent with your thesis. Therefore, you may be able to show that the study, if interpreted properly, does not contradict your thesis. To do so, you need to present enough relevant details so that your readers can see that your interpretation makes sense.

2.6.3 Focus on Facts and Fairness

You want to make strong arguments for your case, but remember that you need to fight fair. Like a crime scene investigator (CSI) testifying in court, you must base your statements on the evidence, consider alternative explanations for the evidence, and be careful not to go too far beyond the evidence.

In everyday life, people often use arguments that are not based on evidence. However, such baseless arguments are inadmissible in court and in a term paper. For example, a judge would object to a CSI using any of the following five tricks:

1. It is true because I feel strongly that it is true (appeal to conviction—how strongly one believes it—rather than to reason): "I really, really feel the defendant is guilty."
2. It is true because most people believe it (appeal to popularity rather than to reason): "Everyone thinks the defendant is guilty."
3. It is true because an authority said so (appeal to authority rather than reason): "A famous prosecutor thinks the defendant is guilty."
4. It is true because a main advocate for the other side is a bad person (attacking the character of the person making the argument—an *ad hominem* attack—rather than the logic of the argument): "The defendant's lawyer is a crook."
5. It is true because our side is morally or intellectually superior (appeal to emotion rather than to reason): "Only a monster would not convict the defendant."

Just as a judge would object to a CSI making arguments not based on logic and evidence, your professor would object to you making such arguments. For example, your professor would object if you wrote any of the following:

1. "Psychoanalysis is correct because I really believe strongly in psychoanalysis."
2. "Psychoanalysis is correct because it is the most rapidly growing division of APA."
3. "Psychoanalysis is correct because Einstein believed in it."
4. "A famous opponent of psychoanalysis was arrested."
5. "You would have to be crazy not to believe in psychoanalysis."

Unfortunately, even if you use facts and logic to support your position, you may still be unfair to the opposing position. To illustrate, if you presented evidence that supported your claim while ignoring the evidence that contradicted your claim, you could make a convincing case for almost any claim, even the following ones: the sun revolves around the earth, the earth is flat, and playing the lottery is a smart way to invest money. Therefore, do not be one-sided: Discuss those inconvenient facts that do not seem to support your position.

2.6.4 Know Your (Facts') Limitations

If you are to be fair, you must stick to all the relevant facts you find. If you are to be accurate, you must stick closely to those facts. Some students, like amateur CSIs, lose credibility by not being careful when interpreting the facts. To be a credible expert, as you will see in the next sections, you must avoid making three types of reckless errors: (a) confusing correlation for causation, (b) overgeneralizing, and (c) making appeals to ignorance.

Correlation is not causality. You can know that two things are related (e.g., depression and television-watching) without knowing the reason for the relationship. The relationship could be due to (a) depression causing one to watch television, (b) television-watching causing one to be depressed, or (c) one of many possible other factors (unemployment, family problems, sleep problems, health problems) causing both depression and television-watching. In such cases, you do not know which possibility is correct: Do not write as though you do know which one is correct.

Generalizing is risky. If you find solid evidence of a relationship, be wary of overgeneralizing those findings. You are supposed to know the risks of generalizing because you are supposed to know that people differ, that situations differ, and that people respond differently in different situations. Therefore, although you can generalize, acknowledge and defend any generalizations you make. For example, suppose the studies you reviewed examined only a certain group (e.g., White, male, university students), but that you are generalizing the results to most people. Your first step would be to acknowledge that because you are generalizing the results to a broader population than was studied, your generalization may be wrong. Your second step would be to defend your generalization, usually by making three related arguments: (a) there are important similarities between the sample studied and the larger population, (b) you do not know of any differences between the studied group and the nonstudied group that would suggest that the findings would fail to generalize to the nonstudied group, and (c) research in related areas tends to generalize from that group to the larger population.

The problem with appeals to ignorance: Failing to find something is not a discovery. If you fail to find evidence of a relationship, remember the saying, "absence of proof is not proof of absence." Put another way, a not guilty verdict is not proof of innocence. Thus, if a study fails to find a relationship between cell phone use and unhappiness, realize that there may be a relationship, but the study failed to find it. Therefore, if you read such a study, do not write, "There is no relationship between cell phone use and unhappiness." Similarly, do not say, "Nobody has disproved psychoanalysis, so it must be true."

2.7 Conclusion

2.7.1 Conclude by Summing Up Your Case

The Conclusion is usually your term paper's closing paragraph, and it will usually parallel your paper's opening paragraphs. In your Introduction, you briefly told your readers what you were going to tell them; in your Conclusion, you will briefly tell your readers what you just told them. Specifically, in one paragraph, review your case by stating your thesis, stating the main evidence for that thesis, explaining how data and criticisms that seem to challenge your thesis do not undermine it, and restating your thesis. Often, the last sentence of your conclusion should essentially say, "I have shown that [my thesis statement] is probably true."

2.7.2 Conclude—Do Not Introduce

Anything you say in the Conclusion must follow logically from the Body of the paper: You are connecting the dots for the reader, but you cannot add any new dots. Therefore, if, as you are writing the Conclusion, you realize that you have left out some important citations or reasons that support your thesis, do not sneak that support into the Conclusion. Instead, go back and insert that support in the Body of your paper. Similarly, if, as you are writing your ending paragraph, you have an insight that leads to a new generalization, you cannot stick that generalization into the Conclusion without rewriting the Body of your paper. Specifically, you will have to insert the citations and reasons that set up your new generalization into the Body of your paper.

To reiterate, you should not sneak new data, new interpretations of previously discussed data, or any other new revelations into your Conclusion. Surprise endings are allowed in mystery stories but not in term papers.

2.8 References

Start the reference list on a new page with the centered heading: "References." All the sources cited in your term paper should appear on this list—with three exceptions. First, do not reference the source if it is a "personal communication" (see 4.3.3) because your reader will not be able to retrieve a conversation you had, a lecture you heard, a letter or an e-mail you read, or an Internet site that you can no longer retrieve. Second, do not reference the original work if you know about it only through a secondary source. Instead, reference only the source you read. For example, suppose the citation in your paper was "Original's study (as cited in Interpreter, 2002)." In that case, you would not put "Original" in your reference list. Instead, you would provide a reference only to "Interpreter"—the source you did read (see 4.3.1). Third, do not reference classic works that are more than 400 years old (e.g., Aristotle's works, the Bible).

Realize that, aside from the three exceptions we just mentioned, the reference list is a list of works you cited. Do not make it a bibliography (a list of works you read). Do not make it a list of suggested readings. Instead, include only those sources that you cited in your paper.

Formatting each reference is tricky. To see examples of acceptable formats for the major reference types and to learn the logic behind formatting references, see 4.10. For an example of how to format your references, see the sample term paper's references (2.10). Once you have each reference properly formatted, you need to make sure each reference is in the right place in your reference list. Looking only at the first author's last name, arrange your references in alphabetical order. Thus, "Alpha, R. T., & Omega, J. B. (2011)" would come before "Omega, J. B., & Alpha, R. T. (2011)." If you need more information on how to put your references in the right order, see 4.10.3.

2.9 Tense

Most of the time, use the past tense (for more information on tense, see 6.1.3). Use the past tense for anything that has a definite date in the past. Thus, when you cite a work published in a given year, you will use the past tense (e.g., "In 2010, Sanders studied"). Use the present perfect tense (e.g., "For many years, researchers have studied") if the activity happened in the past but either (a) cannot be tied to a specific year or (b) is still ongoing. Use the present tense for (a) stating conclusions (e.g., "In conclusion, intelligence does not substantially decline with age.") and (b) anything current, including material in your paper, that you are inviting the reader to consider (e.g., "Cross-sequential designs have two advantages."). Use the future tense when introducing your thesis (e.g., "I will show that").

2.10 Sample Term Paper

On the next few pages, you will find a sample term paper. There are only three aspects of the sample paper that you should not imitate. First, we have used footnotes to make comments so that you can appreciate particular points. In your own term paper, do not use footnotes. Second, we have used only old references so that no one could use this paper in a real class. In your own paper, do not use many old references. Instead, make sure that most of your citations are to recent articles (usually, your professor will want you to use articles published within the past seven years so that your paper is based on up-to-date information). Third, we have not used Times New Roman 12-point font so that the book will cost you less. In your own reports, use Times New Roman 12-point font.

To appreciate this particular term paper, imagine that you were writing a term paper for an adult development and aging course. You narrowed your topic to "Intellectual declines in old age." Your working thesis statement was "Intellectual abilities decline in old age." You found sources by using PsycINFO, *Current Contents*, and *Social Science Citation Index* (see 4.1.1). After reading those sources, you decided your working thesis was wrong. Instead, you now believe that (a) methodological errors may have misled early researchers and (b) old age does not necessarily lead to declines in intellectual ability. You write the Body of your paper, then the Introduction and Conclusion, then the Abstract, title page, and reference page(s). You print out your paper. Then, if your professor allows, you give copies to your friends to get their comments. You write the draft early, so you have some free time before you have to revise, rewrite, edit, polish, and proof it. As a result, when you revisit the draft, you can take a fresh look at it and spot some of the problems a person reading it for the first time might have. You are not under extreme time pressure, so you are calm enough to take your friends' suggestions as helpful advice rather than as hurtful attacks. You use a spelling checker and a grammar checker before printing out the next-to-final version, which you read aloud and proof carefully. You then check your paper against our checklist (2.11), print out a final version, and hand it in on time. You are pleased with your paper—and, when you get it back, you see that your professor is also pleased with it.

Running[5] head: INTELLECTUAL DECLINES IN OLD AGE[6] 1

Intellectual Declines in Old Age: Fact or Artifact?[7]

Ann A. Student[8]

Alpha University

Author Note[9]

Ann A. Student, Department of Psychology, Alpha University.[10]

I[11] thank M. Y. Tutor for guiding my thinking on this topic and I. M. Good for commenting on previous drafts.

Correspondence concerning this article should be addressed to A. A. Student, Department of Psychology, Alpha University, Alpha, CA 97804. E-mail: aastudent@alpha.edu

---

[5]Ann is using APA copy style (also called "APA manuscript format"). If your instructor wants you to use published style (also called "APA final-form format"), see Appendix A. If your instructor asks you to add a cover sheet, do what your professor asks.

[6]Ann was able to verify that her running head was short enough (i.e., it had fewer than 51 characters, including spacing) by using the "Word count" feature of her word-processing software. Note that the running head is in all capital letters.

[7]Note that prepositions such as "in" and conjunctions such as "or" that have fewer than four letters are not capitalized.

[8]If you go by your first name, put your first name, middle initial, and your last name. If you go by your middle name, put your first initial, your middle name, and your last name. Do not put the "written by" or "by" on your title page.

[9]Your professor may not require an Author Note.

[10]We know that this is not a grammatical sentence. However, we are following the format specified by the *Publication Manual.*

[11]Thank anyone who gives you general or editorial help.

Abstract[12]

[13]Researchers using cross-sectional designs found evidence that IQ scores decline with age. Researchers using longitudinal designs, on the other hand, showed that, for healthy participants taking nonspeeded tests, IQ scores do not decline with age. Although both cross-sectional and longitudinal designs have methodological deficiencies, their good points can be combined in a cross-sequential design. An analysis of research using the cross-sequential design confirms that intelligence does not necessarily decline in old age.[14]

Key terms: intelligence, cognitive ability, cross-sequential design, physiological aging[15]

Intellectual Declines in Old Age: Fact or Artifact?[16]

---

[12]The Abstract starts on page 2 and is announced by the centered heading "Abstract." Note that "Abstract" is not boldfaced. To get the correct header on the Abstract and on all subsequent pages, go to page 2 of your document, then go to your word processor's "View" menu and choose "Header and Footer." You will then see the "Header" box. Starting at the left side of the "Header" box, type—in all capital letters—the running head (e.g., "INTELLECTUAL DECLINES IN OLD AGE"). After clicking the "Close" box, go to the "Insert" menu and choose page numbers. Then, choose the "Top of page (header)" and "Position: right" options. Finally, click "okay."

[13]Unlike other paragraphs, the Abstract is not indented (see 2.4). Like the rest of the manuscript, the Abstract is double-spaced.

[14]In 72 words, Ann has introduced the topic, the argument, the evidence, and the conclusion.

[15]Select from two to five terms that are in PsycINFO and relate to your paper's topic.

[16]The Introduction begins on a new page. Its "heading" is the paper's title. Center the title but do not boldface it. Like all of your paper, the Introduction should be double-spaced.

INTELLECTUAL DECLINES IN OLD AGE 3

Growing old involves a decrement in most biological processes (Botwinick, 1973). Some researchers have assumed that growing old also involves a decrement in intellectual function (e.g., Chown, 1972). Research using cross-sectional designs supports this assumption (e.g., Jones & Conrad, 1933). Specifically, Wechsler (1939) thought that intelligence "declines progressively after reaching a peak somewhere between the ages of 18 and 25" (p. 135).[17] Yet studies using longitudinal designs showed a less pronounced rate of decline (e.g., Owens, 1953). I will argue[18] that the two designs' different methodological weaknesses account for why the designs produce different results. Then, I will describe Baltes and Schaie's (1974) technique for combining the two designs into a cross-sequential design that avoids the problems of both the longitudinal and cross-sectional designs (Schaie, 1974). Finally, I will show that the results from studies using the less flawed cross-sequential designs, as well as the results from more flawed designs, are consistent with the view that intelligence does not substantially decline with age.[19]

---

[17]Note the skilled use of quotation to summarize an idea that the writer is going to attack.

[18]Use future tense (e.g., "I will argue") for introducing your argument (see 2.9).

[19]In the opening paragraph, the author has introduced the topic and described what the author plans to prove. The paragraph ends with the author's thesis statement.

Cross-Sectional Research

In the simplest case, cross-sectional researchers compare a group of people of one age (e.g., 45-year-olds) with a group of people of a different age (e.g., 75-year-olds). Researchers using cross-sectional designs have consistently found that older adult groups score lower on IQ tests than younger adult groups (e.g., Jones & Conrad, 1933).

Interpreting the older adult group's lower IQ scores, however, is difficult because of a serious weakness in cross-sectional designs. The weakness, as Botwinick (1967) pointed out,[20] is that the older group is not merely older than the younger group, but also belongs to a different cohort[21] from the younger group. Consequently, with cross-sectional designs, it is hard to separate the effects of age from the effects of generation. In the case of cross-sectional research on IQ, the older group's lower IQ scores are not necessarily due to biological aging. Instead, the older group may score lower because their cohort was less prepared to take IQ tests than the younger cohort was. For example, Botwinick (1967) pointed out that IQ scores are positively

---

[20]Note that Ann used the past tense ("pointed out") rather than the present perfect tense ("has pointed out") because the activity can be tied to a date (1967).

[21]You might wonder why Ann did not use a nontechnical term such as "generation" instead of "cohort" (a term used by developmental psychologists to refer to a group born in a certain year). Ann used "cohort" because it is more precise (a cohort, unlike a generation, usually means that all members are born in the same year). Ann is also demonstrating that she knows an important technical term that her professor would expect her to know.

correlated with amount of education and that younger cohorts receive more education than older cohorts.

Longitudinal Research

Unlike cross-sectional researchers, longitudinal researchers study a single group as it ages. Researchers using longitudinal designs have found[22] little evidence of decline in IQ with age (Bayley & Oden, 1955; Owens, 1953).[23]

Although longitudinal designs avoid confounding age with cohort, they have at least two methodological problems. First, participants with the lowest scores may either die early or refuse to cooperate on subsequent retestings (Riegel, Riegel, & Meyer, 1967). As a result, longitudinal studies may fail to detect age-related declines in IQ. Second, changes observed during the study may be the result of environmental events rather than the result of aging. For example, if the same group of participants performs better on an IQ subtest at 70 years than at 65 years of age, this improvement[24] might be due to aging, but it might be due to new medications, improved nutrition, a new government program, or some other environmental change.

[22]Note the use of present perfect tense ("have found") because the research referred to is continuing.

[23]When you have more than one citation within parentheses, put the citations in alphabetical order and use semicolons to separate citations relating to different authors.

[24]Ann added "improvement" after "this" so that readers would know that "this" referred to improvement.

INTELLECTUAL DECLINES IN OLD AGE 6

Cross-Sequential Designs[25]

To overcome the shortcomings of both cross-sectional and longitudinal designs, Baltes and Schaie (1974) advanced the cross-sequential design. The cross-sequential design starts as a cross-sectional design. Then, researchers add a longitudinal aspect to the study by returning in a few years to retest the groups.

Cross-sequential designs allow the researcher to avoid mistaking either environmental effects or cohort effects for age effects (Mitchell & Jolley, 1988). To illustrate, suppose that both the cross-sectional and the longitudinal parts of a cross-sequential design revealed consistent age-related differences. The longitudinal aspect of the design, in which the researcher compares the same cohort with itself over time, allows the researcher to rule out the possibility that the age-related difference is a cohort effect. The cross-sectional aspect of the design, by allowing the researcher to test the age groups at the same time, allows the researcher to rule out the possibility that the age-related difference is due to recent environmental events. Using the cross-sequential method, Baltes and Schaie[26] (1974) and Schaie and Labouvie-Vief (1974) found

---

[25]Note that (a) subheadings help readers see how the paper is organized and that (b) the heading "Cross-Sequential Designs" is a second-level heading. You can tell it is a second-level heading from its formatting: It is boldfaced and flush against the left margin. To learn more about how to format headings, see 7.2.3.

[26]Note that because the citation is not in parentheses, the two authors' names are joined by "and" rather than by "&."

INTELLECTUAL DECLINES IN OLD AGE 7

virtually no decline in overall intellectual performance with age. Declines were usually limited to tests and subtests in which speed was important.

Reinterpreting Past Research

At first glance, the conclusion that intellectual performance does not decline with age seems to be at odds with previous research. However, one[27] can reconcile this conclusion with past research by considering problems in the following three areas: (a) cross-sectional designs, (b) IQ measurement, and (c) speed tests.[28]

Problems with cross-sectional research.[29] Most evidence for the idea that IQ declines with age comes from the results of cross-sectional studies. However, the results of cross-sectional studies misrepresent the degree to which IQ declines with age because the results of cross-sectional studies are unduly influenced by (a) the low IQ scores of a few individuals suffering from chronic diseases and (b) cohort effects.[30]

Cross-sectional studies provide information about the average IQ of one age group relative to the average IQ of another age group. However, the average IQ of the older age group could be

---

[27]Note the use of "one" because APA style prohibits the use of "you."

[28]This paragraph previews and outlines the next sections. Using the term "speed tests" is an example of the appropriate use of terminology: By using that term, Ann is able to be both concise and precise.

[29]The heading "Problems with cross-sectional research" is a third-level heading. As such, it is boldfaced and indented, ends with a period, and is not capitalized. To learn more about formatting headings, see 7.2.3.

[30]Note how the paragraph prepares the reader for the next two paragraphs.

INTELLECTUAL DECLINES IN OLD AGE 8

unduly influenced by a sharp decline in the performance of a few adults. Riegel and Riegel (1972) made the case that a few individuals in the older age group do suffer such sharp declines and that those individuals' scores mask the fact that most healthy adults do not suffer intellectual declines in old age. Specifically, Riegel and Riegel[31] found that people who die of old age exhibit a complex array of intellectual losses. They named this complex pattern of decline "terminal drop" (p. 306)[32] and detected it up to a year before death (Riegel et al., 1967).[33] They pointed out that if people with terminal drop are included within the older group in a cross-sectional study, those people's low scores would reduce the average IQ of the entire group.

Even if a cross-sectional study includes only individuals whose scores are not declining with age, the older age group may score lower than the younger group because their cohort is, relative to the younger cohort, at a disadvantage on IQ tests. For example, younger people are more likely than older people to have taken an IQ

---

[31]Ann did not follow this reference with a year because (a) she has already provided the year in the earlier reference in this paragraph and (b) she has only one Riegel and Riegel reference, so the reader does not need the year to find the reference in her reference section.

[32]"Terminal drop" is a short quotation, so it is surrounded by quotation marks and followed by the page reference. If Ann had been using "terminal drop" as a technical term rather than as a quotation, she should have italicized it.

[33]Note the use of "et al." Ann can use et al. because this is the second time she has mentioned this study and the study had three authors. Note how tricky the punctuation is (no comma between "Riegel" and "et," no period after "et," but a period and a comma after "al").

test previously (Botwinick, 1967). Furthermore, as Schaie (1974)[34] noted, modern education relies more on problem-solving skills (a major component of intelligence tests) than memory skills, which characterized earlier educational methods.

Problems in measuring intelligence. Another problem that may lead both cross-sectional and longitudinal researchers to overestimate intellectual declines in old age is that IQ tests may not be appropriate for testing older adults. Historically, the function of IQ tests was to predict school performance (Binet & Simon, 1908, as cited in Wechsler, 1939)[35] not to test older adults. Test items involve situations that have little meaning for older adults. According to Schaie (1974), younger people are less fearful of IQ tests and are more highly motivated to do well on IQ tests than older people. These differences in attitudes and motivation—differences that have nothing to do with intellectual ability—may cause older adults to score lower on IQ tests than younger adults (Schaie, 1974).

Problems with speed tests. Older adults are especially likely to score lower than younger adults on IQ tests and subtests in which speed is important. However, there are two problems with interpreting

[34]Note how each major statement of fact is defended with a parenthetical citation (see 4.4.2). The citations not only give credit where credit belongs (thus avoiding plagiarism) but also make Ann's case stronger.

[35]Note the use of a secondary citation (see 4.3.1). This use of a secondary citation rather than the original is excusable because the original article is in French. Ann shows integrity by admitting she did not read Binet and Simon. Note that Binet and Simon do not appear in her reference list.

decreased performance on timed tests as declines in intelligence. First, as Botwinick (1971) pointed out, poor performance on a timed test by older people may represent slowed physical movements and greater susceptibility to fatigue rather than any intellectual decline. Second, mental speed may not be the same thing as intelligence.

Researchers have recognized the problem of what constitutes intelligence. Cattell (1963) differentiated two major kinds of intelligence: (a) crystallized abilities that are maintained with age and are culturally determined and (b) fluid abilities that are innate and subject to the same decrement as other biological processes.[36] Schaie and Labouvie-Vief (1974) showed that crystallized abilities, such as vocabulary and other abilities shaped largely by formal education, increase throughout adulthood but that fluid abilities, such as speed and fluency, decline throughout adulthood.

Conclusion

When researchers compare intellectual performance of widely different age groups, results from traditional cross-sectional studies show older adults to be intellectually inferior to younger adults. When researchers examine age-related changes using the more appropriate

[36]Note how Ann (a) shows that she understands the field's terminology and (b) uses that understanding to make a critical distinction that qualifies her argument. This paragraph will impress her professor.

INTELLECTUAL DECLINES IN OLD AGE 11

cross-sequential design, they find no decisive intellectual decrements over most of the adult life span (Schaie, 1974). I have shown that although older adults might have lower scores on IQ tests than younger adults, their lower scores are primarily due (a) to cohort effects rather than to the effects of age, (b) to attitudinal differences rather than to ability differences, and (c) to items reflecting fluid, rather than crystallized, intelligence.[37]

[37]The Conclusion restates the argument, making appropriate qualifications.

INTELLECTUAL DECLINES IN OLD AGE 12

References[38]

Baltes,[39] P. B., & Schaie, K. W. (1974, July[40]). Aging and IQ: The myth of the twilight years. *Psychology Today,*[41] 10, 35–40.

Bayley, N.,[42] & Oden, M. H. (1955). The maintenance of intellectual ability in gifted adults. *Journal of Gerontology, 10,*[43] 91–107. doi: apa.org/?uid=1956-02583-001

Botwinick, J. (1967). *Cognitive process in maturity and old age.*[44] New York, NY: Springer.

Botwinick, J. (1971). Sensory-set factors in age differences in reaction time.[45] *Journal of Genetic Psychology,*[46] 119, 241–249.

Botwinick, J.[47] (1973). *Aging and behavior.* New York, NY: Springer.

---

[38]Start the reference list on a new page (see 4.10.1) and center the heading ("References"). "References" should not be boldfaced, italicized, or underlined.

[39]In the reference section, the indenting style is the opposite of the indenting for the rest of your paper. Specifically, APA advocates "hanging indent style" in which the first line of a reference is not indented, but additional lines are indented five spaces. To see how to program your word processor to make hanging indents, visit our website.

[40]For a magazine article, put the year, then a comma, and then either the month of publication (for magazines that are published once a month) or the month and day (for magazines that are published more than once a month).

[41]*Psychology Today* is a magazine, not a journal. Your professor will probably require that most of your articles be from journals rather than magazines (see 4.1.3).

[42]Always use a comma between authors' names—even when you have only two authors.

[43]Always italicize volume numbers.

[44]Usually, only the first letter of the first word of a book title is capitalized. The entire title is always italicized.

[45]Usually, only the first letter of the first word of the title of an article is capitalized.

[46]All major words in a journal name are capitalized. (However, major words in a book title are not capitalized.)

[47]Although references are in alphabetical order, in the case of a tie, the more recent references come after the older references.

INTELLECTUAL DECLINES IN OLD AGE 13

Cattell, R. B. (1963). Theory of fluid and crystallized intelligence: A[48] critical experiment. *Journal of Educational Psychology, 54,* 1–22. doi: apa.org/psycinfo/1963-07991-001

Chown, S. M. (1972). The effect of flexibility-rigidity and age on adaptability in job performance. *Industrial Gerontology,*[49] *13,* 105–121. doi: apa.org/?uid=1973-01402-001

Jones, H. E., & Conrad, H. S. (1933). The growth and decline of intelligence: A study of a homogeneous group between the ages of ten and sixty. *Genetic Psychology Monographs, 13,* 223–298. doi: apa.org/?uid=1933-04183-001

Mitchell, M. L., & Jolley, J. M. (1988). *Research design explained* (1st ed.).[50] New York, NY: Holt, Rinehart and Winston.

Owens, W. A., Jr. (1953). Age and mental abilities: A longitudinal study. *Genetic Psychology Monographs, 48,* 3–54.

Riegel, K. F., & Riegel, R. M. (1972). Development, drop, and death. *Developmental Psychology, 6,* 306–319. [51]doi: 10.1037/h0032104

[48]"A" is capitalized because it begins the subtitle.

[49]Note the difference in the rules in capitalization for titles of articles versus the titles of journals, books, or other publications.

[50]The title is italicized, but not the edition.

[51]This article, like most of the articles you will find, has a digital object identifier (DOI). APA requires that you place an article's DOI at the end of the reference. To learn more about DOIs, see p. 150.

INTELLECTUAL DECLINES IN OLD AGE 14

Riegel, K. F., Riegel, R. M., & Meyer, G. (1967).[52] A study of the drop-out rates in longitudinal research on aging and the prediction of death. *Journal of Personality and Social Psychology, 5,* 342–348.

Schaie, K. W. (1974). Transitions in gerontology—from lab to life: Intellectual functioning. *American Psychologist,*[53] 29, 802–807. doi: 10.1037/h0036445

Schaie, K. W., & Labouvie-Vief, G. (1974). Generational versus ontogenetic components of change in adult cognitive behavior: A fourteen-year cross-sequential study. *Developmental Psychology, 10,* 305–320. doi: 10.1037/h0036445

Wechsler, D. (1939). *The measurement of adult intelligence.* Baltimore, MD: Williams & Wilkins.

[52]The fact that this reference occurs after the Riegel and Riegel reference illustrates one rule of alphabetizing: When the first author is the same, look to the second author; if the first two are the same, alphabetize by third, etc. Consequently, all other things being equal, the entry with fewer authors goes first.

[53]The *American Psychologist* is a fine journal meant for a broad audience. It summarizes current thinking and research on a topic. Reading an article from the *American Psychologist* can help you in at least two ways: (a) The article can help you understand a certain theory or issue and (b) the article's reference list can help you identify important articles that you should read. However, your professor may not want you to use the *American Psychologist* because (a) using an article from it may prevent you from doing your own thinking on the topic and (b) reading an article from it, like reading a textbook account, does not allow you to develop skills in understanding and criticizing empirical research. In short, do not base your paper primarily on article(s) from the *American Psychologist* without checking with your professor.

2.11 Checklist for Evaluating Your Paper

☐ My paper addresses the right topic.
- If I was given a question to answer, my paper focuses on answering that question.
- My thesis statement argues that two or more variables are related but is neither an oversimplification nor an overgeneralization (see 2.1).

☐ My paper is well-organized.
- I outlined my paper.
- My paper focuses on the thesis statement.
- My paper's beginning (the Introduction) includes my thesis statement and explains how I will make a case for my thesis statement.
- My paper's middle (Body) portion defends my thesis.
- My paper's end (Conclusion) summarizes the case for my thesis.

☐ I revised all three sections of my paper.
- For the beginning section, I focused on cutting sentences and paragraphs that were not relevant to the main point of my paper.
- For the middle, I emphasized organization: I outlined my paper, reorganized my paper, and re-outlined my paper until I was happy with how the paper was organized. Then, I added subheads and transitions to help readers see how the paper was organized.
- For the end, I worked on (a) making sure that I had not added material that was not set up earlier (sometimes, I cut material from the ending; other times, I added material to the middle section) and (b) cutting irrelevant material.
- I reread my paper, making sure that I could answer, for each paragraph, the question, "How is this paragraph advancing my argument?"
- I made sure there were transitions between each paragraph so that my readers will not say, "What is this paragraph doing here?" and that each paragraph has a clear topic sentence so that my readers will not say, "What is the point of this paragraph?"

☐ My conclusions are based on a balanced and thoughtful consideration of the relevant evidence.
- I found many recent journal articles that were (a) empirical (articles in which authors reported their own research) and (b) related to my topic.
- I presented evidence that supported my thesis statement by paraphrasing, summarizing, critiquing, and synthesizing journal articles (see Chapter 4).

— I addressed evidence that seemed to counter my position.

— I adhered to the standards of academic honesty (see 1.2.4).

☐ I proofed my paper for errors in grammar, spelling, punctuation, and usage (see Chapter 6), as well as for inappropriate and biased language (see 1.3.4).

☐ My paper is free of formatting errors.

— I compared my paper against the checklist in 7.4.

— I cited and referenced my sources according to APA style (for citations, see 4.4–4.6; for references, see 4.10).

— My title page adheres to APA format because I compared my title page to the model in 2.10 and the checklist in 7.4.

2.12 Summary

1. Usually, the first step in writing a term paper or an essay is to choose a narrow topic.
2. After selecting a narrow topic, you should write a *working thesis statement:* a brief, clear statement of what you think your paper will show to be true.
3. In the first section of your paper (Introduction), you will present both your thesis statement and an overview of how you plan to defend it. In the second section of your paper (Body), you will defend your thesis statement. In the third section of your paper (Conclusion), you will summarize your defense of your thesis and then restate your thesis statement.
4. If your professor requires an Abstract, you must write a one-paragraph summary of your paper (see 2.4).
5. The Introduction should foreshadow the rest of the paper.
6. The main challenge many students face when writing the Body of the paper is organizing and integrating the material they have read. If you are having trouble organizing the Body of your paper, see 2.6.1.
7. Anything you say in the Conclusion must follow logically from the Body of the term paper.
8. All the sources in your reference list should be cited in your paper. To see an example of how to format your References, see the sample term paper's References (2.10). To learn more about formatting your reference page, see 4.10.
9. If your professor wants an Author Note, put the Author Note on the title page. Start by typing the heading "Author Note" one double-spaced line below your school's name.

CHAPTER

3

Writing Research Reports and Proposals

In Chapter 2, you learned how to write term papers and essays that synthesize the results of other people's research. In this chapter, you will learn how to write research reports and proposals—papers that, in addition to synthesizing other people's studies, describe studies that you either did or will do.

3.1 General Strategies for Writing Your Paper: Presenting, Writing, and Planning Its Different Parts

Research proposals and reports both require that you adhere to a standard format. For example, a research report must contain the following seven sections in the following order: Title page, Abstract, Introduction, Method, Results, Discussion, and References. (Research proposals, because they are written before data collection, typically lack both Results and Discussion sections.) In addition to these seven sections, research papers often contain one or more of the following three sections: Appendixes, Tables, and Figures. Consequently, many research papers have 10 sections.

3.1.1 Main Headings and Sections: Formatting the Research Paper's 10 Sections

As you can see from Figure 3.1, each of the research paper's 10 major sections begins with a centered heading. The first three sections—Title page (page 1), Abstract (page 2), and Introduction (page 3)—each begins on a new page, as do all the sections that follow the Discussion: References, Appendixes, Tables, and Figures. Only the Method, Results, and Discussion sections do not begin on new pages.

3.1.2 The Value of Writing Your Paper out of Order

Ideal order of writing up a research report. Although we will discuss each of the sections in the order that they should appear in your paper, you probably should write the sections in a different order. For example, suppose you are writing a report on a study you did. It is easiest to start with the Method section because (a) you can write it before you have even started analyzing your data, (b) all you have to do is describe what was done in the study, and (c) you can write it while the details of what you did are still fresh in your mind.

After writing the Method section, you may want to write the Introduction, a section that examines what is known about the research problem and that should set up both the Method and Discussion sections. Then, you may want to write the Results section. In the Results section, you should focus on whether the data supported the hypothesis. Having written the Introduction and Results sections, you should have a relatively easy time writing the Discussion, in which you discuss implications of the results.

Once you have written the body of your paper, write the Abstract, which summarizes the paper. Next, write the title, which summarizes the Abstract, and type up the Title page. If you then add the References, the Appendixes (if you have any), and all the tables and figures that you refer to in your paper (if you have any), you have completed your rough draft.

Ideal order of writing up a research proposal. If, on the other hand, you are writing a research proposal, write the Introduction first: Once you have described what hypothesis you plan to test, you can describe how you will collect data to test that hypothesis (the Method section), and, if your professor wants, you can describe how you will analyze those data (the Results section). Next, write the first sections of your paper: the Abstract, Title, and Author Note. Finally, complete your paper's first draft by writing the end parts of the paper: the References and any other end material (Appendixes, Tables, Figures) that you have.

3.1.3 The General Plan of Your Paper

Regardless of the order in which you write the paper, you should understand the structure of a research paper (see Figure 3.2). The structure of the Introduction is like a funnel. The wide mouth of this funnel represents the beginning of the Introduction. In this beginning section, rather than introduce your specific research question, attract the reader by highlighting interesting aspects of the broader topic. As you highlight

FIGURE 3.1 The Research Paper's Main Section Headings (Centered) and Subsection Headings (Flush left, Boldfaced)

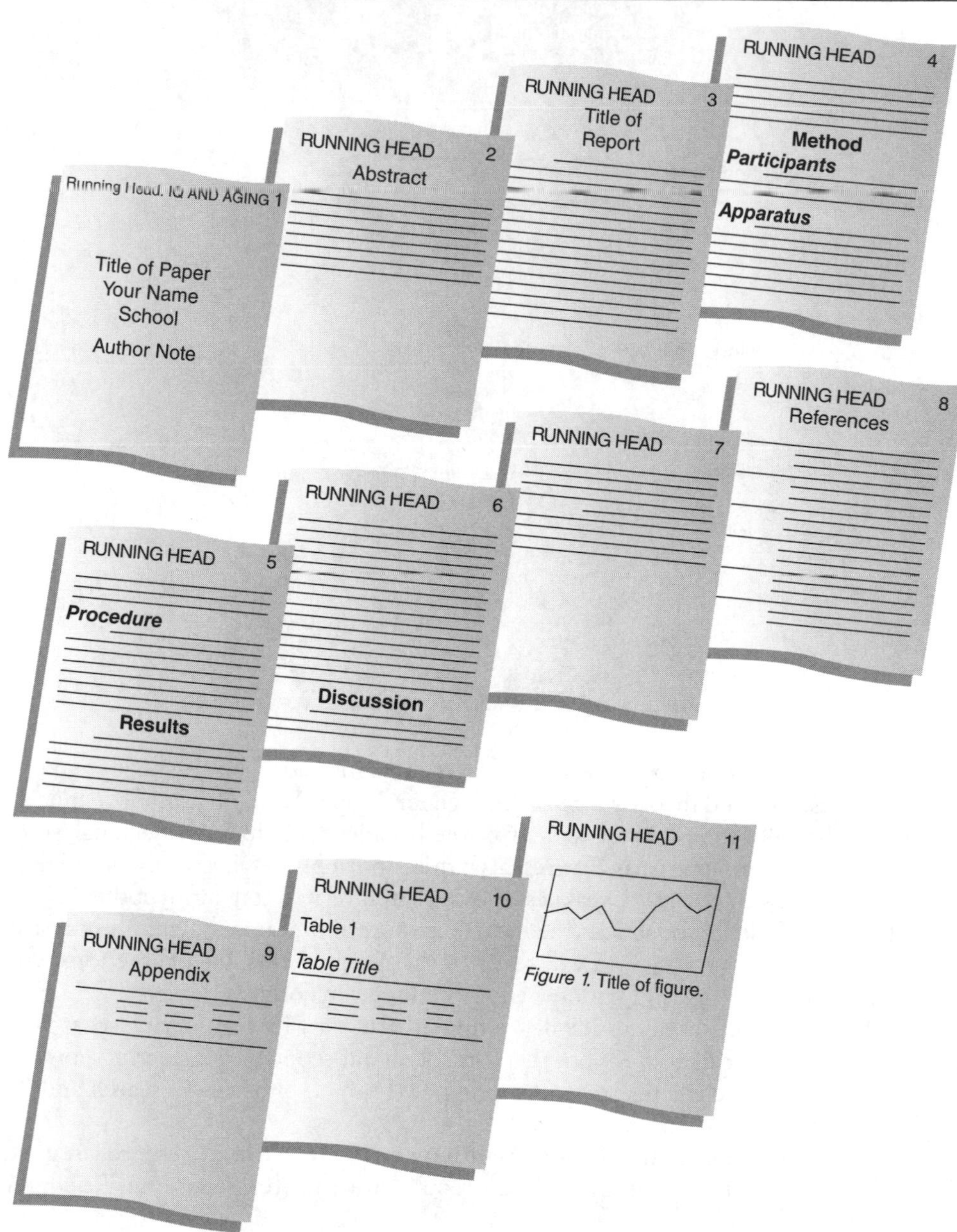

FIGURE **3.2** The Basic Structure of a Research Paper
© Cengage Learning 2013

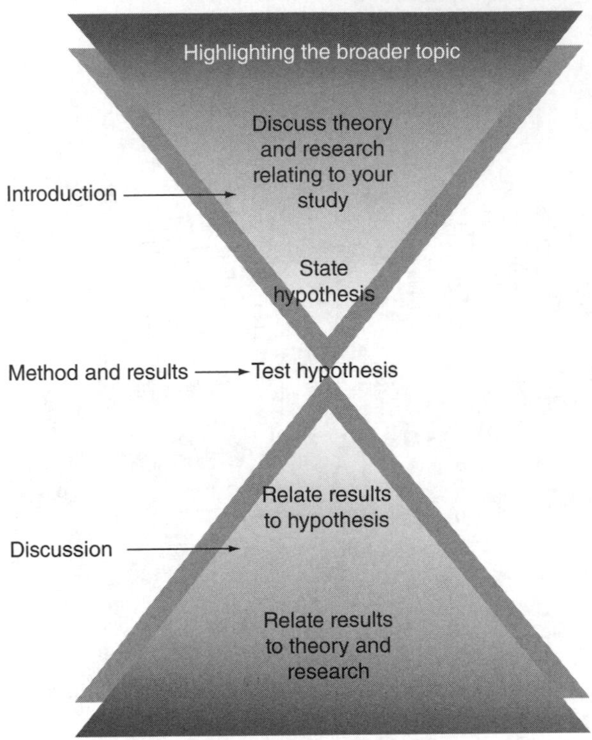

the broader topic, do not critique studies or theory; instead, do little more than cite important research and theory related to that general topic. Your job is to move quickly but gracefully from the general overview of the broader topic to a detailed analysis of what is known about your particular research question. This detailed analysis will usually focus on the strengths and weaknesses of research related to your hypothesis.

At the end of the Introduction (the narrowest part of the funnel), you must clearly state the specific hypothesis you will test.[1] In the Method and Results sections, you focus narrowly on the specifics of how you tested your hypothesis.

The Discussion is like an upside down funnel. You start by considering what your results mean for your hypothesis but then broaden your scope by considering how the results of your study challenge, extend, or support both (a) published research and (b) published theories.

Whereas using the funnel analogy will help you write a solid research report, Roediger's (2007) story analogy will help you write an interesting one. Roediger

[1]In some cases, rather than concluding your Introduction by stating your hypothesis, you might merely state a research question.

stresses that the key to writing a good research paper—like the key to almost any good writing—is to tell a good story. He says you should start your story with an interesting or important phenomenon, discuss possible ways to make sense of that puzzling phenomenon, make a case for one explanation being the most likely, describe a clever test of that explanation, and reveal the results of your test. Roediger suggests you end your story by explaining (a) how the results help us make sense of this previously puzzling phenomenon and (b) why we will all be better off because you did this work.

To see how you can use this advice to write a research report, imagine a class exercise that starts with you and your classmates reading four adjectives that supposedly describe a person. Unknown to you, some of your classmates have been randomly assigned to get the adjectives in this order: humorous, cold, intelligent, and polite; whereas others have been randomly assigned to get the adjectives in a different order: cold, intelligent, polite, and humorous. After reading the adjectives, students individually rate how much they like the person described by those adjectives. Then, the professor leads a discussion about the study. As a result of this discussion, you realize that (a) the independent (manipulated) variable was the position of "humorous" in the list (first vs. last), (b) the dependent (measured) variable was how much participants liked the described person, and (c) the experimental hypothesis was that a person will be liked more when a favorable adjective describing the person comes first in a list than when the same adjective comes last in a list. In the next few sections, we will look at how you would write a report on such a study.

3.2 Formatting the Title Page, Wording the Title, and Writing the Author Note

3.2.1 Formatting the Title Page

As you can see from Figure 3.1, page 1 of your paper should be the Title page. The Title page contains four components: the header, your paper's title, your name, and your school's name. In addition, the title page may also contain the "Author Note."

The title page's header has two parts. The first part starts in the top, left corner of the page and consists of the phrase "Running head:" followed by the ***running head***: a two- to six-word description of your paper's topic.

Be sure your running head follows these rules:

- It is in all capital letters (e.g., "PRIMACY EFFECTS").
- It is fewer than 51 characters.
- It includes either the names of the two main variables you studied (typically joined by the word "AND") or the name of your topic. If the title is short enough, the title could be the running head. More often, the running head is a shortened form of the title. For example, if the title is "The Primacy Effect in Impression Formation," PRIMACY EFFECTS could be the running head.

The second part of the page header is the page number ("1"). It should be near the top, right corner of the page. Thus, if your title was "The Primacy Effect in Impression Formation," the top of your title page could look like this[2]:

Running head: PRIMACY EFFECTS 1

Alternatively, the top of your title page might look like this:

Running head: DESCRIPTOR ORDER ON LIKING RATINGS 1

You will center the title page's next three components: your paper's title, your name, and your institution's name. Start each component on a new line and capitalize the first letter of each line and of each *major word*: a word that either has more than three letters or is an adjective, adverb, noun, pronoun, or verb. (Thus, do not capitalize the articles "a," "an," and "the"; prepositions such as "of," "in," and "on"; and conjunctions such as "and," "but," and "or.")

Begin by putting the title about a third of the way down the page. On the next line, put your name—including your middle initial. On the following line, put your school's name. Thus, the middle third of your title page might look like this:

The Primacy Effect in Impression Formation

Ann A. Student

Alpha University

To verify that you have formatted your title page correctly, do two things. First, compare your title page to the sample paper's title page (3.11). Second, compare your title page to our title page checklist (7.4.6).

3.2.2 Wording the Title

Although the format of your title page is the first thing the reader will see, the title is the first thing your reader will read. The title should be tantalizing enough to lead the reader on to the next, more substantial morsel: the Abstract. To keep the reader's attention, the title should be both short—no longer than 12 words—and informative: It should summarize the main point of the report and identify the crucial variables or issues. Thus, if you are reporting on an experiment, your title should contain both the independent variable(s) and the main dependent variable.

---

[2]Specifically, go to the "View" menu of your word processor and select "Header and Footer." On the left side of the header box, type "Running head:" followed by, in all capital letters, your running head. Then, near the right edge of the box, insert the page number by selecting (from the "Insert" menu) the "insert page number" command. Then, click on the "Page Setup button" (it looks like a book) and select the box titled "Different front page." Then, go to your second page and delete "Running head:"—and, if necessary, space your page number back to the right. Now that you have formatted your headers, return to the text of your paper by choosing "Normal" under the "View" menu.

To practice judging titles, suppose you had written the following four titles for our example experiment:

- ✗ An Investigation of a Psychological Phenomenon
- ✗ Influences on Liking Ratings
- ✔ Effects of Descriptor Order on How Much a Person Is Liked
- ✔ Favorable First Descriptors Produce Favorable Impressions

Which title did you prefer? The last title is perhaps the best of the four because it communicates the most about the results of the experiment. The third title, however, is the most common sort of title, and its small mystery (what was the effect?) may make it more tantalizing.

Note that because this study was an experiment, you can and should put words in your title that reflect cause-effect relationships such as "affect," "influence," and "impact." If, however, you do a correlational study, you should not use such words. Instead, you should stick to words—such as "association" and "relationship"—that do not imply a cause-effect relationship. (If you are not sure why you need to be careful about claiming that you have established a cause-effect relationship, see 5.6.1.)

3.2.3 Writing the Author Note

If your professor wants an Author Note, the bottom of your title page will look like this:

Author Note

Ann A. Student, Department of Psychology, Alpha University.

I thank M. Y. Tuder for guiding my thinking on this topic and I. M. Goode for commenting on previous drafts.

Correspondence concerning this article should be addressed to Ann A. Student, Department of Psychology, Alpha University, Alpha, CA 97804. E-mail: an@al.edu

As you can see, the Author Note has four parts: (a) the centered heading "Author Note" (this heading starts one double-spaced line below your school's name); (b) an indented "paragraph" consisting of your name, your department's name, and your school's name; (c) the acknowledgments paragraph; and (d) the line starting "Correspondence concerning this article should be addressed to" that is followed by your name, your mailing address, and your e-mail address.

For your papers, the most important section is the acknowledgments section. In that section, be sure to disclose (a) who, if anyone, helped you with your paper and (b) what part of your paper, if any, was used in another class.

3.3 Abstract

3.3.1 Writing the Abstract

The Abstract is a short (although some publications allow the Abstract to be 250 words, many publications and professors insist that it be fewer than 151 words), one-paragraph, self-contained summary of your report. Start the Abstract by stating the research hypothesis or question. Then, if you are writing a research report, describe the number, gender composition, and age of the individuals you tested; the design and procedures; the main results of your statistical tests; and the main conclusion. If you are writing a research proposal, describe the number, gender composition, and age of the participants or subjects to be tested; the design and procedures; how you plan to analyze your data; and how you will be interpreting your results.

Some writers omit some of required information, as in the following case:

✗ Based on the primacy effect in serial recall, it was hypothesized that a target person would be better liked when positive information was presented first rather than last. This hypothesis was tested in a simple experiment in which half the participants were exposed to a description of a person that began with an extremely positive adjective whereas the other half received the identical description except that the positive adjective ended the description. Consistent with the hypothesis, participants whose descriptions began with a highly favorable adjective rated the described person as more likeable than participants who learned the favorable adjective last. The results are consistent with the primacy effect being due to participants' assumptions about the order in which people present descriptive information.

Although the previous example is consistent with both what you will find in journals and with the sample Abstract in the *Publication Manual*, it is not consistent with the guidelines on page 26 of the *Publication Manual*. Specifically, it does not contain detailed numerical information about the number, gender composition, and age of the sample; and it does not contain details about the results of statistical tests. The advantage of omitting specific numerical information from the Abstract is that it allows room to provide a broad overview of the study. However, as you can see from the 108-word sample Abstract that follows, you can provide your readers with a general overview of a study, supplement that overview with the specific details necessary to meet the *Publication Manual's* guidelines, and still stay within a 150-word limit.

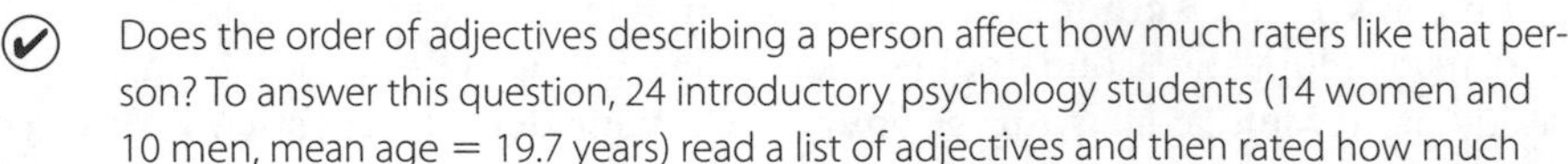

✓ Does the order of adjectives describing a person affect how much raters like that person? To answer this question, 24 introductory psychology students (14 women and 10 men, mean age = 19.7 years) read a list of adjectives and then rated how much

> they liked the described person. Participants were randomly assigned to 2 groups. Those receiving "humorous" as the first adjective in a 4-item list rated the person as more likeable than those receiving the identical list except with "humorous" last, $t(22) = 5.62, p < .001, d = 1.17$. The results are consistent with the explanation that the primacy effect is due to participants assuming that people present the most important descriptive information first.

You should wait to write your Abstract until after you have written the rest of your report because it is easier to write a summary of something you have written than of something you have not written. Once you have written your report, you can produce a draft of the Abstract by stringing together the following seven sentences:

1. the sentence from the Introduction that states the hypothesis;
2. the sentence from the Participants section that states the number of participants and describes any other relevant participant characteristics (e.g., age, gender);
3. the sentence from the Materials or Procedure section that describes the dependent measure task;
4. the sentence from the Method section that states what research design you used (e.g., a survey, a simple experiment, a factorial experiment);
5. the sentence from the Procedure that outlines the manipulation (if you had a manipulation);
6. the sentence from the Results that states whether the results supported the hypothesis (e.g., the sentence that starts, "As hypothesized"); and
7. the sentence from the Discussion that summarizes what the findings mean for theory, previous research, or real life (e.g., the sentence that starts, "These findings suggest" or "These findings have implications for").

You can often condense the first three sentences into one by following this model: To test the hypothesis that [insert hypothesis], [insert number] participants ([insert number] men and [insert number] women) did [describe or name the dependent measure task]. For example, O'Shea, Moss, and McKenzie (2007, p. 36) wrote, "To test the hypothesis that exposure to violence on television promotes mistrust of strangers, participants (24 men and 24 women) rated the extent to which a stranger in a photograph seemed hostile." You may even be able to condense the first four sentences into one by writing, "In a [insert name of design, such as simple experiment], [insert number] participants ([insert number] men and [insert number] women; M_{age} = [insert average age], *SD* = [insert standard deviation of ages]) were measured on [describe or name the dependent measure task] to test the hypothesis that [insert hypothesis]."

In short, although you have some flexibility in how you write your Abstract, you must include four elements. First, you must state the hypothesis that you tested. Second, you must state how you tested that hypothesis (what design you used, who you studied, what you did to them [the manipulation], and what they did [the dependent measure task]). Third, you must state whether your results supported that hypothesis—and include key statistics such as *p* values that back up that statement. Fourth, you must briefly state what your results mean in the larger scheme of things—or promise that your paper will discuss your study's importance (e.g., "The importance of these results for theory and practice are discussed").

3.3.2 Keywords

Below your Abstract, indent five spaces and type "*Keywords*:" in italics. After the colon, put words and phrases that (a) might be used as search terms by someone who was trying to find an article on your topic and (b) are in the *PsycINFO* thesaurus. You can get these terms by (a) remembering the search terms you used to find studies related to yours and (b) putting key words from your title and Abstract into the *PsycINFO* thesaurus. (To learn how to use search terms and *PsycINFO*, see 4.1.1.)

3.3.3 Finishing and Formatting the Abstract Page

Begin the Abstract on page 2. Give that page the centered heading "Abstract" and follow that heading with an unindented paragraph. Without exceeding 250 words, provide a complete, self-contained summary of your report. Avoid making the following formatting mistakes: (a) indenting the Abstract, (b) making the Abstract longer than a paragraph, (c) single-spacing the Abstract, (d) boldfacing the title "Abstract," and (e) not properly formatting the keywords section (for help on the keywords section, see 3.3.2).

If you are still unsure about how to format your Abstract, see 2.4. In addition, consult the model in 3.11 and the checklist in 3.12.

3.4 Introduction

Begin the Introduction at the top of page 3. Announce it by using its centered heading: your paper's title. Do not make the mistake of using the word "Introduction" as its heading.

In the Introduction, you must first introduce the general research area and then your specific hypothesis. As readers read the first sentence, they should be saying, "Yes, I know about that." As they read the rest of the first paragraph, they should be thinking, "Yes, that is an interesting and important research area." As they move through the rest of the Introduction, they should be thinking, "That hypothesis makes sense. It really should be tested. I wish I had thought of that hypothesis."

In addition to preparing readers for your hypothesis, you are also trying to prepare readers for your way of testing the hypothesis. If you prepare them well, when they read the **Method** section, they will think, "Yes, that is a good way to test the hypothesis."

To write a good Introduction, you must make the case for your hypothesis (O'Shea et al., 2007). Many students fail to make a good case for their hypothesis because their Introduction is either too short to do the job (usually, you will need at least two pages) or too disorganized. You, however, can avoid such problems by taking two steps:

1. To organize your introduction, outline it (for sample outlines see Box 3.1 and our website). If you are still having trouble organizing it, refer to section 2.6.1's hints on organizing essays and term papers.
2. To have enough of the right content, follow the advice in the next sections.

3.4.1 Introduce the General Topic

Do not start your Introduction by discussing your specific hypothesis. Instead, devote your first paragraph to convincing the reader that the general topic is important. If you are having trouble writing that paragraph, try to start it with a sentence resembling one of the following.

- People often feel [insert name of your topic].
- [insert name of your topic] is a major problem in [insert name of your country].
- Because [insert name of your topic] often has an effect on people, . . .
- Despite centuries of interest in [insert name of your topic], researchers have not yet identified . . .
- [insert name of your topic] is a core assumption of [insert name of a theory].
- Although more than 100 studies have examined [insert name of your general topic], researchers have paid little attention to [your particular aspect of that topic].

3.4.2 Review Relevant Research and Theory

In the first paragraph, you introduced the reader to your paper's topic by showing how the general topic relates to what the reader already knows. In the second paragraph, you gently take the reader's hand and guide him or her down the path to your study by summarizing the major research and theory bearing on the specific question you are going to study. To avoid startling your reader, move slowly, explain where you are going, and use examples and simple words before—or while—you present technical terms and theories.

To gain your reader's trust, show that you know what you are doing by finding and citing articles that will put your study in context (for tips on how to find such studies, see 4.1; for information on how to cite those articles, see 4.4–4.5). Ideally, you should establish your expertise by citing three types of research on the topic: the first study, the most important studies, and the most recent studies (Wegner, 2007). If, however, no studies relate to your specific topic, cite studies that relate to the general research area.

If you follow the advice in Chapter 4, you will probably be able to find enough related studies; the trick is presenting the studies in a way that tells a story. One way to organize this section is to describe a study that describes a relationship between two variables (e.g., cell phone use and unhappiness), to discuss possible explanations for why the variables are related (e.g., unhappiness may lead to cell phone use, cell phone use may lead to unhappiness, or insecurity may lead to both unhappiness and cell phone use), and to point out that research is needed to identify which explanation is more likely to be correct. The more general approach is (a) to discuss the relationship between what has been found and what relevant theories would have predicted, (b) to explain how previous research—because it was flawed, obtained conflicting results, or failed to investigate a key question—has left a gap in our knowledge that must be filled, and (c) to show how your study fills that gap. You might begin one of your paragraphs in this section with a topic sentence that resembles one of the following:

- To date, existing research has been correlational. Thus, it has not been possible to determine whether [insert name of your independent variable] and [insert name of your dependent variable] are causally related.
- [insert name of your first independent variable] and [insert name of your second independent variable] have been studied separately, but previous research has never examined how they operate together to affect [insert name of your dependent variable].
- What is striking, however, is the extent to which data revealing ____________ differences derive almost exclusively from ____________ (a single research paradigm, a limited sample of participants, laboratory studies, one specific measure, etc.).
- If [insert name of theory] is true, one can predict [insert your hypothesis].
- Existing research has not tested whether [insert name of variable] moderates the effect.
- Existing research has not tested the theory's assumption that ____________ is true.
- Despite growing research in [insert name of your topic], all researchers implicitly assume that [insert untested assumption].
- Almost all previous research has assumed a linear relationship between [predictor variable] and [outcome variable].
- However, systematic research on [your specific topic] is lacking.
- With one notable exception, there have been no studies of [your specific topic].
- Little research has been done on [your specific topic].
- Although there is much research on [general topic, related topic], there is very little research on [your specific topic].
- Existing research has failed to distinguish between several possible explanations for these results.
- An often overlooked explanation for these findings is [your hypothesis].
- Existing research has not studied ____________ population.
- Existing research has failed to make a distinction between types of ____________.
- However, [last names of the study's author(s)] study did not allow a direct test of this hypothesis because ____________.
- The studies that find ____________ are flawed because ____________.
- The findings with respect to ____________ have been inconsistent. The inconsistencies may be due to methodological problems with the studies that find ____________.

The focus of your literature review should be on showing how past studies relate to, make a case for, and demand your study. You will show that those other studies have—or should have—used your procedures and have—or should have—obtained results consistent with your predictions.

As you write and revise your Introduction, take two steps to maximize the chances that your reader benefits from your Introduction. First, think about your hypothesis and your study; then follow Meyer and Meyer's (1993) advice: "put yourself in the reader's place and ask: What would I need to know. What would I want to know?" (p. 76). Following this advice will often lead you to delete much of your Introduction.

Second, think about what you want your reader to be thinking. As your professor reads your literature review, you want your professor to be thinking the following:

"The research cited in the literature review clearly relates to the student's hypothesis."

"This student is summarizing and commenting on—rather than quoting from—research articles."

"This student has read and understood the recent research."

"I see why this hypothesis is important and worth testing."

"This student, like a good prosecutor, has a made a convincing case that leaves little room for objections: The facts that are presented are relevant and backed up with citations to reliable sources, and when opinions are presented, those opinions are stated as opinions (rather than being passed off as fact) and are supported by logic and facts." Keeping these thoughts in mind will help you include critiques of relevant research and remind you to explain how those critiques are relevant to your study.

3.4.3 Introduce the Hypothesis

Your literature review should lead readers to your Introduction's climax: your hypothesis. Even before you state the hypothesis, the reader should know what the hypothesis is, how your hypothesis follows logically from past research and theory, and why it is important to test your hypothesis.

As you prepare your Introduction, adopt the mindset of a prosecuting attorney preparing an opening statement. Begin by asking, "What would help the audience see how I came to my conclusion?" Then, just as a prosecuting attorney should spell out how logic and evidence lead to the conclusion that the defendant is guilty, you should spell out how logic and evidence lead to the conclusion that your hypothesis is a reasonable and important one.

Like the prosecutor, you must state your conclusion. For the attorney, the conclusion is that the defendant is guilty; for you, the conclusion is your hypothesis. As you can see from the following hypotheses, a hypothesis is a prediction about how a measured variable is related to one or more other variables.

- Visual acuity will improve with increases in lighting level.
- When a person thinks that several others have witnessed an accident, the person will be slower to give help than when the person thinks he or she is the sole witness.
- Adults over age 65 in good health will score better on the XYZ test of crystallized intelligence than adults between the ages of 25 and 35.
- Performance on the ABC test of IQ will predict school performance.

To introduce your hypothesis, use words such as, "In view of [the logic and research findings I outlined earlier], I predicted that [my hypothesis]," or "If [the logic I spelled out earlier] is the case, it should follow that [my hypothesis]." When you state your hypothesis, be specific about which variables are involved and about whether you are making a cause-effect hypothesis.

After you introduce the hypothesis, you could provide an overview of how you plan to test it; doing so would provide a preview of the next section of your report: the Method section (Bem, 1987). That is, just as you want to show that your hypothesis makes sense, you will probably want to show that your way of testing it makes sense. For example, if you are testing a cause-effect hypothesis, you would point out that you are using a method that allows you to test a cause-effect hypothesis: an experiment. However, previewing the Method section is optional; what is mandatory is that your Introduction leaves your reader with clear answers to these four questions:

1. What was the hypothesis? Note that your hypothesis must be testable. Therefore, you must predict a relationship, not an absence of a relationship (to understand why, see 5.6.2).
2. Why would anyone think that the hypothesis would be supported?
3. What does this study have to do with previous research or theory?
4. Why is it important to do this study?

3.5 Method

You use the Introduction to explain why you conducted your study; you use the Method section to describe how you conducted (in a research report) or will conduct (in a research proposal) your study. In this "how to" section, do not describe everything you did or plan on doing. Instead, describe your procedures in just enough detail that a casual reader could evaluate your study and an experienced researcher could replicate your study. To avoid boring both audiences, omit details such as, "I recorded participant's responses using a number two pencil." In addition, to avoid boring the casual reader, omit details that are necessary only for replicating the study. Instead, refer the reader who wants those details to other sources that provide those details, such as your Appendix or, if possible, other articles.

Start the Method section one double-spaced line below the Introduction. Label it with the centered, boldfaced heading: "**Method**." Divide the Method section into its appropriate subsections, such as one describing participants and one describing procedures.

Start each subsection with a label (e.g., "**Participants**") that begins at the far left margin and is boldfaced. If any of these labels consist of more than one word (e.g., "Apparatus and Stimuli"), capitalize the first letter of each major word.

If you subdivide one of those subsections into smaller subsections (e.g., you subdivide a "**Measures**" subsection into "**Personality tests**" and "**Physiological measures**"), start each of those smaller subsections with a label (e.g., "**Personality tests**") that is indented and boldfaced with only the first letter of the label capitalized (see 7.2.3). Be sure to end that label with a period and to start the next sentence immediately after that period.

Make sure to use complete sentences. One mistake that beginning writers often make is treating a section's heading as if it were the beginning of the first sentence of that section. As a result, the first line of their "**Participants**" section might be the incomplete sentence: "were 20 students." To avoid making that mistake, write complete sentences that repeat the information contained in the headings. For example, follow the heading "**Participants**" with the complete sentence: The participants were 20 students.

3.5.1 Participants or Subjects

Usually, you should devote the first subsection of your Method section to describing your sample. You are answering the questions: Who were these individuals, and how did they get into your study? Specifically, you should describe (a) the general characteristics (e.g., how many women, how many men, average age, range or standard deviation of ages) of the individuals you studied or plan on studying, (b) when, where, and how you recruited and selected those individuals, and, if applicable, (c) how you assigned those individuals to different conditions. In this first subsection, provide information that will help (a) researchers who want to repeat your study, (b) reviewers who want to be sure your study was conducted ethically, and (c) readers who want to evaluate how representative your sample was. The way you write and label this section depends on whether you studied a sample of humans or a sample of nonhuman animals.

If you studied people who gave informed consent to participate in the study, label this section "**Participants**" and refer to the individuals you studied as "participants." Although the editors of the latest edition of the APA Manual have allowed you to call such participants "subjects," you should probably reserve the term "subjects" for individuals who are incapable of giving informed consent (e.g., children and nonhuman animals).

State how many participants you studied, how many were women, and how many were men. State the average age of the participants, as well as either the age range or standard deviation. You may need to provide additional background information about the participants (e.g., ethnicity, religion, political affiliation, socioeconomic status, visual acuity) if (a) you are doing an analysis using one of those background variables or (b) that information is necessary for assessing the generalizability of your results.

To give the reader the ability to evaluate the representativeness of your sample and the ability to replicate your study with an equivalent sample, you must do more than describe the characteristics of your sample. You must also describe (a) how you selected your sample (e.g., "were a random sample of university students" or, more commonly, "were students in an introductory psychology class"); (b) where the participants came from and when you studied them (e.g., "Participants were students at Clarion University during the Fall 2012 semester"); (c) any requirements potential participants had to meet (e.g., "had to be native English speakers"); and (d) what incentives, if any, you used to encourage participation (e.g., participants received money, received extra credit, received no compensation). In addition, either here or in the Results section, you must state (a) the number of participants who dropped out, (b) the number of participants whose data you excluded from analysis, and (c) the reasons for these dropouts and exclusions.

If you divided your participants into different groups, describe how you made these assignments. You may include this information at the end of the **Participants** subsection, in a **Design** subsection, or in the **Procedure** subsection—just be sure to include it. For example, in a simple experiment, you would state that you randomly assigned participants to groups; in a correlational study, you might state that you assigned participants who scored above a certain score to one condition and those who scored below that score to the other condition.

If, rather than studying adults, you studied or propose studying individuals incapable of giving informed consent, use "**Subjects**" as the heading for this section. In the case of children, provide the number of subjects, their ages and sexes, and how their involvement in the study was negotiated (usually with the informed consent of each child's parents or guardians). In the case of animals, provide the number of subjects, their ages, sexes, and weights as well as the species name, strain, and supplier. Describe how you treated these animals: how much they were handled, their feeding schedules, the temperature of their environment, and the lighting conditions. In addition, provide any other information about how you treated your subjects that would be necessary to replicate the study.

Whether you had participants or subjects, provide assurances that you conducted the study ethically. If the experiment involved individuals from whom informed consent is difficult or impossible to obtain (such as children or animals), you should state the ethical standards under which the study was conducted. For example, if you had read APA's ethical principles, you might include the following statement:

> Animals were treated in accordance with the American Psychological Association's ethical code (American Psychological Association, 2002).

Often, authors suggest that participants were treated ethically by stating that participants were volunteers. However, according to the Publication Manual, authors must state, rather than merely suggest, that participants were treated ethically. Thus, for our example study, a Participants section might look like the following:

> **Participants**
>
> Participants were 24 students (14 women and 10 men; $M_{age} = 19.34$, $SD_{age} = 2.11$; 88% White) enrolled in an introductory psychology class at Clarion University in Spring of 2012 who volunteered as part of a class exercise. Participants were randomly assigned using a random number table to one of two conditions. All participants were treated in accordance with the American Psychological Association's ethical code (American Psychological Association, 2002).[3]

3.5.2 Apparatus

If you used (or plan to use) equipment to present or record information (e.g., computers, slide projectors, or stopwatches), you could describe that equipment briefly in a subsection called "**Apparatus.**" Provide brand names and numbers for complicated equipment (e.g., computers, skin-fold calipers) but not for simple, standard equipment (e.g., stopwatches). Do not even mention everyday materials, such as rulers or pencils.

If, in addition to equipment, you also used pencil-and-paper materials, you could describe those materials here. Whether you describe those materials here, in a

[3]Include this citation only if you read the *Principles*. If you did get approval from your school's IRB, you might state, "The (name of your school) Institutional Review Board gave approval for this research."

Materials section, in the Procedure section, or in some other section, describe your materials well enough so that another researcher could reproduce your stimuli (e.g., "Memory lists were printed on standard-sized (23 × 28 cm) sheets of white, bond paper in 12-point Courier font. Distractor material was printed on every alternate line in a 10-point Courier font.").

3.5.3 Materials or Measures

If you used (or plan to use) only pencil-and-paper tests, you should not have an Apparatus subsection. However, you might have a subsection entitled "**Measures.**" If your pencil-and-paper tests are well known, just name, abbreviate, and cite them—for example, "Beck Depression Inventory (BDI; Beck, Ward, Mendelssohn, Mock, & Erlbaugh, 1961)"; if they are not well known, name, cite, and briefly describe the test(s). If you created a test for the research study, put a copy of that test in an appendix (to learn how to format that material and put it in the appendix, see 3.9). If you borrowed questions from other measures, you must state that fact: If you do not cite those other measures, you are plagiarizing.

For most tests or questionnaires, you should define each subscale, include a sample question from each subscale, and include the response options. For example, The scale ranged from (1) *strongly disagree* to (5) *strongly agree.* If possible, either here or in the Results section, you should provide evidence that the measure is reliable and valid.

If you constructed the materials yourself, include enough detail to ensure that another researcher could reproduce your stimuli. Specifically, you should state the number of stimuli per condition, describe the stimuli, describe how they were presented to the participants, and indicate any control procedures that you used such as randomizing or counterbalancing the order of the stimuli. In our example study, a Materials section might look like the following:

> **Materials**
>
> Each participant received a single sheet of white, 8.5 × 11 in. (22 × 28 cm) bond paper with these words printed on it:
>
> Imagine you are about to meet a person for the first time. You know nothing about the person, except that this person's friends describe her as humorous, cold, intelligent, polite [or cold, intelligent, polite, humorous]. How much do you think you would like this person? Rate your answer on a 7-point scale where 1 means that you would dislike this person a lot, 4 means that you would neither dislike nor like this person, and 7 means that you would like this person a lot.

3.5.4 Design and Other Optional Subsections

If your design is too complicated to describe in a single paragraph, put information about the design in a separate subsection called "**Design.**" Indeed, consider setting off any aspect of your Method section that requires more than a paragraph to describe (e.g., your coding scheme, your manipulation checks) in a separate subsection (e.g., "**Coding**," "**Manipulation Checks**"). In addition, if your procedure is complex enough or long enough that the reader might get overwhelmed, consider beginning the Method section with a general "**Overview**" subsection.

3.5.5 Procedure

Whereas you can choose whether to have an Overview or Design section, you must have a Procedure section. The Procedure section is a step-by-step, first-to-last account of what important events happened (or, in the case of a proposal, will happen) to the participants during the study. This section should focus on participants to such an extent that readers should be able to imagine themselves as participants in your study. To focus on participants, consider making participants the subject of most sentences. For instance, rather than writing, "I read the stimulus words," you might write, "Participants heard the stimulus words." The following example illustrates how to keep the focus on the participants:

> **Procedure**
>
> Participants received a randomly distributed response sheet. They had 2 min to read it and write their responses on it.

In addition to helping readers visualize what it would be like to be a participant in your study, you need to include information that will help readers replicate your study. Thus, in addition to telling the reader what tasks participants did, in what order the participants did those tasks, and how long participants had to complete each task, you need to include information about instructions and methodological wrinkles.

Although you should include information about instructions, do not state all your instructions word-for-word. Instead of quoting your instructions, summarize them (e.g., Participants read standard instructions that can be found in Appendix B.). Quote only the key instructions, such as those instructions that are different for the different experimental groups.

Include any methodological wrinkles that boost the study's validity. Thus, if you used a double-blind procedure, be sure to mention that you did. If you used a sophisticated procedure to control for order effects, describe that procedure (e.g., "Order and serial position of the six conditions were counterbalanced using Latin squares."). If you did not have a separate "**Design**" or "**Participants and Design**" subsection, at the end of the Procedure section, tell the reader what design you used (e.g., survey, within-subjects design) and, if you used an experimental design, tell the reader what your independent and dependent variables were. Thus, for our example experiment, you might end your Procedure section with the following paragraph:

> The study was a two-level, between-participant experiment with sequence of information ("humorous" first vs. last) as the independent variable. The dependent variable was the liking ratings.

3.6 Results

The Results section starts one double-spaced line after the end of the Method section. It begins with the centered, boldfaced heading: "**Results.**"

In a research proposal, you might not have a Results section. If your proposal does have a Results section, use it to tell readers how you plan to analyze your data. For example, you might write, Data will be analyzed using an independent groups *t* test and a .05 significance level.

In a research report, start the Results section by telling the reader exactly which data you analyzed—if those data differ from the measured variable you described in the Method section. For example, you would need to say whether you had transformed data in any way (e.g., percentage correct in a memory test rather than number of items recalled), and if you omitted any data (e.g., data from practice trials).

Once the reader knows what data you are analyzing, you can describe how you analyzed those data. If you did any significance tests, tell the reader the following:

- Why you did the test (e.g., To test the hypothesis that the sequence of presenting the information had an effect on likeability, I performed . . .).
- What test you performed (e.g., an independent-groups *t* test).
- What your two-tailed significance (alpha) level was (e.g., using an alpha level of .05 or the probability of a Type I error was .05 [or whatever level you used] for all analyses.)—unless you are using a one-tailed test. If you are using a one-tailed test, tell the reader (e.g., Using a one-tailed test and an alpha level of .05).
- What the result of the test was, both in terms of statistical criteria such as statistical significance and in terms of your hypothesis (e.g., As hypothesized, participants who received "humorous" first rated the person as significantly more likeable than those who received "humorous" last, $t(22) = 3.46, p = .002$.). APA journal editors also want authors to include a measure of effect size and a confidence interval for that effect size (Cooper, 2011). Thus, you might write, As hypothesized, participants who received "humorous" first rated the person as significantly more likeable than those who received "humorous" last, $t(22) = 3.46, p = .002, d = .72$, 95% CI [0.13,1.09]. For information on how to calculate confidence intervals and effect sizes, see the book's website.
- What the relevant summary statistics (averages and measures of spread) are for the important conditions. These descriptive statistics help readers see the pattern in your data. For example, you might write, Specifically, the mean rating from those receiving "humorous" first was 5.6 ($SD = 1.04$), whereas the mean rating from those receiving "humorous" last was 5.0 ($SD = 0.65$).

If you present the previously listed information skillfully, you will give (a) the casual reader a clear understanding of whether the results support the hypothesis, (b) the skeptical reader evidence that your results support your claims, and (c) the reader doing a meta-analysis the information necessary to combine your results with those of related studies. To present the information skillfully, you need to organize the information so that it tells a story. The most important element of that story is whether the hypothesis was supported.

One way to emphasize your results—and their implications—is to state your conclusion (e.g., the results support the hypothesis) first. Then, use the rest of the paragraph to provide support for that conclusion, as in the following paragraph:

> As hypothesized, participants who received "humorous" first rated the person as more likeable than those who received "humorous" last. The mean rating from those receiving "humorous" first was 5.6 (SD = 1.04), whereas the mean rating from those receiving "humorous" last was 5.0 (SD = 0.65). Using a between-subjects t test, this difference was significant, $t(22) = 3.46, p = .02, d = .72$, 95% CI [0.13,1.09].

The previous approach puts the verbal summary of the results into a headline role, the summary statistics into a supporting role, and the inferential statistics almost off the stage. Try it for your first draft. If you do not like it, you can write your final draft in a more conventional way. For example, to use simple words to announce your results, simple descriptive statistics to echo those results, and statistical tests to hum supportively in the background, you might organize the information from the sample study like this:

> To test the hypothesis that participants receiving "humorous" first would rate the person as more likeable than participants receiving "humorous" last, I used a between-subjects t test on the likeability ratings. As hypothesized, participants who received "humorous" first rated the person as more likeable ($M = 5.75, SD = 1.06$) than those who received "humorous" last ($M = 4.50, SD = 0.67$), $t(22) = 3.46, p = .02$, $d = .72$, 95% CI [0.13,1.09].

3.6.1 Statistical Significance

If your results are statistically significant, the editors of the *Publication Manual* encourage you to supplement significant tests with both (a) effect size estimates and (b) confidence intervals. Check to see whether your professor wants you to provide those additional statistics. If so, the Chapter 3 section of this book's website can help you calculate and incorporate those statistics into your Results section.

If, on the other hand, your results are not statistically significant, the editors of the *Publication Manual* encourage you to report your study's power. That is, tell the reader that if the variable had an effect of a certain size, what the chances of your study finding that effect statistically significant would be. Check to see whether your professor wants you to do a power analysis and, if so, what form that power analysis should take (for additional help on power analysis, see the Chapter 3 section of the text's website).

Note that in the traditional approach to significance testing, results are either statistically significant or they are not statistically significant: There is no middle ground. Thus, according to the traditional view, it would be considered misleading to refer to results that were not significant as either "just short of significance" or as "marginally significant."[4]

---

[4]If your professor is one of the many professors who are dissatisfied with the traditional approach to significance testing, your professor may allow you to use the term "marginally significant." However, unless you are sure your professor approves of the concept of marginally significant, avoid that term.

Note also that you should use the adjective "significant" only when you mean that the null hypothesis has been rejected. You should not use "significant" as a synonym for "important" or for "large." Therefore, do not use the phrase "significant result" when you mean "important result," and do not use the phrase "significant effect" when you mean "substantial effect."

Finally, note that you can use "insignificant" only when you mean unimportant. Therefore, if you mean that the results fail to disprove the null hypothesis, do not refer to the results as "insignificant." Instead, refer to results either as "not significant" or as "nonsignificant"—even if your spell-checker hates "nonsignificant."

3.6.2 Formatting Statistical Information

As you saw from the examples of Results sections in 3.6, formatting statistical information is different from formatting regular text. Some letters are italicized, some numbers below one are expressed with a leading zero in front of the decimal point (e.g., 0.20), some numbers below one are expressed without a leading zero (e.g., .20), some material is in parentheses, and some commas are used in unusual ways. Fortunately, there are rules:

- Italicize any statistical abbreviations based on the 26 letters of the alphabet (e.g., *t, p, F, N, df, M, SD*).
- Do not italicize any Greek letters (e.g., Σ, β, μ).
- For any inferential statistical test, give, at a minimum, its name or the abbreviation for its name, the degrees of freedom in parentheses, an equals sign, the statistic's value, and "*p* =" followed by the probability (*p*) value to two or three decimal places—unless that would mean writing "*p* = .00" or "*p* = .000." For a *t* test, for example, you might write *t* (24) = 2.73, *p* = .011. If, however, *p* was less than .001, you would give the probability value as "*p* <001."
- For chi-square test, provide the abbreviation for its name (χ^2), the degrees of freedom and the sample size (*N*) in parentheses. For example, you might write, $x^2(1, N = 92) = 4.05, p = .04$.
- Use a comma to attach the detailed results of statistical tests to the end of a sentence.
- State percentage and integer data as whole numbers. For any other numbers, go to no more than two decimal places, except for probability values. With probability values, you can go to three decimal places.
- Do not put zeros in front of the decimal point for either (a) probabilities (*p* values) or (b) correlation coefficients (*r* values).

To see these rules in practice, study the following four examples:

✔ The increase in mean confidence ratings was significantly greater in the experimental condition (*M* = 5.01, *SD* = 3.52) than in the control condition (*M* = 3.84, *SD* = 3.02), *t* (26) = 2.66, *p* = .013.

✔ As predicted, the experimental group recalled significantly more words (*M* = 5.75, *SD* = 0.72) than the control group (*M* = 5.00, *SD* = 0.65), *t* (31) = 3.10, *p* = .004, *d* = 1.13, 95% CI [0.85, 1.39].

✔ There was a significant interaction, $F(1, 62) = 14.24, p < .001, \eta^2 = .06$, plotted in Figure 4.

✔ The distribution of preferences shown in Table 6 was not significantly different among the four categories, $\chi^2(3, N = 300) = 8.00, p = .046$.

3.6.3 When Not to Use Either a Table or a Figure

Three rules will help you decide whether to add a figure or a table to your Results section. First, if you can incorporate your key statistics into the text of your Results section without overwhelming your reader with numbers, do that rather than adding a figure or a table. Thus, if you only have two means, you do not need a figure or a table because you can easily insert those two numbers in text. Second, if a table or figure is merely going to duplicate what you have already said in text, omit that figure or table—unless your professor requires one. (Your professor may require figures or tables so that you can learn how to format them.) Third, if you do not refer to the table or figure in your paper, it is not important: Delete it.

3.6.4 When to Use Tables

Sometimes, you must include many numbers in your Results section. However, if you include all those numbers in text, you may overwhelm and confuse your reader. In such a case, you should use either a table or a figure. If your goal is to show that the data fit a general pattern (e.g., to show that performance increases over time, to illustrate that the relationship between two variables can be described with a straight line, or to show that an interaction is X-shaped), use a figure to paint that general picture (see 3.6.6). If, on the other hand, you want to focus on the exact values of specific numbers, use a table—especially, if you are presenting the following:

- between 4 and 10 means (and their standard deviations)
- more than four correlation coefficients

3.6.5 Creating Tables

Your goal in using a table should be to summarize information for your reader. For your table to accomplish that goal, your reader should be able to understand your table without reading the accompanying text. However, the table is not supposed to stand by itself, waiting for the interested reader to absorb it. Instead, refer to it in text. (Indeed, as we mentioned earlier, if you do not refer to the table in your Results section, delete it because it is unnecessary.) When you refer to the table, refer to it by its number and highlight the table's most relevant numbers or patterns of numbers. For example,

> As can be seen in Table 2, the treatment group scored higher than the control group on every dependent measure.

One reason it is important to refer to a table by number is that the tables in a manuscript submitted for publication do not appear next to the text that refers to them. Instead, tables must be placed, one per page, after the References. (You may wish to ask your professor if you can deviate from APA manuscript style and put the table in the text near where it is discussed.)

Main elements of a table. All tables consist of three parts: (a) a caption appearing above the rest of the table, which includes a table number and title; (b) headings for the table's columns and headings for the table's rows; and (c) the table's data. In addition, some tables contain a fourth part: explanatory notes. We will now discuss each of these four parts. To follow our discussion, you will find it useful to refer to Exhibit 3.1.[5]

Caption. As you can see, the first line of our table identifies the table by its table number ("Table 2"). Number your tables using Arabic numbers (e.g., "2") rather than Roman numerals (e.g., do not use "II"), and number the tables according to the order in which you refer to them in text. Thus, the second table you refer to will be "Table 2."

EXHIBIT **3.1** An Example of a Table

Table 2

Mean Differences in Reaction Time (in ms) Between No-Noise and Noise Conditions

Noise level (dB)	Mean difference[a]		t
	Simple RTs		
60	-7.21_z	(9)[b]	2.62*
70	-7.45_z	(8)	3.55**
80	-9.15_z	(10)	4.49**
90	-9.72_z	(9)	3.85**
	Choice RTs		
60	-11.05_y	(5)	2.82*
70	-11.92_y	(9)	9.90***
80	-4.91_x	(10)	3.61**
90	0.33_w	(10)	1.41

Note. This table is made up. If it had been previously published, we would have cited the study here. Numbers having different subscripts differ significantly at $p < .01$ by *t* test. [a]Negative numbers indicate noise RT was slower than no-noise RT. [b]Number in parentheses is the number of participants in each condition.
$^{*}p < 0.5$. $^{**}p < .01$. $^{***}p < .001$.

[5]Exhibit 3.1 is a good example of an APA-style table. Note that tables can be single-spaced or double-spaced.

The second line of the table is the table title. The title should be a short but meaningful description of the relationship between (a) the data in the table and (b) the variables or statistics identified by the column and row headers. If your data can be expressed in units (e.g., milliseconds, liters), the title should also include the abbreviation for that unit of measurement.

Italicize the table title and capitalize the first letter of each major word. Be sure the unit of measurement is abbreviated and in parentheses.

Once you make sure that your table number line is not italicized but that your table title is italicized, be sure that the table caption is above the table. Thus, as you can see from Exhibit 3.1, the top of a table might look like this:

Table 2

Mean Differences in Reaction Time (in ms) Between No-Noise and Noise Conditions

Column and row headings. As you can see from Exhibit 3.1, the column and row headings tell the reader what the data in the table represent. The left-most column heading identifies the major manipulated variable (i.e., noise level). Under that column header are the row headings. The row headings label the levels (amounts) of the major manipulated variable (e.g., 60 dB). Other column headings can specify almost anything: values of other manipulated variables (e.g., "Unpredictable noise" and "Predictable noise"), values of predictor variables (e.g., "Men" and "Women"), different information about each condition (e.g., "Mean," Standard deviation," or "Sample size"), or even comparisons between conditions (e.g., "Mean difference").

Lines. Often, your tables will have three horizontal lines. Near the top of the table, put a horizontal line right below the table caption to separate it from the column headings. Next, put a line right below the column headings to separate them from the body of the table. Finally, put a line at the bottom of the body of the table to separate the table body from the explanatory notes. Use other horizontal lines sparingly. Never use vertical lines.

Data. If numbers have decimal points, the decimal points in a column should line up with each other. Realize that decimal points make it harder for the reader to decipher your table. Therefore, consider whether you can eliminate the decimal points. For example, you may be able to turn decimal numbers into whole numbers by changing proportions into percentages (e.g., convert .67 to 67) or by changing the unit of measurement (e.g., convert .34 meters into 34 centimeters). In addition, consider how many decimal points you need. If you are reporting means and all your groups differ by more than two units, you do not need to go beyond one decimal point. With any numbers other than p values, you should probably never go beyond two decimal places. Make sure that all numbers in a column have the same number of decimal points.

Notes. Set any notes that you have at the bottom of the table in unindented paragraphs. The first paragraph would be *general notes* relating to the entire table (e.g., "Numbers having different subscripts differ significantly at $p < .01$ by t test."). Start this general notes section with the italicized word *Note* followed by a period. Make each note a complete sentence, and end each note with a period (see Exhibit 3.1).

Table 3.1
Superscripts for Probabilities of Two- and One-Tailed Statistical Tests

p <	Two-Tailed	One-Tailed
.05	*	†
.01	**	††
.001	***	†††

Your second paragraph would start on a new line and would contain *specific notes* applying to particular entries, columns, or rows (e.g., "[a]Negative sign indicates noise RT was slower than control RT."). Identify those notes, both in the table and in the notes, with superscript letters (e.g.,[a]).

The third paragraph would start on a new line and would explain *probability notes*. You use probability notes when you use symbols, such as asterisks (*) and daggers (†) to indicate that a result is statistically significant. Probability notes spell out the connection between your symbols (e.g., *) and the significance level (e.g., $p < .05$) they represent. Table 3.1 shows a common way of using superscripts to express probability levels. Exhibit 3.1 provides an example of probability notes in action.

3.6.6 When to Use Figures

A figure is a picture that helps your reader see the point you are trying to make. In the Results section, figures can be useful to illustrate the shape of a relationship between two variables, to illustrate an interaction among variables, and to present a large number of data points. You might also use a figure in the Method section to illustrate anything that would otherwise be hard to describe, such as what the apparatus or stimuli looked like. Although figures can be useful, if you do not refer to a particular figure in your paper, do not include that figure in your paper.

3.6.7 Creating Figures

As is the case with tables, the following guidelines apply:

- Your reader should be able to understand your figures without reading the accompanying text.
- Figures should do more than duplicate information already in the accompanying text.
- The text should draw the reader's attention to the important aspects of your figure.
- The text must refer to the figure—and must refer to it by number (e.g., "As can be seen in Figure 1, ...").

In referring to figures, note three points. First, regardless of whether your "figure" is a graph, a photograph, or a diagram, always refer to it by the word "Figure" followed by the figure number. Second, as is the case with tables, it is important to refer to the correct figure number because the figure is not next to the text to which it refers. Instead, the figures are put, one per page, at the end of the paper (after the References, after any appendixes, and after any tables). Third, software packages, such as Excel®, SPSS®, and DeltaGraph® can help you construct graphs. However, when using such programs, realize that (a) using them may be extremely time-consuming, (b) using them may result in figures that violate APA standards, and (c) using them to construct appropriate graphs is easier if you know the terminology associated with the four parts of a graph:

1. the graph's axes—the "x" (horizontal) axis and the "y" (vertical) axis;
2. the data—the data points and lines joining them or the bars representing them;
3. the figure legend—a box within the figure that describes what the different lines, symbols, and bar shadings represent; and
4. the figure caption—a heading that includes the figure's number, the figure's title, and explanations of what the figure's lines, symbols, and abbreviations represent—if those explanations (a) are necessary for understanding the figure and (b) could not fit in the legend box.

We will now discuss each of these four components. To follow this discussion, you will find it helpful to refer to Exhibit 3.2 on page 87.

Axes. Choose scale values for each axis that spread out the data and allow the figure to fit comfortably on one page. For example, you should not need to resort to using a small font to fit your figure onto the page.

Make the horizontal (x) axis by drawing a line that starts near the left, bottom side of the page and goes straight across the page. If you conducted an experiment, this horizontal axis will represent your independent variable. If you conducted a nonexperimental study, this horizontal axis will represent your predictor variable.

Make the vertical (y) axis by starting at the far left end of your horizontal axis and drawing a straight line up toward the top of the page. Make this vertical line about as long as your horizontal axis. This vertical line will represent your dependent variable (in an experiment, this variable is your measured—not your manipulated—variable; in a nonexperimental study, this variable is your outcome—your predicted—variable).

Thus far, your graph has two lines for the two axes. The two axes are two sides of an incomplete rectangle. Complete the rectangle by adding the top and the right side.[6]

Inside that rectangular box, place ***tick marks:*** small marks that will indicate values of the variables on your axes (see Exhibit 3.2). Then, outside of the box, place labels (usually numbers) corresponding to the tick marks (e.g., in Exhibit 3.2, on the vertical axis, the axis labels are the "0," "2," "4," "6," "8," and "10"). Print those numbers (called "scale values") left-to-right as you would ordinary text.

[6]If you are making a scatterplot or a bar graph, you will remove both the line that forms the top of the rectangle and the line that forms the right side of the rectangle from the final draft of your figure. If you are making a line graph and the final graph looks better without those two lines, remove them.

EXHIBIT **3.2** An Example of a Line Graph

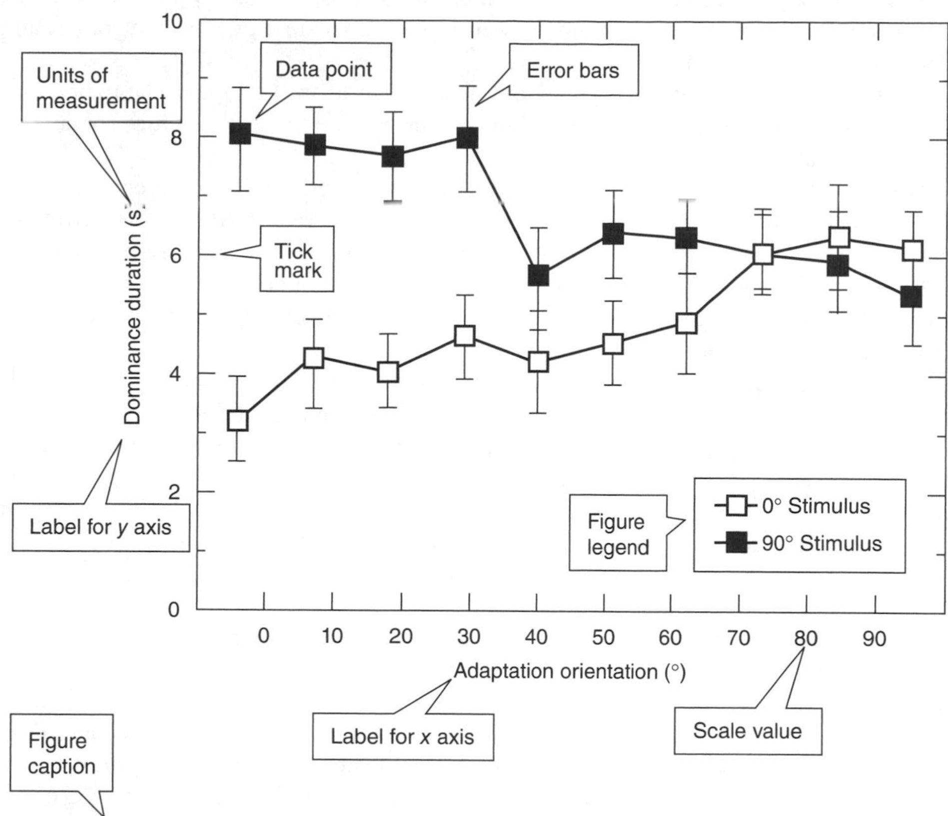

Figure 2. Mean duration of binocular-rivalry dominance of vertical (0°) and horizontal (90°) stimuli following adaptation to a monocular grating of various orientations. Vertical lines show ±1 standard error of the mean.

You now need axis labels (e.g., in Exhibit 3.2, the labels "Dominance duration" and "Adaptation orientation") to help the reader understand what those numbers represent. The two axis labels (one for the vertical axis, one for the horizontal axis) should be meaningful but brief. To make the labels meaningful, let the reader know the units to which the numbers are referring (e.g., meters, milligrams, seconds) by including that information in the axis labels. To help make the axis labels brief, try to abbreviate the name of those units (for a list of abbreviations for common units, see 3.6.8). Put the unit abbreviation in parentheses (e.g., in Exhibit 3.2, we used "(s)" for seconds as part of the vertical axis label). If you were unable to use an abbreviation, put the unit name in parentheses. For example, in Exhibit 3.3 on page 89, we used "(% correct)" as part of the vertical axis label. Once you have your axis labels, center them and print each one parallel to its axis.

Data and Three Types of Graphs. Although you could use a computer to create pie charts, multicolored graphs, and 3-dimensional (3-D) graphs like the ones you see in newspapers, you should not. Instead, limit your graphs to these three types of black and white (and sometimes, gray), two-dimensional graphs: line graphs, bar graphs, and scatterplots.

Which of these three graphs you should use depends on the type of data you have. In the next section, we will show you how to choose the type of graph that matches the type of data you have.

Line graphs. Use a line graph when you have conducted an experiment and at least one manipulated variable involves three or more conditions that differ in amount (e.g., amount of drug given) or number (e.g., number of onlookers, or, as in Exhibit 3.2, orientation in degrees). If you have one such variable, put it on the horizontal axis and put your measured (dependent) variable on the vertical axis. Plot your data as points and join the points with lines.

If you have more than one manipulated variable, put the one that has more levels (values) on the horizontal axis. Thus, in Exhibit 3.2, we had 10 levels of adaptation orientation and only two types of stimuli, so adaptation orientation was on the horizontal axis (that way, instead of having 10 lines, we only had two). Putting a variable on the horizontal axis means that as you go from the left side of the graph to the right side, you are going from lower levels of that variable to higher levels. In Exhibit 3.2, for example, you are going from 0° adaptation on the far left side of the graph to 90° adaptation on the far right side of the graph.

Distinguish the different levels of the second variable by using a different line for each level. If, for example, as in Exhibit 3.2, you had two levels of the second variable, you would draw two lines—one line for each level. Specifically, use different shapes for each level's data points (e.g., circles for the first level, squares for the second level, or filled and unfilled squares as in Exhibit 3.2) and then join each level's points with different kinds of lines (e.g., solid lines for the first level, dotted lines for the other level). If you have a third manipulated variable, consider drawing a separate graph for each level of that variable.

If your data are means, you can give your reader some idea of the variability of scores around each mean by creating error bars. Error bars are usually vertical lines above and below a point with a length equal to the standard error of the mean. More rarely, error bars can be the length of the standard deviations or of the confidence interval. Therefore, you need to be clear which unit your error bars represent.

If you use standard errors, follow these three steps. First, compute the standard error of the mean (SE; it is the standard deviation divided by the square root of the number of participants contributing to the mean).[7] Second, draw a line that starts one SE directly above the point representing your first mean, continues down through that point, and stops one standard error below that point. (You should now have a line that is 2 SEs in length and has the mean as its midpoint.) This line is an error bar.

[7]For help on computing standard error bars or confidence intervals, see this text's website.

Third, draw error bars for each of your means. To see what these standard error lines look like, see Exhibit 3.2.

If you wish to use standard deviation lines instead of standard error lines, follow the three preceding steps but use standard deviations instead of standard errors. If you wish to use confidence intervals—or if you have any questions about how to calculate the standard deviation or standard error—see this book's website.

Bar graphs. Use a bar graph, like the one in Exhibit 3.3, in two situations. First, use a bar graph when you have conducted a study and all your predictors involve distinct categories (e.g., men versus women) or different kinds—rather than amounts—of treatments (e.g., yoga versus aerobics, or, as in Exhibit 3.3, experimental vs. control). Second, use a bar graph (or a table) whenever you are tempted to use a pie chart.

In making your bar graph, put the measured (dependent) variable on the vertical axis. If you have one manipulated (independent) variable, put that variable on the horizontal axis. If you have two manipulated variables, only one can be on the horizontal axis. The levels of the other one will be expressed by differently shaded bars (e.g., black, white, gray). To determine which manipulated variable you should express with bars, make one graph putting one manipulated variable on the horizontal axis and make another graph putting the other manipulated variable on the horizontal axis. Then, compare the graphs to see which graph makes your conclusions clearer.[8]

EXHIBIT **3.3** An Example of a Bar Graph

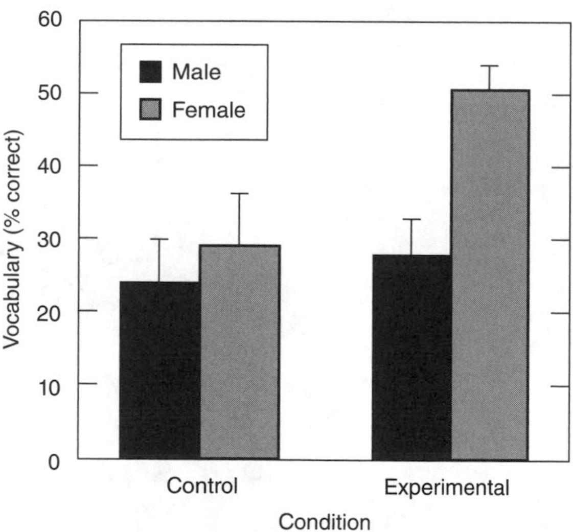

[8]Sometimes, changing which variable you put on the horizontal axis will make no difference in how easy your graph is to read; other times, changing which variable you put on the horizontal axis can make your graph much easier to grasp. To see examples of both cases, go to our website (http://www.writingforpsychology.com).

Once you have your bars, consider adding standard error lines above the bars to show the variability in your data (see Exhibit 3.3).

When working with your bars, obey the following three rules. First, use differently shaded bars (i.e., black, white, gray) rather than differently colored bars. Second, do not use diagonal lines to shade the bars because diagonal lines will create the illusion that your bars are tilted. Third, do not add 3-D effects because those effects make it more difficult for readers to understand your graph.

Scatterplots. If you do not have a manipulated variable, you may want to use a scatterplot (also called a scattergram; see Exhibit 3.4). A scatterplot is especially useful when you have given two tests to your participants. Put the variable you consider the predictor variable on the horizontal axis and put the variable you are trying to predict (the criterion variable) on the vertical axis. Then, use dots to plot your data on the graph. If you want to provide more information than a swarm of dots can convey, add a regression line to your scatterplot (see Exhibit 3.4).

Figure legend. In the figure's legend, provide information to help the reader understand any abbreviations, bar shadings, symbols, and lines that you are using. Put that legend in a rectangular box inside the graph (see, e.g., the legend in Exhibit 3.2). If there is not enough room within the borders of the graph to write out all the necessary explanatory information, place the explanatory information in the figure caption instead. Thus, in Exhibit 3.2, if we had been unable to fit "unfilled squares designate the 0° stimulus; filled squares designate the 90° stimulus" in the legend, we would put that information in the figure caption: the figure's heading.

EXHIBIT **3.4** An Example of a Scatterplot

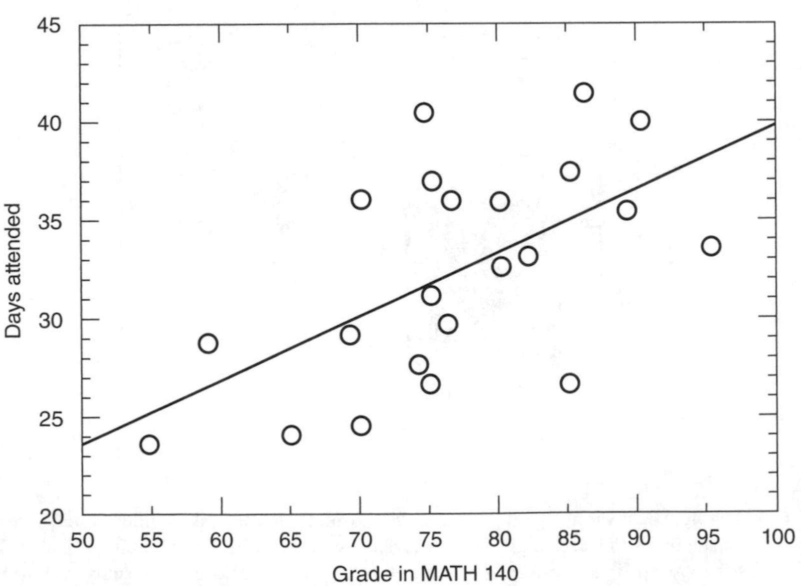

Figure 4. Grade in introductory math class correlates with attendance.

Figure caption. Put each figure caption directly under its figure, as we have done in Exhibit 3.2. Specifically, start the caption on the far left margin and treat the caption like an unindented paragraph that contains two parts.

The first part of the caption is the figure number ending with a period (e.g., "*Figure 1.* "). Note that this first part is italicized.

The second part of the caption is the figure title. In the title, describe the figure in a brief sentence or phrase. Note that (a) only the first letter of the figure title is capitalized and (b) the figure title is not italicized.

Right after the figure title, some figure captions contain a third part. This third part consists of information that the reader needs to understand the figure—such as what the different lines, symbols, and abbreviations represent—that did not fit in the legend. For example, in Exhibit 3.2, because the explanation of the vertical lines would not fit in the legend, the caption contains that explanation ("Vertical lines show ±1 standard error of the mean").

3.6.8 Units

Both the APA and the international scientific community use the metric system. Specifically, they conform to a set of metric system standards called the International System of Units (SI). Units of measurement in any part of your report should almost always be expressed using SI. If you originally took your measurements in non-SI units (e.g., inches), you can report those measurements in non-SI units—but you must also report the measurements in SI units (e.g., centimeters). To be more precise, you "must report the SI equivalents in parentheses immediately after the nonmetric units" (APA, 2010, pp. 114-115). In the rare instances in which non-SI units of measurement are universally used (e.g., decibels), you can use the non-SI unit.

Regardless of whether you use an SI or non-SI unit, abbreviate the unit (to see how to abbreviate some common units, see Table 3.2). When abbreviating the units, omit periods from the abbreviation—except for the abbreviation for inch. The abbreviation for inch has a period ("in.") to prevent readers from confusing it with the preposition ("in").

You may find that some SI units are too big or too small for your purposes. For example, suppose that you were trying to report the smallest bump that participants could reliably detect in an otherwise flat surface. In this case, putting the size of this bump in meters (e.g., "0.0005 m") would be clumsy and confusing. Therefore, instead of putting the size of the bump in meters, you would put the size of the bump in millimeters (e.g., "0.5 mm"). That is, you would add the prefix "milli" to your original unit of measurement. Table 3.3 can help you find the best prefix for expressing your measurements.

3.7 Discussion

The Discussion section follows immediately after the Results section and starts with the centered, boldfaced heading: "**Discussion.**" In the Discussion section of a research report, you review your findings and show how they relate to the literature. The Discussion provides you with the opportunity to interpret, reinterpret, qualify, and explore the importance of your results. If your Discussion makes up less than one-fourth of the body of your paper, be concerned: You may not have thought enough

Table 3.2
*Accepted Units of Measurement and Their Abbreviations**

Quantity	Unit	Abbreviation	SI Unit
Acceleration	meter per second squared	m/s^2	same
Angle	radian	rad	same
Area	square meter	m^2	same
Concentration	molecules per cubic meter	mol/m^3	same
Density	kilogram per cubic meter	kg/m^3	same
Electric current	ampere	A	same
Electric potential	volt	V	same
Electric resistance	ohm	Ω	same
Force	newton	N	same
Frequency	hertz	Hz	same
Length	meter	m	same
Luminance	candela per square meter	cd/m^2	same
Mass	kilogram	Kg	same
Power	watt	W	same
Pressure	pascal	Pa	same
Sound pressure level	decibel	dB	N/m^2
Temperature	degree Celsius	°C	°Kelvin
Time	second	s	same
Velocity	meter per second	m/s	same
Visual angle	degree	°	radian
Volume	cubic meter	m^3	same
Weight	see Mass		

*If you need help making these abbreviations in your word processor, see this book's website (http://www.writingforpsychology.com).

about your results—or you may have been too eager to finish your paper. However, do not ramble on merely to lengthen this section: Ultimately, your Discussion section will be judged not on how long it is but on how well organized and meaningful it is.

Remember that you have taken your reader on a journey though the Introduction, Method, and Results sections. In the Discussion section, you should convince your reader that the journey was worthwhile because you have arrived somewhere interesting.

3.7.1 Briefly Restate the Results

To convince your reader of the journey's importance, you must start by telling your reader whether you found what you expected to find. Therefore, begin the Discussion of

Table 3.3
Common SI Prefixes

Factor	Prefix	Symbol	Example
billion times (10^9)	giga	G	Gb (gigabyte)
million times (10^6)	mega	M	MV (megavolt)
thousand times (10^3)	kilo	k	kHz (kilohertz)
one tenth (10^{-1})	deci	d	dB (decibel)
one hundredth (10^{-2})	centi	c	cm (centimeter)
one thousandth (10^{-3})	milli	m	mA (milliamp)
one millionth (10^{-6})	micro	μ	μm (micrometer)
one billionth (10^{-9})	nano	n	nm (nanometer)

a research report by letting the reader know whether your results are consistent with your original hypothesis. Briefly inform the reader whether the obtained results are (a) statistically significant and consistent with your hypothesis, (b) statistically significant but inconsistent with your hypothesis, or (c) not statistically significant. Be sure that your summary is accurate and reflects what you found in the Results: As Wegner (2007) warns, results that were not significant in your Results should remain nonsignificant in your Discussion.

To keep your description of the results brief, (a) leave out means, probability values, and other numbers and (b) focus solely on whether the results support the hypothesis. However, do not be so brief that you fail to remind the reader what it was you set out to test. Do not make a vague statement such as, "The results of this study confirm the hypothesis." Instead, say something specific such as this:

> As predicted, when students rated the likeability of a person described by a list of adjectives, they rated the person more favorably when the most positive adjective was the first item on the list than when that adjective was the last item on the list.

Recap your results at the beginning of the Discussion section for three reasons. First, some readers will read this paragraph first before deciding whether to read the rest of the paper (Wegner, 2007). Second, if readers have made it this far, you do not want to risk losing them now. Third, as Roediger (2007) points out, "once we know what the results are, we can discuss them" (p. 20).

3.7.2 Relate Results to Other Research

After relating the results to the hypothesis, you should relate the results to the work of other researchers—a step that often involves reviewing some of the literature you discussed in the Introduction. If other researchers have found similar results, explain how your work supports and extends their findings. If other researchers obtained different results, explain why your findings are different from theirs. In short, explain whether your study filled the hole in the literature that you identified in the Introduction.

3.7.3 State Qualifications and Reservations—And Use Them to Propose Future Research

If the results of your study were significant, at least three major questions arise (see 5.6). First, can the results be generalized to a broader population? For example, if your results were based on a sample of students, those results might not generalize to all adults. Second, are the methods you used to measure and manipulate variables valid? For example, if you tried to induce stress by making participants answer math problems within a certain number of seconds, is that a valid manipulation of stress? Third, can you legitimately make a cause-effect statement from your results? You probably cannot if (a) you did not manipulate the treatment or (b) there were any other variables that varied along with the manipulated variables (see 5.6.1).

Although you should mention limits to the generalizability and validity of your results, try to be positive. Otherwise, your readers (including the professor grading your report) will feel that they have been taken for a ride rather than taken on a useful journey. Therefore, instead of downplaying your research because you studied only students, for example, you could suggest that students are more suspicious of psychological testing than other people, so any effect that students show is likely to be even stronger in other people. Similarly, rather than deriding your study because you used a weak stressor, you could say that the effects of stress on performance must be quite strong if a weak stressor managed to produce a significant effect.

You should mention any defects in the method or design of the study (e.g., some participants did not follow instructions, the measuring device was difficult to use, the apparatus was unreliable). Do not dwell on these defects, however, unless they were systematic. If the defects were unsystematic, they reduced the chances of obtaining significant results. Consequently, the fact that you obtained significant results in spite of these unsystematic defects is a tribute to the strength of the hypothesis.

If the method or design defects were systematic (e.g., only participants in the experimental group misinterpreted the instructions, the difficulty in using the measuring device led to more errors in one condition than in the others, the apparatus was unreliable for only one of the conditions, participants were not randomly assigned to conditions), you should admit that those errors make it impossible for you to come to a firm conclusion about the effect of your treatment. For example, suppose your experimental group, which was taught to use a special memory strategy, recalled more words than your control group of students who were not using such a strategy. However, suppose that you also discovered that you tested the experimental group in a quiet room and the control group in a noisy room. In that case, you should admit that your experiment is flawed. Point out that the memory strategy may not have increased learning in the experimental group; instead, the noise may have decreased learning in the control group.

If there are alternative explanations for your results—and there probably will be—do not hide these alternative explanations from your reader. Instead, tell the reader about these alternative explanations and briefly propose a type of study that might help determine which explanation is correct. Thus, instead of turning off your reader by having your reader say, "Oh, it is terrible that the study is imperfect," turn on your reader by making the reader say, "Hey, I can answer an important question by following up on this research!"

If your results were not significant, there are going to be a variety of possible explanations for your results. Spend part of your Discussion considering why you obtained nonsignificant results. You can guard against making the reader feel that your study has arrived at a dead end if you write about the validity and potency of your manipulations and measures and how they could be improved in future studies.

3.7.4 Explain the Research's Implications

Once you have satisfied the reader that your results should be taken seriously, you can go on to discuss the implications your results have for understanding research (and, ideally, theory) in this area and, possibly, for improving the world. When discussing these implications, some speculation is allowed. However, such speculation should be (a) closely related to your results, rather than wild speculation; (b) brief, rather than long-winded; and (c) clearly indicated as speculation, rather than being disguised as fact.

3.7.5 Conclude

Sometimes, your last paragraph will be a brief mention of the practical implications of your results or some suggestions for future research. You should always end by stating a conclusion that will make readers believe that your report has important implications for theory, research, or practice. The following are examples of how you could begin your concluding paragraph:

- Results from the current study suggest several promising directions for future research.
- The results raise serious questions about [name of a theory].
- This study is an important step in understanding [your topic].
- The effects reported in this article have two important practical implications.
- Practitioners should be aware of [these findings] when they ____________.
- Two important findings from this study are ____________.
- The present findings lend new support for the [name of theory] explanation of [your topic or the phenomenon you studied].
- The results presented here should lead psychologists to take a serious look at [your theory or independent variable] and its potential impact on [your dependent variable].
- Future research should [be like your study but make the following changes].
- This study will help fill in an important gap in our knowledge about [your topic].

The conclusion can be longer than a paragraph. In journal articles, the conclusion is often several paragraphs long and is labeled with a subheading titled "**Conclusions**." If you are writing a long report, you will probably have more than a one-paragraph conclusion. However, if your report is as short as the typical student research report, you can probably conclude with a single paragraph that follows the O'Shea et al. (2007) three-step formula:

1. In conclusion, this study, consistent with [name of theory], found that [the results supported the hypothesis].
2. Nevertheless, future research is needed to answer one question that this study failed to answer definitively: [state the question].
3. Such research could help [better understand the causes of the phenomenon you studied or solve a practical problem related to this phenomenon].

In the case of a proposal, you should conclude with why the study is needed and what different patterns of results would indicate. Thus, you might state

1. In conclusion, this study is needed because it will ...
2. If the hypothesis is supported, this will mean ...
3. If the hypothesis is not supported, it will mean....

3.8 References

Every journal article you cite in your paper should appear in your reference list. The citations should be in alphabetical order according to the last name of the work's primary author. The reference list should start on a new page with the centered heading: "References" typed in a normal font, not bolded. To see how individual references are formatted, you can look at the reference list of the sample research report (3.11) as well as at the reference list of the sample term paper (2.11). To learn the rules for the reference list, see 4.10; to verify that you are following those rules, compare your reference section with the reference list checklist (4.11.4).

3.9 Appendixes

In published articles, appendixes are rare. When an appendix appears in a published article, it presents important material, such as unpublished test materials and details of specially constructed equipment that, if presented in the paper's method section, would interrupt the paper's flow. In research proposals and in student reports, on the other hand, appendixes are much more common because professors want you to show your work by having you present raw data, stimulus materials, questionnaires, consent forms, data summary sheets, and statistical calculations. Raw data should be presented in a table, using the same directions as for tables in the text (to see those directions, see 3.6.5). The only difference is that, rather than being labeled with a number (e.g., "Table 1"), each data table will be labeled with a capital letter (e.g., "A" if the table is in Appendix A, "B" if it is in Appendix B), followed by a number (e.g., "Table A1" for the first table in Appendix A, "Table A2" for the second table in Appendix A).

Your appendix will begin on a new page after the references. If you have only one appendix, it will have the centered heading "Appendix." If you have more than one, the heading for the first one will be "Appendix A"; the heading for the second one will be "Appendix B." Unless your professor states otherwise, you must refer to appendixes in the body of your paper. For example, suppose you had appendixes that contained (a) data about your three participants' vision from their eye doctors, (b) your three participants' scores on the task ("raw data") that you later analyzed, and (c) analysis of variance summary tables for all four measured variables. You would need to refer to all three appendixes. You might refer to them as follows:

> The participants were three men with normal visual acuity. Appendix A presents the details of their optometric characteristics.
>
> Results
>
> Raw data for the three participants are presented in Tables B1, B2, and B3. Analysis of variance summary tables for reaction times to hits, misses, false alarms, and correct rejections are shown in Tables C1–C4, respectively. Consistent with the hypothesis. . .

3.10 Tense

If you are writing a report on a study you performed, most of your report involves describing what you did or reviewing what others did. Not only are you reviewing past findings and conclusions but you are reviewing past findings and conclusions that may be contradicted or revised. What is found in one study, may not be found in later studies. What an author believed when writing one article, may be different from what that author believes now. Thus, for most of your article, you are not talking about timeless truths; instead, you are talking about what seemed to be true at one moment in the past. Therefore, for most of your report, use the past tense.

- Jones (2010) found [past tense] …
- Use the present tense only when you are (a) referring to an existing, permanent condition (e.g., "Dissonance is a state of arousal."), (b) referring to a figure or other part of your report (e.g., As Figure 1 shows, . . .), or (c) referring to conclusions (e.g., "The results support the hypothesis.").
- Smith (2011) argued that attribution is [present tense for a situation that exists and will continue to exist] internal…
- As can be seen in Figure 3 [present tense for part of a report], the means differ [present tense for an existing and continuing condition]…
- In conclusion, X appears [present tense for conclusion] to affect Y.

If you are writing a proposal, you are proposing what you will do, so you will use the future tense much more than you would in a report. For example, whereas the Method section of a report should be in the past tense (e.g., "Participants played a video game."), the Method section of your proposal should be in the future tense (e.g., "Participants will play a video game."). For more information about tense, see 6.1.3. For more information on how research reports and proposals differ, see Table 3.4.

Table 3.4
Differences Between Research Reports and Research Proposals

	Reports	Proposals
Abstract	Past tense for what was done, present tense for implications of results.	Future tense
Method	Past tense	Future tense
Results	Essential	Often omitted or replaced with an "Analysis of Results" or "Plan for Analyzing Results" section.
Discussion	Essential	Often omitted
Appendix	Often omitted	May be more important in proposal than in report. For example, institutional review boards (IRBs) may require that your proposal have an appendix containing copies of all your measures and stimulus materials.

3.11 Sample Research Report

Imagine that you are sitting quietly in class one day, waiting for the lecture to begin. However, instead of announcing the day's lecture topic, the professor announces that the day will be devoted to conducting an experiment. The professor tells you that a list of 12 digits will be read aloud, and after 30 seconds, you are to write down as many as you can remember in order. Then, the instructor repeats the procedure with a list of 12 letters. The professor then hands out the lists and asks you to count how many entries you matched on each list. Next, the numbers of digits and letters that each student recalled are collated, and a statistical test is performed. Finally, the instructor tells the class that a report, in APA style, on the experiment just conducted is worth 20% of the course grade and is due in a week.

At first, such a writing assignment might seem overwhelming. Eventually, however, you might come up with something resembling the following report. Your report should differ from our report in only three significant respects. First, we have annotated our report with footnotes so that you can appreciate particular points. In your own report, do not use footnotes. Second, we have used only old references. In your own report, cite current research. Third, we have not used Times New Roman 12-point font so that the book will cost less. In your own report, use Times New Roman 12-point font.

Running[9] head: DIGITS VS. LETTERS IN SERIAL RECALL[10] 1

Memory for Digits and Letters in a Serial Recall Task[11]

Ann A. Student[12]

Alpha University

Author Note[13]

Ann A. Student, Psychology Department, Alpha University.[14]

I thank[15] M. I. Tuder for guiding my thinking on this topic and I. M. Goode for commenting on previous drafts.

Correspondence concerning this article should be addressed to Ann A. Student, Department of Psychology, Alpha University, Alpha, CA 97804. E-mail: an@al.edu

---

[9]Ann is using APA copy style (also called APA-manuscript format). If your instructor wants you to use published format, see Appendix A. If your instructor asks you to add a cover sheet, do so.

[10]Ann was able to verify that her running head was short enough (had fewer than 51 characters, including spaces) by using the "Word count" feature of her word-processing software.

[11]For the title, if a word has fewer than four letters and is (a) a preposition (e.g., "of" and "in"), (b) an article (e.g., "a"), or (c) a conjunction (e.g., "and"), that word—unless it is the first word of the title or the first word of the subtitle—is not capitalized.

[12]Include your middle initial. Do not include the word "by."

[13]Your professor may not require an Author Note, but APA style does.

[14]We realize that the first line of the Author Note is not a sentence, much less a paragraph. It is, however, in the form prescribed by the *Publication Manual.*

[15]Thank anyone who gives you general or editorial help. (For more on giving proper credit and on academic honesty, see 1.2.4.)

[16]DIGITS VS. LETTERS IN SERIAL RECALL 2

Abstract[17]

[18]To test the hypothesis that letters would be more easily recalled than digits, the professor of an undergraduate research methods class read a 12-digit list and then a 12-letter list to 72 members of that class (50 women and 22 men, mean age = 20.40 years) during a regularly scheduled class meeting.[19] The results did not support the hypothesis: Letters were not recalled significantly more than digits, $t(71) = -1.21$, $p = .60$. Perhaps letter stimuli have no memory advantage, or perhaps design problems, such as always presenting the digits before the letters, having a small sample size, or using only one set of letters, obscured the effect.[20]

Keywords: nonsense syllable learning, association, rote learning, serial verbal learning, retention

---

[16]The words "Running head" appear only on page 1.

[17]Begin the Abstract on page 2. Announce it with the centered—but not boldfaced—heading "Abstract."

[18]Do not indent the Abstract (but indent all other paragraphs).

[19]Double-space your entire paper.

[20]In only 107 words, Ann stated her hypothesis and described her method, participants, findings (including significance levels), and conclusions.

DIGITS VS. LETTERS IN SERIAL RECALL 3

Memory for Digits and Letters in a Serial Recall Task[21]

Ebbinghaus[22] (as cited in Woodworth & Schlossberg, 1954)[23] considered memory[24] to consist of the formation of associations between stimuli. In attempting to test the capacity of memory, researchers should therefore control prior associations between stimuli.[25]

Ebbinghaus (as cited in Woodworth & Schlossberg, 1954)[26]controlled for prior associations by inventing nonsense syllables and discarding any that reminded him of real words, were well-known initials, or had any emotional tone. When Ebbinghaus memorized a list of nonsense syllables, he seemed to be tapping pure memory, uncontaminated by any prior associations. However, prior associations may contaminate current memory tests.[27,28]

One current memory test[29] is rote memory for digits. Researchers sometimes treat rote memory for digits as a test of pure

---

[21]The introduction begins on a new page. Its heading is the paper's title.

[22]According to the *Publication Manual*, when you cite a source you have not read, you name the source, but you do not date it.

[23]Note the use of a secondary citation. Ann will not put Ebbinghaus in her reference list because she did not read Ebbinghaus's work.

[24]The first sentence introduces the general area of investigation. (For more on beginning the introduction, see 3.4.1.)

[25]This sentence prepares the reader for the next paragraph. (For more tips on helping the reader navigate your paper, see 6.4.2.)

[26] Citations, even name citations, do not carry over from one paragraph to the next. Thus, even though Ann cited the date and author of the work in the previous paragraph, she has to cite them again in this paragraph.

[27]The first two paragraphs briefly set the theoretical scene (as we advised in 3.4.1).

[28]The last sentence of this paragraph introduces the next paragraph.

[29]Repeating a phrase from the previous paragraph helps the reader make a connection to the previous paragraph.

memory and incorporate it into IQ tests (Wechsler, 1939). The usual method is to present a few digits on the first trial and then to increase the number until learners reach their limit and cannot repeat all of the digits (Woodworth & Schlossberg, 1954).[30]

Rote memory for words or letters is less commonly tested. The reasons for not using such stimuli follow from the work of Hilgard and Bower (1966), who established (a) that individuals have prior associations to words and letters and (b) that one individual may have a stronger prior association to a particular word or letter than another individual. That is, the problem of individuals having prior associations to word and letter stimuli cannot be solved by using nonsense syllables. Glaze (1928)[31] found[32] that using nonsense syllables did not entirely eliminate prior associations and thus associative value.[33]

Even though the associative strength of letter stimuli is weaker for some individuals than for others, the average associative strength of letter stimuli should be stronger than the average associative strength of

---

[30]Note that "&" instead of "and" is used to join authors' names inside parentheses.

[31]Whenever possible, you should use recent citations. This paper's sources would have been recent enough about 40 years ago.

[32]Ann used the past tense because Glaze's study was performed in the past and it can be tied to a specific date (1928). In most of your paper, you will use the past tense.

[33]Always review the literature—even when writing a lab report. For papers that are more involved than a lab report, your literature review will be longer. For a research proposal, for example, your professor will probably expect you to have one paragraph that briefly touches on studies done in the area and then one paragraph for each study that you analyze in depth—and your professor will expect you to analyze several studies in depth.

DIGITS VS. LETTERS IN SERIAL RECALL 5

digits. Letters can be formed into words, rich with associative strength, whereas[34] digits can be formed only into numbers, poor in associative strength.[35] Consequently, if no other variable is operating to favor the retention of digits,[36] people should have better recall for letters than for digits. Therefore, I[37] predicted that when participants tried to memorize a set of digits and a set of letters, participants would[38] remember more letters than digits.[39]

---

[34]Ann wisely used "whereas" instead of "while" so that readers would know she meant "but" rather than "during."

[35]Ann used parallel structure to help the reader note and remember the difference between the rich associative strength of words and the poor associative strength of numbers. (For more on what parallel structure is and how you can use it to improve your writing, see 6.4.3.)

[36]Ann wisely admits flaws in her argument, questionable assumptions she made, and qualifications to her argument before her readers think they have discovered a problem that she overlooked.

[37]The use of "I" is proper. The experiment did not make the prediction. "We" did not make the prediction. Ann made the prediction—and said so.

[38]When stating her prediction about what she predicted would happen, Ann used the past tense ("I predicted") and the conditional tense ("would remember").

[39]The last paragraph of the Introduction develops the logic of the study and ends by stating the hypothesis. (For more about how to write the last part of your Introduction, see 3.4.3.) Note also that a main problem students have with the Introduction is organizing it. To make sure that your Introduction is organized, outline it. To help the reader see that your Introduction is organized, use some of the techniques Ann used (see footnotes 24, 25, 27, and 29).

DIGITS VS. LETTERS IN SERIAL RECALL 6

Method[40]

Participants[41]

Seventy-two[42] members of an introductory psychology class (50 women and 22 men,[43] mean age = 20.4 years,[44] *SD* = 2.1) participated voluntarily as part of a class exercise. All participants were treated in accordance with the American Psychological Association's ethical code (American Psychological Association, 2002).[45]

---

[40]The Method section does not usually start on a new page. Instead, it usually starts right after the Introduction with **Method** as its centered and boldfaced heading. It should, however, start on a new page if there is not room to start the text of the Method section on the bottom of the page. In other words, do not put headings at the bottom of a page.

Major sections, such as **Method, Results,** and **Discussion**, begin with centered, boldfaced headings. Subdivisions within these sections have boldfaced headings (e.g., "**Participants**") that start on the left margin. Note that the section's text is not on the same line as the heading. Instead, it begins as an independent paragraph, one double-spaced line below and five spaces to the right of the heading.

[41]When studying adults, use the term "participants." Adults give informed consent to participate in a study, so it is proper to call them "participants." Children and animals are subject to the wishes of others or of the researcher, so it is proper to call them "subjects."

[42]Usually, you should express numbers 10 and above as digits. However, express any number that starts a sentence in words.

[43]Do not use the terms "females" and "males" as nouns unless the age span for participants includes both children and adults. Furthermore, do not use one term (e.g., "girls") to describe female participants while using a nonequivalent term (e.g., "men") to describe male participants. (For more tips on avoiding sexist language, see 1.3.4.)

[44]According to the Publication Manual, you must be specific about the age of your participants.

[45]According to page 247 of the Publication Manual, you should state that participants were treated ethically.

DIGITS VS. LETTERS IN SERIAL RECALL 7

Materials[46]

The list of letters was[47] *G, U, X, K, P, M, B, T, C, S, L,* and *F.* The list of digits was 3, 5, 9, 4, 1, 0, 5, 3, 6, 2, 5, and 0.[48] Thus, neither list contained any meaningful combinations.[49]

Procedure

Participants heard the set of 12 digits at 1 digit per s. After another 30 s,[50] participants were asked to write down as many digits as they could remember, in order. Participants then heard the set of 12 letters and, after a 30 s delay, wrote down as many letters as they could remember, in order.[51] Finally, participants scored their own lists, giving themselves

---

[46]If the experiment had used any specialized equipment (not standard laboratory equipment such as stopwatches), Ann might have added an Apparatus section. The **Apparatus** section, like the **Materials** section, would probably have come before the **Procedure** section.

[47]Note that "list" is the subject of the sentence. It is singular and requires a singular verb. Therefore, Ann wrote that the list "was" rather than that the list "were." In other words, "of letters" is a prepositional phrase, not the subject of the sentence.

[48]The letters were italicized because letters, when they are examples, are italicized. If including the stimulus materials had taken up much more space, Ann would have probably put them in an appendix.

[49]Always mention any steps you took to improve the validity of your study. These steps not only boost your credibility but also help others replicate your study.

[50]Abbreviate standard units and omit periods. (For more on abbreviations, see 3.6.8.)

[51]Note that the Procedure section is organized around when things happened to participants: First, Ann stated what happened first; second, she stated what happened second; and lastly, she stated what happened last. To keep the focus of the Procedure section on the participants, Ann made "participants" the subject of most of the sentences of this paragraph.

one point for each item that they had recalled in the correct position. They summed the number correct for each list to get a total for each list.[52]

Thus, the design was within-subjects with two levels (letters vs. digits). The dependent measure was how many items participants correctly remembered from each list.[53]

Results

The number of items correctly remembered from each list was analyzed using a within-subjects t test and an alpha level of .05.[54] The hypothesis was not supported: Participants did not recall significantly more letters (M = 6.22, SD = 7.92) than digits (M = 6.44, SD = 8.04),[55] $t(71) = -1.21$, $p = .23$, d = -.04.[56,57,58]

---

[52]Ann needed to provide this information so that (a) readers could understand how Ann obtained the scores that she entered into the analysis, (b) other researchers could replicate the study, and (c) readers could evaluate the possibility that the results would have been different if someone other than the learner had scored the recall. Sometimes, an author will put this information in a separate section called "Data scoring."

[53]Ann could have put the last two sentences in a separate Design section.

[54]According to page 248 of the Publication Manual, you should state the significance (alpha) level of your statistical test(s) (see 3.6.1).

[55]Note the use of summary statistics describing the typical score (using means) and the spread of the distribution (using standard deviations). Note also that the abbreviations for these statistics are italicized. These descriptive statistics are included to help the reader understand the pattern of the results and to help investigators who might want to include your study in their meta-analysis of related studies.

[56]In the Results section, limit your discussion of the results to whether the results of the statistical test support or do not support the hypothesis; do not discuss methodological problems that may account for the results. Such discussions belong in the Discussion.

[57]There is no need for either a table or a figure of these results because Ann has only two means to discuss. With such simple results, the reader does not need a table or a figure to understand the results. However, your professor may still require you to make a table or a figure to give you practice in making tables or graphs.

[58]APA now wants you to state what the p value equals (to two or three decimal places).

Discussion

The results did not support the hypothesis that letters would be easier to remember than digits.[59,60] There are at least four explanations for the failure to support the hypothesis.

First, perhaps the hypothesis that people recall letters better than digits is wrong. Letters may not be better recalled than digits because any associative advantages letter stimuli might enjoy are offset by other advantages of digit stimuli. For example, digits may be easier to recall because (a) there are fewer digits than letters (10 as opposed to 26) and (b) digits are more commonly used in isolation than are letters.

Second, although letters, as a rule, have more associative strength than digits, perhaps this general rule did not hold for the particular list used in this experiment. It seems likely that a set of letters such as *U N I V X Y Z B S* would be relatively easy for some people to remember because they might realize that *UNIV* begins the word university, that *XYZ* is in alphabetical order, and that BS is a commonly used abbreviation. Future research should take into account a wider range of possible association values in the letters (cf. Glaze, 1928).[61]

---

[59]The first sentence summarizes the results (3.7.1).

[60]Note that participants actually recalled more digits than letters. However, because the difference was not significant, Ann wisely does not discuss the difference as though it were significant (3.6.1).

[61]The abbreviation "cf." means "compare." The abbreviation, rather than the whole word, is used because the comment is inside parentheses. (For more on abbreviations, see 7.2.5.)

Third, even if most people show a memory advantage for letters over numbers, this advantage might not have held for the particular participants in this study. For example, university students may be more experienced than the general population at remembering numbers.[62]

Fourth, procedural problems in this study could have obscured the advantage of memory for letters. For example, the experimenter always presented letters second. Consequently, participants could have experienced fatigue that reduced their recall for letters (see Woodworth & Schlossberg, 1954, for a review of fatigue effects). In addition, the sample size of 72[63] may have been insufficient to detect the superior recall for letters, especially if the effect is small.[64]

The question about the advantage of letter stimuli in memory is still open. Researchers could seek a more definitive answer by modifying this study (a) to include larger and more varied samples of both learners and of stimuli and (b) to balance order of presentation of letter and digit stimuli. From this experiment, however, one can tentatively conclude[65] that any effect of letters being better recalled than digits is weak.[66]

---

[62]As we stressed in 3.7.3, point out weaknesses and limitations of your study.

[63]Usually, numbers above 10 are expressed using digits.

[64]Normally, if you have nonsignificant results, you need to discuss the statistical power of your study. However, Ann did not have the statistical background to present detailed information about power. For information about how to calculate power, see the book's website.

[65]Note the use of the present tense for conclusions. (For more on tense, see 3.10 and footnotes 32 and 38.)

[66]Despite the nonsignificant results, Ann has come up with a conclusion likely to reassure a reader that he or she has learned something useful from reading the report.

DIGITS VS. LETTERS IN SERIAL RECALL 11

References[67]

[68]American Psychological Association.[69] (2002). Ethical principles of psychologists and code of conduct. *American Psychologist,*[70] *57,*[71] 1060–1073. doi:10.1037/0003-066X.57.12.1060[72]

Glaze, J. A. (1928). The association value of nonsense syllables.[73] *Journal of Genetic Psychology*, *35*, 225–269.

[74]Hilgard, E.,[75] & Bower, G. H. (1966). *Theories of learning.* New York, NY: Appleton-Century-Crofts.

Wechsler, D. (1939). *The measurement of adult intelligence.*[76] Baltimore, MD: Williams & Wilkins.

Woodworth, R. S., & Schlossberg, H. (1954). *Experimental psychology* (Rev. ed.).[77] London, England: Methuen.

---

[67]Start the reference section on a new page and center—but do not bold—the heading ("References"). (For more on the reference section, see 4.10.1.)

[68]In the reference section, the indenting style is the opposite of the indenting for the rest of the paper. Specifically, APA advocates "hanging indent style" in which the first line of a reference is not indented, but additional lines are indented five spaces. To see how to program your word processor to make hanging indents, see the Chapter 4 section of our website. Use the hanging indent feature rather than tabs at the start of each line because any subsequent correction you might make to the citation could move the five-space gap into the middle of a line.

[69]This is an example of a reference for which the author is an organization.

[70]All major words in a journal name are capitalized; the entire journal name is italicized.

[71]Volume number and journal title are italicized. The issue number is usually not mentioned.

[72]This article, like most of the articles you will find, has a digital object identifier (doi). APA requires that you place an article's doi at the end of the reference. To learn more about dois, see p. 150.

[73]Usually, only the first letter of the first word of the title of an article is capitalized. The article title is not italicized.

[74]List references in alphabetical order according to the last name of the first author. Thus, this reference comes after, rather than before, Glaze.

[75]In the reference list, always use a comma between authors' names—even when there are only two authors.

[76]Usually, only the first letter of the first word of a book title is capitalized. However, the entire title is always italicized.

[77]The title of the book is italicized, but not the information in parentheses informing the reader that it is a revised edition.

BOX 3.1 How to Outline a Research Report

Type the major sections of your research report: Title, Abstract, Introduction, Method, Results, Discussion, and References. Next, add subheadings under the relevant headings. In most cases, the start of your outline will look like this:

I. Title (should contain key predictors, should name the main outcome measure, and should imply a cause-effect conclusion only if you have done an experiment)

II. Abstract
    A. Hypothesis
    B. Method
        1. Participants
        2. Procedures
            a. Dependent measure task
            b. Experimental conditions
    C. Results relating to hypothesis (in a proposal, how data will be analyzed)
    D. Implications of the study

III. Introduction (Remember that the heading for the Introduction is not "Introduction"; instead, it is your paper's title.)
    A. Overview of research area (why the area is important)
    B. Review of past studies (questions raised by past research)
    C. Overview of your study (how your research will answer questions raised by past research; in this section, you will state your hypothesis)

IV. Method
    A. **Participants**
        1. Number, gender, age, ethnicity, and other key characteristics
        2. Where recruited from (e.g., Clarion University students enrolled in General Psychology, residents of Columbus, Ohio)
        3. When recruited (e.g., during Fall, 2012)
        4. How recruited (e.g., no compensation, course credit, $5) and who was excluded (e.g., Participants had to be native English speakers.)
        5. How assigned to condition
        6. What the design was (may be put elsewhere)
        7. Ethically recruited (e.g., The Clarion University Institutional Review Board gave approval for this research.)
    B. **Materials, Measures, or Apparatus** (optional: may be integrated into **Procedure** section)
    C. **Procedure**
        1. Where study was done (e.g., lab, field)
        2. Independent variable manipulation (if you had an independent variable)

(*continued*)

BOX 3.1 (*Continued*)

a. Name of manipulation(s)
b. Description of the manipulation—how long it took, what the differences between conditions were, reference to a source that provides more detail about the manipulation
c. Techniques that you used to make the manipulation valid (e.g., training experimenters, making experimenters unaware of the hypothesis)

3. Dependent measure task
   a. Name of what you are trying to measure
   b. How you are trying to measure it (e.g., name of instrument, sample questions, reference to a source that provides more detail about the measure)
   c. Techniques used to make the measure valid or evidence supporting the measure's validity (e.g., training observers, making observers unaware of experimental condition, presenting evidence of interrater agreement)
4. Participants were treated ethically (e.g., "Participants were then thanked and debriefed.")

V. **Results**

A. What your data are (data preparation, how behaviors were converted into scores ["To get a score for each participant, . . .]")—if this is not obvious and was not already described in the Method section
B. Statistical evidence that the "data are trustworthy" (Silvia, 2007, p. 86)—if you have collected evidence that the measure is reliable or that the manipulation is valid
C. What analysis was done
   1. Name of analysis ("Data were analyzed using . . .")
   2. Reason for using this analysis (may involve explaining the analysis or explaining how the data met the analysis's underlying assumptions)—often optional
   3. What the hypothesis to be tested is (often, which conditions should differ from each other or from zero)
D. What the results were
   1. In terms of supporting the hypothesis
   2. In terms of the average score and standard deviation for each condition
   3. In terms of the numbers generated from the statistical test
      a. Usually, the degrees of freedom for the test, the value of the test statistic, and the *p* value: the probability of getting the obtained results if the variables were not related.
      b. In terms of an effect size statistic such as Cohen's *d* and a confidence interval for that effect size statistic—may be optional.
   4. In terms of whether the results were statistically significant.

VI. **Discussion**

A. Summary of the results relating to the hypothesis
B. How the results fit—or challenge—existing research and theory (Citations will be necessary here. Some of these citations will come from your introduction.)

BOX 3.1 (*Continued*)

C. Strength of research (optional)
D. Limitations of the research (Speak for skeptics who might argue that the results may not provide as much support for the hypothesis as it first appears. Consider—and if possible refute—interpretations of the results that would not be as supportive of your hypothesis as you might like. Take care not to overstate how definitive your study is or to overgeneralize your findings.)
E. Need for future research (to build on the research's strengths and to expand beyond its limitations. For example, you might increase the generalizability of the findings by repeating the study with a broader sample of participants or a broader sample of stimuli.)
F. Conclusions: As Roediger (2007) put it, the "take home message: What we did not know before, why the study is important" (p. 20)

VII. References

If you start with the preceding outline, you will still need to add subheadings to have a complete outline for your paper. Adding subheadings is especially important for the Introduction and Discussion sections. To illustrate the difference between a general outline and one that will provide enough detail to guide your writing, study the outline of this chapter's sample paper:

I. Title: Memory for Digits and Letters in a Serial Recall Task

II. Abstract
  A. Procedure and participants used to test the hypothesis
  B. Results did not support the hypothesis
  C. Possible explanations for the results

III. Introduction: Memory for Digits and Letters in a Serial Recall Task
  A. If memory is the ability to form associations between stimuli, stimuli that already have prior associations between them should be easier to remember.
  B. Ebbinghaus believed that letter combinations that are words, remind people of words, or remind people of initials have prior associations.
  C. Most tests of rote memory use digits because experts assume digits do not have prior associations.
  D. Few tests of rote memory use letters because research indicates that words and letters (Hilgard & Bower, 1966)—and even nonsense syllables (Glaze, 1928)—have prior associations.
  E. If, as seems likely, the prior associations between letters are stronger than the prior associations between digits (and no other factor is operating to give digits an edge over letters), memory for letters should be stronger than memory for digits.

IV. Method
  A. **Participants**
  B. **Materials**
  C. **Procedure**
  D. **Design**

(continued)

BOX 3.1 (*Continued*)

V. Results
   A. Statistical tests used
   B. Hypothesis was not supported

VI. Discussion
   A. The hypothesis was not supported
   B. Four explanations for why the hypothesis was not supported
      1. The hypothesis is wrong.
      2. The hypothesis holds for most lists of letters but not for the particular list used in this experiment.
      3. The hypothesis holds for most people but not for the particular participants studied in this experiment.
      4. Methodological problems—order effects and lack of power—prevented this experiment from detecting the effect.
   C. Conclusions and recommendations for future research

VII. References

3.12 Report and Proposal Content Checklist

- ☐ My title is short, simple, and to the point. It contains the names of the relevant variables (in an experiment, the independent [manipulated] and dependent [measured] variables; in a correlational study, the predictor and criterion [to-be-predicted] variables).
- ☐ My Abstract begins on page 2 with the centered title "Abstract." It consists of an unindented paragraph followed by the indented and italicized text "*Keywords:*" followed by key terms related to my paper.
- ☐ My Abstract is a brief summary of the following sections of my paper: the Introduction—what I studied and why, the Participants section—who the participants were, the Procedure section—what the participants did, the Results section—whether the data supported the hypothesis, and the **Discussion** section—the meaning of the results.
- ☐ I cited any source from which I got ideas—even if I did not directly quote that source.
- ☐ My citations are free of the following common content errors:
   — When citing authors, I limited myself to stating authors' last names. I did not mention authors' first names, professional titles (e.g., "Dr."), or professional affiliations.
   — When citing sources, I did not use footnotes to cite sources.
   — I did not mention any article titles in the text of my paper.

- [ ] Most of my citations are from recent journal articles describing actual research studies rather than from secondary sources (e.g., textbooks, magazines, newspapers).

Introduction

- [ ] My Introduction starts on page 3 with the title of my paper centered on the top of the page.
- [ ] The beginning of my Introduction engages the reader by illustrating why my topic area is interesting and important.
- [ ] When I suggested that a statement was a fact, I made sure that I was not just expressing my opinion.
- [ ] If I stated a fact that was not common knowledge, I cited a credible source for that fact.
- [ ] I cited several studies related to my topic.
- [ ] I explained why testing my hypothesis is important: I showed how my study builds on previous work or fills a gap in previous work.
- [ ] I explained why I believe that the hypothesis might be true. To make the logic behind my hypothesis clear, I explained relevant concepts and theories.
- [ ] My hypothesis is clearly stated.
- [ ] My Introduction foreshadows the rest of the paper (especially, the essence of the Method section).

Method

- [ ] I did not start this section on a new page. Instead, I began this section immediately (one double-spaced line below) after the Introduction with the boldfaced and centered heading "**Method**"—not "Methods."
- [ ] I used complete sentences: I did not list information as I might for a recipe or for a chemistry experiment.
- [ ] I used the metric system (e.g., centimeters instead of inches, kilograms instead of pounds).
- [ ] I used the past tense—unless I was writing a research proposal, in which case, I used the future tense.
- [ ] I did not misuse the terms experiment, sample, population, or random.
- [ ] I boldfaced all the headings in the Method section.
- [ ] I divided the Method section into at least two subsections (**Participants** [if I studied adult humans, **Subjects** if I studied children or nonhuman animals] and **Procedure**).

Participants or Subjects Section

- [ ] I specified how I selected or recruited my sample.
- [ ] I indicated how participants were compensated (if they were compensated).

- ☐ I included the number of participants of each gender.
- ☐ I specified the age of participants (average age and either standard deviation or range of ages).
- ☐ I included other demographic characteristics, when appropriate.
- ☐ I specified the number of participants who dropped out of the study or whose data I did not analyze and the reasons for not having data from all my participants.
- ☐ I explained, in this section or elsewhere in the Method section, how I assigned participants to condition.
- ☐ I made it clear that I treated participants ethically.

Procedure

- ☐ I focused on what happened to participants and what participants did—and presented the information in order from the first thing that happened to the last thing that happened (e.g., "Participants were thanked and debriefed.").
- ☐ I left out any details that had nothing to do with replicating the study and instead focused on details that, if changed, might change how participants acted or the study's results.
- ☐ It is clear how (under what conditions) I tested each participant.
- ☐ If I used standard laboratory equipment, I identified the manufacturer and model number.
- ☐ If I asked participants questions that I borrowed from other sources, I made that clear—and cited those sources.
- ☐ It is clear how I turned each participant's response into a score.
- ☐ It is clear how I assigned participants to conditions (this explanation might be in another subsection of the Method section).
- ☐ It is clear how a control or comparison group ruled out an alternative explanation for a difference between groups.
- ☐ It is clear that the measure I used is reliable and valid because
  - — If I used a published measure, I cited evidence of the measure's reliability and validity.
  - — If I collected data related to the measure's reliability or validity, I reported those data. For example, if I had data related to the extent to which two different observers' scores agreed when scoring the same response, I reported those data.
- ☐ After a researcher read my Method section, that researcher could replicate my study.
- ☐ It is clear from my paper that my study is a good way to test my hypothesis.
- ☐ It is clear what I did to reduce bias.
- ☐ I described all my measurements in metric units (e.g., I used centimeters rather than inches).

Results

- ☐ I did not start this section on a new page. Instead, I began this section immediately (one double-spaced line below) after the Method section with the centered and boldfaced heading "**Results**."
- ☐ I included enough information about descriptive statistics to help readers know more than just the outcome of the statistical significance test. For example, if I used a *t* test, I presented means and standard deviations for the two conditions.
- ☐ I determined my professor's views about reporting analyses beyond that of significance tests. Thus, I know whether my professor required me to follow the *Publication Manual's* suggestions that I include a confidence interval or report an estimate of effect size, such as Cohen's *d.*
- ☐ I made it clear to the reader what data I used in the analyses (how behaviors were turned into scores), if it was not obvious, and if I had not included this information in the Method section.
- ☐ I made it clear what analyses I used on those data and what the purpose of each analysis was (e.g., "I did a *t* test to test the hypothesis that . . .").
- ☐ I specified what significance level I used (if I used a significance test).
- ☐ I indicated which groups scored significantly higher than others. To help readers visualize the pattern in the results, I supplemented the significance test with summary statistics (usually means and standard deviations for each group). If I had fewer than four conditions and my professor did not require a table or a figure, I put the all the means in the text of the Results section. Otherwise, I put them in a table or a graph.
- ☐ I indicated whether the results supported my hypothesis.
- ☐ I wrote what *p* value I obtained by writing "$p =$" rather than just saying "$p <$"—unless p was less than .001.
- ☐ If I used a graph, I used a standard one: I did not use color, 3-D effects, or pie charts.
- ☐ If I used a graph, I plotted the outcome (dependent) measure on the y (vertical) axis.
- ☐ If I used tables, I made sure that each table added meaningful information beyond what I presented in the text of my Results section.
- ☐ I made sure that I referred to each table and figure in the text of my paper (e.g., "As Table 1 indicates").
- ☐ I expressed numbers relating to my results in digits (e.g., "5") rather in words (e.g., "five").

Discussion

- ☐ I did not start this section on a new page. Instead, I began this section immediately (one double-spaced line below) after the Results section with the centered heading "**Discussion**" in bold text.
- ☐ I started the text of this section by stating whether the results supported my hypothesis.
- ☐ I compared my Discussion against the citation checklist (4.11.2).
- ☐ I interpreted my results in the context of the theory, past research, and practical issues that I noted in my Introduction. For example, I compared my results to what other researchers found.
- ☐ I tried to explain results that did not fit my predictions.
- ☐ I addressed alternative explanations for my results. I tried to rule out these alternative explanations, but when I could not, I admitted that I could not.
- ☐ I pointed out the weaknesses and limitations of my study. I even sketched out future research that researchers could do to correct these weaknesses or overcome these limitations.
- ☐ If possible, I made a case for generalizing my results (I had a representative sample, the results were similar to what others had found, etc.).
- ☐ I treated nonsignificant results as inconclusive.
  - — I did not use nonsignificant results as proof that a treatment had no effect.
  - — I did not use nonsignificant results that were almost significant as evidence that the treatment had an effect.
- ☐ I ended with a brief paragraph that (a) restated the main findings, (b) highlighted how those findings filled a gap in existing research, and (c) suggested directions for future research.

References

- ☐ I started this section on a new page with the centered heading "References" in plain (normal) text.
- ☐ I cited in the main text of my paper all the references listed in this section. If a reference was not cited, I either added that citation to the main text of my paper or deleted the reference.
- ☐ All the sources cited in my paper are also listed in this section except for "personal communication" citations (see 4.3.3); original works that I did not read, but which I learned about through a secondary source (see 4.3.1); and ancient works, such as the Bible.

3.13 Summary

1. The sections of a research report or proposal should appear in this order: Title and Author Note, Abstract, Introduction, **Method, Results, Discussion,** References, Appendixes (optional), Tables (optional), and Figures (optional).
2. The title should be short. For an experiment, it should usually include the independent (manipulated) variable(s) and the dependent (measured) variable(s).
3. If your professor wants an Author Note, put the Author Note on the bottom of the title page. Start it with the centered heading: "Author Note."
4. The Abstract is a short, unindented paragraph that summarizes the paper.
5. In the Introduction (the "why" section of the paper), you should introduce and state the hypothesis.
6. The Method section (the "how" section of the paper) usually has at least two subsections: a Participants section (called a Subjects section if you studied nonhuman animals) and a Procedure section.
7. In the Results section, for each analysis, tell the reader what the analysis was, why you did it, and whether the results of that analysis support your hypothesis.
8. You may be able to present your results without a figure or a table. If you have a table or a figure, refer to it in text.
9. Line graphs are allowed when you are summarizing the results of an experiment in which you manipulated the amount of a variable. If, on the other hand, your experiment involves comparing different types of treatments or comparing a treatment group to a control group, you should use a bar graph. Scatterplots are most appropriate when your study does not involve manipulating a variable (e.g., you correlated scores on two tests). Never use pie charts.
10. Usually, you must express units of measurement in any part of your report in metric units.
11. Begin the Discussion by relating the results to the hypothesis. Next, relate your results to previous research. Then, discuss limitations of your study that may qualify your conclusions. Finally, discuss the implications of your study for future research.
12. All the sources listed in your reference section should be cited in your paper. To see an example of how to format your references, see either the term paper's reference list (2.11) or the sample research report's reference list (3.11). To learn more about formatting your reference list, see 4.10.

CHAPTER 4

Finding, Reading, Citing, and Referencing Sources

Sources—information that others have produced—are the raw material from which you build your paper. You must find, extract, refine, cite, and reference that raw material. Thus, to write a strong paper, you must first find high-quality sources so that you can base your paper on the best information available. Next, you must extract material that provides solid support for your claim. Then, you must refine that material: Quoting it is not enough. Finally, you must correctly cite and reference your sources so that you show how your work builds on the work of others.

4.1 Finding Information

4.1.1 Starting Your Search: Databases, Search Terms, and Secondary Sources

Your professor will expect you to read current journal articles related to your paper's topic. To find current articles, you can use two strategies.

The first strategy is to use PsycINFO, PsycARTICLES, *Psychological Abstracts*, *Social Science Index*, *Current Contents*, *Social Science Citation Index*, or some other database designed to help researchers find recent articles on a topic. The two keys to using these databases are to know (a) what search terms you should use and (b) how to combine search terms.

If you are using a computerized database such as PsycINFO, finding the right search terms is often easy. For many databases, if you enter the name for the concept you want to study (e.g., "aggression"), you can select the "Index Terms" search field, and the computer will automatically convert your term into several appropriate search terms and conduct a search under those terms.

The real power of computerized searches comes when you combine search terms. For example, in less than a minute, you can find all review articles published in APA journals in the past 10 years involving recovered memory of sexual abuse in men. Despite the potential advantages of a computerized search, after you do such a search, you may have one or more of the following problems.

First, you might get too many references. In that case, see Table 4.1.

Second, you may have too few references. If that is the case, after making sure you have spelled your search terms correctly, consult either Table 4.2 (page 121) or a reference librarian.

Table 4.1
*What to Do if a PsycINFO or PsycArticles Search Produces Too Many Sources**

Modify Your Quick Search	**Example**
Use quotation marks to search for an exact phrase.	In the search box, type the exact phrase you want and surround that phrase with quotation marks (e.g., "cell phones on driving").
Limit your search to a publication type.	Under the "Publication Type" menu, scroll down and select "All Journals."
Limit your search to peer-reviewed journals.	Under "Publication Type," scroll down and select "Peer Reviewed Journal."
Limit the number of articles by selecting specific publication dates.	Next to "Published Date," fill in the date boxes so that your search includes only articles from the past two years.
Limit your search to a specific population.	Select a specific age group (e.g., "Childhood") or population group (e.g., "Human" or "Male") by scrolling down and selecting your choice in the appropriate menu.
Conduct a Fielded Search	**Example**
Narrow your search by adding a search term. For instance, rather than searching for all articles on Alzheimer's, you might search for only those articles on Alzheimer's that deal with resilience.	1. Original search term: "Alzheimer's." 2. Select "and" in the scroll bar located below "Look for." 3. Add a second search term: "resilience."

Table 4.1
What to Do if a PsycINFO or PsycArticles Search Produces Too Many Sources—continued*

Modify Your Quick Search	Example
Limit your search by excluding concepts not related to your paper.	1. Original search term: "Alzheimer's." 2. Select "not" in the scroll bar located below "Look for." 3. Term to exclude: "depression."
Limit your search to certain search fields.	Instead of searching "any field," select the "Title" or "Author" field.
Limit your search to journals.	Under the "Publication Type" menu, scroll down and select "All Journals."
Limit your search to peer-reviewed journals	Check the option "Peer Reviewed," or under "Publication Type," scroll down and select "Peer Reviewed Journal."
Limit your search to a specific journal, preferably one that is both highly respected and owned by your library.	Type in the journal's name next to "Publication Name" (e.g., "*Developmental Psychology*").
Limit your search to recently published articles.	Next to "Published Date," fill in the date boxes.

*Most of this advice is also relevant for computer searches in EBSCO, Education Resources Information Center (ERIC), ProQuest, and other databases.

Table 4.2
*What to Do if a PsycINFO or PsycArticles Search Retrieves an Insufficient Number of Sources**

Expanding Either a Quick Search or a Fielded Search	Example
Expand your search by selecting additional publication types.	Select "All" under "Publication Type."
Combine search terms with the word "OR."	Search term: "aging OR older."
Rather than include the entire search term (e.g., "adolescence"), type the first part of it (e.g., "adolescen") followed by an "*" (e.g., "adolescen*").	A search for "moral*" will find articles that include "moral," "moralistic," and "morality."
Special Tip for Expanding a Fielded Search	**Example**
In addition to the preceding tips, expand your search to include similar search terms by checking "Also search for related words."	If your search term is "aging," the search will include similar terms that are contained in APA's *Psychological Thesaurus* such as "older," "elderly," and "mature."

*Most of this advice is also relevant for computer searches in EBSCO, ERIC, PROQUEST, and other databases.

Third, your library will probably not have all the references you have found. Fortunately, you may be able to get some of those articles by using Google Scholar, going to the home pages of the articles' authors, or, as a last resort, using interlibrary loan. Unfortunately, interlibrary loan takes time—so if you put off your library search, you may not receive key material in time.

Fourth, you may be tempted to read abstracts (summaries) of articles (especially if you are using PsycINFO, which gives you abstracts rather than entire articles) rather than reading the actual articles. Although reading abstracts can help you separate the articles that are relevant to your paper from the articles that are irrelevant, you will not get enough detail from the abstracts to allow you to analyze the articles. You will learn far more if you read the papers themselves. Therefore, when the abstract of an article suggests that the article is relevant to your paper, take the time to find and read the entire article.

In addition to using databases, there is a second strategy for finding journal articles—consulting secondary sources for secondhand accounts of research. After reading about a potentially relevant article in a secondary source such as a chapter in a textbook; a chapter in the *Annual Review of Psychology;* or a review article in a journal, such as *Psychological Science;* you can use the secondary source's reference list to find that article.

4.1.2 Using One Reference to Find More References

Once you find one relevant article, you can use that article to find other relevant articles (see Table 4.3). For example, imagine that you have found only one reference relevant to your assignment: Researcher (2012). When you read Researcher's paper, you may discover that (a) the topic was first identified by Originator (2003), (b) much of the important work was conducted by Refiner (2007), and (c) some recent work is being done by Current (in press). You can find those three references in Researcher's reference list.[1] After you find and read those sources, look for additional useful references in those sources' reference lists.

Although tracking down sources listed in reference lists can educate you about the history of the topic, it will not get you the recent references you need. Fortunately, you can get an older source to lead you to newer ones by using the following two tactics.

First, because recent articles that build on your older source should cite that source, do a PsycINFO citation search, a *Social Science Citation Index* search, or a Google Scholar search for recent articles that cite your older source. To see how you would use this strategy, suppose that your valued, older source is Refiner (2007). To search in PsycINFO for articles that cite Refiner (2007), click on "citation search" and then type the Refiner (2007) reference in the "search" box. You would then get a list of papers that cited Refiner (2007), and those papers would probably be relevant to your assignment. To search in the *Social Science Citation Index* for articles that cite Refiner (2007), go to the most recent volume (e.g., the 2012 volume) of the *Social Science Citation Index* and look up Refiner (2007). The index will give you a list of papers written in that year whose authors cited Refiner (2007). To do a Google Scholar search for

---

[1]If the reference list refers to a website that no longer exists, you may be able to find that website by looking it up at http://web.archive.org.

articles that cited Refiner (2007), go to Google Scholar (http://scholar.google.com), type the article's title into the search box, click "Search," find the entry for your article in the search results, and click on the "Cited by . . ." link.

A second way you can use an older source to find more recent sources is to search for recent work by the original article's author (e.g., in Google Scholar, click on "Advanced Scholar Search," and then type in the author's name in the "Author" box; in

Table 4.3
A Five-Step Plan for Literature Searches

Step	Task	Notes
1A	Browse secondary sources (magazine articles, newspaper articles, books, encyclopedias, dictionaries, and blogs).	The main purpose is to get a general understanding of your topic and to get leads to articles that might be worth reading.
1B	Find search terms.	Remember that search terms will usually refer to nouns that represent your main variables—and that the question you are addressing will involve between two and five variables (e.g., video games lead to aggression in adolescents). Look up your main variables in the *Psychological Thesaurus*—and pay special attention to the entries for "Related terms," "Narrower terms," and "Scope notes." If you are still having trouble coming up with search terms, talk to a reference librarian.
2	Search for journal articles.	Use the authors and key words you found in Steps 1A and 1B to guide your search. If your search yields too many sources, see Table 4.1; if your search yields too few sources, see Table 4.2.
3	Read articles.	Once you find a relevant article, find its key words (the key words will be listed after the phrase "key words:" on the article's first page, just below the article's abstract), and use those key words to do a key word search. In addition, use the authors it cites to search the literature by author.
4	Consult reference lists of your articles to find relevant older articles.	This strategy will get you old, but important, articles.
5	Conduct a citation search (e.g., using Google Scholar or the *Social Science Citation Index*) to find recent articles that cite the older, key article you found.	This strategy will help you locate newer resources.

PsycARTICLES, select the "AU" or "Author" field and type the author's name in the relevant box). In addition to tracking down that author's published papers, you may want to track down that author's website. The author's website may provide links to relevant unpublished work (e.g., papers presented at conferences that were written by the author or by the author's graduate students) and to the websites of other researchers doing work relevant to the topic.

4.1.3 Deciding What to Read: Choosing Acceptable Sources

An important part of understanding your assignment is understanding what sources your professor will accept. Although different sources of information have their uses (see Table 4.4), most professors, as well as the editors of the *Publication Manual*, expect that you will read, cite, and reference *empirical articles* (articles in which authors report

Table 4.4
Different Sources of Information: Strengths, Limitations, and Warnings

Sources	Strengths	Comments and Limitations	Warnings
General psychology textbook, encyclopedia, psychological dictionary	Overviews of the topic	Not as recent or as detailed as journal articles	You might cite these sources at the very beginning of a paper to introduce a topic or term. If you are introducing a psychological term, use a psychological dictionary rather than a regular dictionary.
	Peer-reviewed (and therefore usually accurate) information		
	Leads to classic articles		
Magazine article, newspaper article	Overviews of the topic Leads to recent journal articles	Not as accurate or as detailed as journal articles; not as accurate as textbooks	You will probably cite these sources only to introduce some interesting fact or story that is not based on psychological research. If the story describes some interesting research, read—and cite—the original research report.
Books devoted to theory or topic	Detailed, historical views of the theory or topic	Not as current as journal articles; may be promoting a particular point of view	Books will vary in quality and depth. Some books will be written for a popular, rather than a professional, audience. Check to see whether the book's author is an expert in the field.

Table 4.4
Different Sources of Information: Strengths, Limitations, and Warnings—continued

Sources	Strengths	Comments and Limitations	Warnings
Review articles	Coherent summaries of recent research and may tell you about other relevant articles	May be promoting a particular point of view; not as detailed as research articles	Ask your professor whether you can use review articles.
Empirical articles	Details about recent and classic studies that you can critique or replicate	Difficult to read	Read the abstract before deciding whether to invest in reading the entire study. Some journals are more extensively reviewed than others. For example, articles submitted to journals published by either the Association for Psychological Science (APS) or the American Psychological Association (APA) tend to go through a more rigorous review process than articles submitted to most other journals. The more reviewed the journal, the fewer flaws the studies will have, and the more likely the authors are to confess those mistakes in the Discussion section. Thus, reading Discussion sections of high-quality journals can help you learn how to look for flaws in research.
Conference papers	Recent information on topics	Not as thoroughly reviewed as journal articles	Be very cautious about trusting these papers because their final versions, in many cases, have not been peer reviewed.
Web	You can find almost anything on the Internet.	You can find almost anything on the Internet—including "proof" that the sun revolves around the earth.	Usually, ".edu" sites, ".org" sites, sites of established authors, and sites of databases you have to pay for (e.g., PsycARTICLES and EBSCOhost) are more reliable than ".com" sites.

their own research) from high-quality journals. Unfortunately, students often violate this expectation. These violations come in three forms.

The most serious violation is reading an article in a magazine (e.g., *Psychology Today*, *Time*, *Newsweek*) rather than a journal article. (If you are unsure of the difference between magazines and journals, see Table 4.5.) At worst, magazine articles may misrepresent and misinterpret research findings. At best, magazine articles provide few details about how the research was conducted. In any case, reading secondhand accounts of research in magazine articles does not help you develop the ability to read and critique the firsthand accounts of research that you find in empirical journal articles.

The second most serious violation is reading review articles (in which authors discuss other people's research) instead of reading empirical articles (in which researchers provide firsthand reports of their own research).[2] Although review articles integrate

Table 4.5
How Psychological Journals Differ From Magazines

Journal Articles	**Magazines**
Follow APA format. For example, they have an Abstract and a Reference list.	Do not follow APA format.
Usually list reviewers or consulting editors—and their professional (usually university) affiliation inside the front or back cover.	List the magazine staff (but no affiliations) somewhere in the first few pages of the publication.
Usually have instructions on how to submit papers for publication.	Usually do not provide instructions on how to submit articles.
The title of the journal often includes the word "Journal," "Research," or "Bulletin." If the publisher is not the APA, the APS, or another scientific organization, the journal describes itself (usually on the cover, inside the cover, or on a page before the articles start) as the journal of a certain scientific society or organization.	The title usually does not include the word "Journal." The magazine is rarely affiliated with a professional organization. For example, *Psychology Today* is not affiliated with any group of professional psychologists.
In journals, there are no discontinuous pages for an article: Once a reader starts an article, the reader does not have to skip any page to continue reading the article.	Articles in magazines often have discontinuous pages: To continue reading an article, the reader may have to follow directions such as "continued on page 121."
Journals have a more serious look: They usually do not have color pictures. Ads are usually for professional books and other products of interest only to professionals in the field. There are no ads for consumer products.	Most magazines have a less serious look than a professional journal does. Magazines may contain color pictures and ads for consumer products.

[2]Your professor may want you to read review articles in addition to—but not instead of—empirical articles. Note also that because a review article will cite and reference empirical articles, a recent review article may help you find relevant empirical articles.

many research studies, they are still secondhand accounts of research. These secondhand accounts may be slanted by their authors' theoretical positions. Furthermore, reading secondhand accounts of research does not give you practice in critiquing firsthand accounts of research studies. (To learn about a few of the journals that specialize in firsthand accounts of research, see Table 4.6.)

The third most serious violation is failing to use articles from high-quality journals. There are three main reasons students fail to use articles from elite journals.

First, students may not appreciate that journals vary in quality. Journals vary in quality because journals vary in how likely they are to accept an article. For journals that most professors consider high-quality (typically journals sponsored by the APA or the APS), many manuscripts are submitted but few are published.[3] Usually, manuscripts are rejected because the study had methodological flaws or because the study was not considered as important as the studies that were published. Whereas the articles that are published in a high-quality journal have survived a rigorous screening process, articles published in journals that professors consider low quality (typically, journals not sponsored by a professional psychological organization and that publish the majority of the manuscripts submitted to them) have not been as extensively prescreened.[4]

Second, students may fail to use articles from a high-quality journal because they are using Internet sources instead of journal articles. Unfortunately, the Internet is

Table 4.6
A Sample of Journals That Publish Research Articles

Journal	Brief Description
Developmental Psychology	Journal that primarily reports research relating to child and adolescent development.
Journal of Abnormal Psychology	Articles focus on the treatment and diagnosis of psychopathology. Occasionally reports experimental studies on humans or animals related to emotion or pathology. Sometimes reports studies that test hypotheses derived from psychological theories.
Journal of Applied Behavior Analysis	Articles report a sizable effect on an important behavior, usually employing a single-participant design.

(continued)

[3]To see a list of all the APA journals, go to http://www.apa.org/journals/by_title.html; to see a list of all the APS journals, go to http://www.psychologicalscience.org/journals/.

[4]Usually, the organization sponsoring the journal will be prominently mentioned on either the front or the back of the journal's cover. If you do not have access to the journal, you can usually find the sponsoring organization by doing a Google search to find the journal's home page. Usually, the home page will mention the sponsoring organization, and its URL (e.g., "apa.org") will often reveal the sponsoring organization. If, after looking at the home page, you still do not know what organization is sponsoring the journal, click on the "About the Journal" link.

Table 4.6
A Sample of Journals That Publish Research Articles—continued

Journal	Brief Description
Journal of Applied Psychology	Reports research relating to industry, government, health, education, consumer affairs, and other applied areas.
Journal of Comparative Psychology	Articles may include both laboratory and field observation of species. Emphasis is on relating findings to the theory of evolution.
Journal of Counseling Psychology	Publishes research articles evaluating the effectiveness of (a) counseling and (b) techniques for selecting and training counselors.
Journals of Experimental Psychology	Publishes research on fundamental mechanisms and processes. There are four different journals: *Journal of Experimental Psychology: General;* *Journal of Experimental Psychology: Animal Behavior Processes;* *Journal of Experimental Psychology: Learning, Memory, and Cognition;* and *Journal of Experimental Psychology: Human Perception and Performance.*
Journal of Experimental Social Psychology	Almost all articles report the results of social psychological experiments.
Journal of Personality and Social Psychology	Contains three sections: (a) attitudes and social cognition, (b) interpersonal relations and group processes, and (c) personality and individual differences.
Journal of Social Psychology	Source of relatively short articles.
Memory and Cognition	A good source of articles related to human experimental psychology. See also *Journal of Experimental Psychology: Learning, Memory, and Cognition.*
Personality and Social Psychology Bulletin	Contains short articles that are often easy to understand.
Psychological Assessment: A Journal of Consulting and Clinical Psychology	Publishes research that assesses the validity of a variety of tests and measures.
Psychological Record	Source of short articles.
Psychology and Aging	Source of easy-to-read articles on physiological and behavioral aspects of aging during older adulthood.

often a questionable source. Some of the information presented as fact on the Internet has little research support, and much of it is not of sufficient quality to be published in a reputable academic journal. Although there is some trustworthy information on the Internet, that information is often trustworthy only because it already appeared in a reputable, reviewed, printed journal.

Third, students may not use an article from a high-quality journal because they do not see how that article is relevant to their paper. Thus, students investigating a specific topic (e.g., discrimination against students who smoke) often fail to realize that articles in an elite journal that study a more general topic (e.g., discrimination) as well as articles that study a slightly different topic (e.g., discrimination against lesbians) are probably relevant to their particular topic. As a result, students may ignore a journal article published in a highly regarded journal that discovers a general principle (e.g., a way to reduce discrimination) but treasure an article in a lower-quality journal that applies that general principle to a specific case (e.g., seeing whether that principle works to reduce discrimination against people who smoke).

In short, your sources should include articles from elite journals. The following three tips will help you include such articles.

1. Realize that the particular phenomenon you are investigating probably represents a particular example of a more general phenomenon. Consequently, principles that affect other attitudes also affect the attitude you are studying; principles that affect other behaviors probably also affect the behavior you are investigating; and principles that apply to one group often apply to another group. Therefore, do not exclude an article from your paper merely because it does not study exactly the same behavior, attitude, or population that you are investigating.
2. If you find an article that does focus on the specific behavior or attitude you are examining, check its reference list for articles from elite journals that investigated a more general topic.
3. Make sure that at least some of your sources come from journals sponsored by APA or APS.

4.2 Reading

4.2.1 Read Purposefully

As we have discussed, you should find recent journal articles that contain first-hand reports of research. Before you start reading those articles, be sure you are clear about the questions you are trying to answer. Your questions should relate to your thesis statement (if you are writing a term paper) or to your hypothesis (if you are writing a research report). Focusing on the questions you are trying to answer will help you decide which articles to read: You will know, after reading an article's abstract, whether you should read the rest of that article. As you read the article, focusing on the questions you are trying to answer will help you take useful notes on the article.

4.2.2 Take Thoughtful, Useful Notes—And if You Copy, Be Careful

To take useful notes—and to avoid plagiarism—resist the impulse to jot down notes as soon as you find an article. Before you start taking notes on the article, record the full reference as it should appear in your paper's reference list (to see how to format a reference in APA style, see 4.10.10). Recording the full reference will allow you to return to the source if you need to and will prevent you from needing to return to the source (often the night before the paper is due) merely to complete your reference list.

Before taking any notes, read the article at least once and reflect on how it relates to your paper. Taking notes as you read, although giving the illusion of progress, will hurt you more than help you. At best, you have copied material that you will eventually have to think about, rephrase, and summarize to put in your paper. At worst, you have set yourself up to plagiarize.

To prevent yourself from merely copying information, use a system of note taking that encourages you to think. The following system might work for you: Precede each "fact" you note with an "S" if it is the author's own idea, conclusion, theory, or opinion ("S" because the author Stated it); a "C" if it is another's fact the author has Cited; or an "R" if it is a Result of the author's research. Alternatively, you might try using Exhibit 4.1 as a guide for note taking. Using a system such as the one described in Exhibit 4.1 will help you spot common flaws in research. (For more help on spotting flaws in research, see Chapter 5.)

Even if you use a note-taking system, you will sometimes copy material from a source. When you do copy three or more consecutive words from a source, (a) place quotation marks around those copied words and (b) write down the page number next to the quotation.

In short, whereas thoughtful note taking can prepare you to write a great paper, careless note taking can set you up to plagiarize. Given that the costs of carelessness are so high, be sure to (a) record the full reference to the source before taking notes and (b) put quotation marks around any words, phrases, sentences, or paragraphs that you copy.

4.2.3 Reread

You will have to read articles more than once. Your job is not to scan them but to dissect them. Many professors spend hours studying a single article. Do not expect to gain an in-depth understanding more quickly than professors can. To help you understand what you will get by reading an article more than once, study Table 4.7.

As you can see from studying Table 4.7, the first time through the article, your focus is on understanding what the author is saying. The second time through, your focus is on questioning what the author is saying.

4.2.4 Revise Your Notes

Revising your notes before you start writing can help you in at least two ways. First, it will help you understand the material better. Whereas your original notes will probably consist largely of copied phrases, your rewritten notes should consist

EXHIBIT 4.1 Note-Taking System to Encourage Critical Thinking

1. APA-style reference of the article
2. Short description of study
   - Type of study (correlational/experimental)
   - The results support (do not support) my hypothesis/thesis because
   - This study is related to the following other studies
   - I will use this study in my paper to
   - The study's main strength is
   - The study's main weakness is
3. In-depth analysis
   - Measure's quality
     - How is measure consistent with accepted definitions of the concept?
     - What evidence is there for the measure's validity?
     - Is there potential for subject bias?
       - How likely is it that participants knew the hypothesis or knew to which condition they had been assigned?
       - Was it easy for participants to play along with the hypothesis? (If the researchers used a self-report measure, the answer will probably be "yes.")
       - If a behavioral measure (rather than a self-report) measure was used, was that behavior scored objectively and reliably?
   - Manipulation's quality
     - Was it strong enough?
     - Could it have been biased?
       - Was the manipulation of the treatment sufficiently standardized?
       - Were double-blind techniques used?
   - Sample quality
     - Size
     - Age (average age and range or standard deviation of ages)
     - Number of men and number of women
     - Diversity
     - How recruited
     - Who was excluded?
     - Was it a randomly selected sample of some group?
   - Were the author's cause-effect statements justifiable (see 5.6.1)? For example, was random assignment used?
   - Were the author's generalizations justified (see 5.6.5)?
   - Were null results properly interpreted (see 5.6.2)?
   - What other explanations are there for the results?
4. Notes taken from individual pages of the source

Source page number	Note from that page	Type of note: (Q = quotation, P = paraphrase, SU = summary, MR = my reaction)	Reason for note: I took that note because ___ (e.g., the passage supports [contradicts] my thesis).

Table 4.7
What to Look for in a Journal Article

	First Time Through	Second Time Through
Introduction	Why do we care about this area of research? Do I understand the theory or the studies that set up this research? If not, what references do I need to read? What are the hypotheses? Why do the authors expect their hypotheses to be supported? If this study cures a weakness in previous research, what was wrong with previous research? If this study fills a gap in previous research, what was that gap?	Do I agree with the authors' arguments? Does the hypothesis really follow from theory or previous research? If the authors had obtained different results, what would they have changed in their Introduction?
Method	How were participants selected? What was the age of the sample? Are men and women both adequately represented in the sample? What population did the sample represent? What was done to the participants? If there were manipulated variables, how were those variables manipulated? What did participants do? What was the measured variable? What was the design? Do I understand how the study's method allowed the researcher to test the hypothesis?	Are there any reasons to expect that the researchers might have obtained different results with a different population of participants? Were groups equivalent before the study began? Were there enough participants? Did many participants drop out of the study? Are there any variables that the researchers should have controlled or manipulated? If I had been a participant, would I have (a) guessed the hypothesis? (b) taken the task seriously? Were the control groups adequate? Would it have been better to use a different measure?
Results	How were participants' responses turned into the scores used in the analyses? What are the average scores for the different groups? Do the results support the hypothesis?	Do the statistics directly test the predictions made in the Introduction? Do the statistical tests match up with the verbal descriptions? That is, if the authors say that Group 1 scored better than Group 2, do they have an analysis that directly compares Group 1 against Group 2? Are the statistics appropriate? Did the researchers correctly report that their null (nonsignificant) results failed to reject the null hypothesis?

Table 4.7
What to Look for in a Journal Article—continued

	First Time Through	Second Time Through
Discussion	Do the authors think the results matched their predictions? How do they explain any discrepancies? What additional studies do they recommend?	What are other explanations for the results? Other explanations could come from (a) a problem with their study that the authors did not mention or (b) a theory or a hypothesis that the author did not mention. Are there additional studies I would recommend? Did the authors make cause-effect statements on the basis of correlational evidence? Did the authors state something that was not supported by the results? For example, did they treat a nonsignificant result as significant or talk about a comparison that they did not statistically test?

EXHIBIT **4.2** A System to Help See Connections Among Studies

	Research Study	
	Study 1	Study 2
Reference (in APA style)		
Type of study (experimental or correlational)		
Measures used		
Sample (number and type of participants)		
Precautions used to prevent bias		
Results of study (supported hypothesis, contradicted hypothesis, or null results)		

of paraphrases, summaries, and critiques. Second, revising your notes will help you organize your paper by helping you see relationships among studies. For example, reorganizing your original notes by using the scheme presented in Exhibit 4.2 should help you organize your paper and help you get insights into how studies fit together.

4.3 Citations: What to Cite and Why

You must take thorough notes so that you can support the claims you make in your paper. Whenever you make a claim, you should provide evidence (e.g., a study, a statistic) to support your claim. Whenever you provide evidence, you must cite the source of that evidence, unless (a) your evidence is a well-known fact or (b) your paper is the source of that evidence (i.e., you reported it in your Results section).

You must also use citations whenever you present someone else's ideas (e.g., words, concepts, criticisms, theories, methods). If you fail to give a source's authors credit for their ideas, you are guilty of plagiarism. To avoid plagiarism, obey three rules. First, if you borrowed ideas from a source, cite that source—even if you did not quote that source. Second, if you are in doubt about whether to cite a source, cite it. Third, if you go more than a paragraph without citing (except for the Method and Results sections of a research paper), review that section to make sure you have not left out a citation.

In conclusion, citing boosts your credibility in three ways. First, you are telling the readers that you are not making stuff up—if they do not believe you, you are telling them how to look it up for themselves (Lipson, 2006). Second, you are showing that you have done your homework: You know what others have done, and you have built your argument on the newest and best evidence available. Third, you are showing the reader that you are honest: Rather than stealing others' words or ideas, you are giving credit where credit is due (Lipson, 2006).

Now that you know why you should cite, we will tell you what you should cite. As you will see in the next few sections, although you should cite any source from which you get information or an idea, most of your citations should refer to recent journal articles rather than to secondary sources, websites, or personal communications.

4.3.1 Citing From Secondary Sources

Citing from secondary sources refers to citing what one person has done or said after reading a second person's account of what the first person did or said. As a student, you may be tempted to use secondary citations for two reasons. First, after reading a secondhand account of an article and therefore believing you already know what the article is about, it may be hard to motivate yourself to track down that article. Second, reading about an article in a magazine, newspaper, or textbook is easier than reading the original article.

Although you might be tempted to use a secondary source, resist temptation. Instead, read, study, understand, and cite the original source. The only times APA journal editors will allow you to cite secondhand, hearsay evidence are when the primary source is in a foreign language or when the primary source is unavailable. The reason for editors' distrust of secondary sources is clear: A secondhand account is an incomplete account—and it may also be an inaccurate account.

Your teacher may be more lenient than a journal editor. You might ask your teacher if you can use one or two secondary sources.

If you are allowed to cite secondary sources and you do cite a secondhand account of an original source, start by stating the last name of the original source's author.

Then, immediately state that you are citing a secondary source by typing "(as cited in" followed by (a) the last name(s) of the author(s) of the secondary source, (b) a comma and a space, (c) the date the secondary source was published, and (d) a closing parenthesis. For example, if you read about Original's work in Interpreter's article, then your citation would be

Original (as cited in Interpreter, 2011) found . . .

In your reference section, omit the article you did not read (i.e., "Original"). Instead, provide a reference only to the article you read (i.e., "Interpreter, 2011").

To reiterate a point that is very important if you are to benefit from (and do well on) your assignment, do not substitute secondary sources (hearsay) for primary sources (direct evidence). Take the time to find the original article, even if you have to get it from interlibrary loan.

4.3.2 Citing Information Obtained From the Internet

Although you can use the Internet to retrieve articles that appear in paper journals (by using PsycARTICLES, Proquest, EBSCOhost, InfoTrac® College Edition, and other full text article retrieval services), you can also use the Internet to retrieve information that has never appeared in a paper journal. For example, you may find information on an individual's or an organization's website. However, be very skeptical about information from such a source. The information on the website may not have been evaluated by outside experts. Even if an Internet source does report original research, a paper journal's description of the same research may provide a more complete and more permanently retrievable source.

If your readers will probably be able to access your Internet source, cite that source the same way you would cite any other source (to learn how to cite sources, see 4.4 and 4.5). Thus, if you were citing a 2012 work by Jolley, your citation would be either "Jolley (2012)" or "(Jolley, 2012)," regardless of whether the work was a book, a journal article, or an Internet source. Often, thanks to websites, such as http://www.archive.org, that back up and preserve copies of websites, if a source was once on the Internet, that source probably can still be retrieved today. If, however, you have reason to believe readers would not be able to retrieve your Internet source, cite and reference it as you would a personal communication (to learn how to cite personal communications, read the next section [4.3.3]).

4.3.3 Citing Personal Communications

From a lecture, a conversation, an e-mail, or an Internet source that is no longer publicly available, you may get an idea from someone and put it in your paper. If so, give that person credit by using a *personal communication* citation. For such a citation, write the *person's initials*, last name, the words "personal communication," and the *exact date* the communication occurred. As you can see from the examples that follow, you can either (a) put both the person's name and the date of the communication inside parentheses or (b) make the name part of the sentence and put only "personal communication" and the date inside parentheses:

✔ . . . is an alternative explanation (I. B. Hepfl, personal communication, May 13, 2012).

✔ I. B. Hepfl (personal communication, May 13, 2012) proposed . . .

Omit personal communications from your list of references because the reader will be unable to access that lecture, conversation, or electronic communication. Note also that few of your citations should be personal communications. Instead, most of your citations should be from sources that could be accessed either by visiting a major university library or by logging on to a reputable electronic database such as PsycARTICLES.

4.4 General Rules for How to Format Citations

4.4.1 What Your Citation Should Include: Usually, Only Name and Date

Most of your citations will be to sources you have referenced in your reference list. The main goal of those citations is to provide the reader with enough information about the source so that the reader can use your citation to find the complete reference to the source in your reference list. To lead the reader to the right place in the reference list, citations usually need to include only two things: (a) the last name(s) of the author(s) followed by (b) the year the source was published.

Providing the author's last name for a single-author publication is usually straightforward. If the work has two authors, there is only one added complication: You have to make sure that you put the authors in the correct order (i.e., you should put the authors in the same order as they appear on the source's title page).

If the work has three to five authors, there are only two added complications from the single-author case. First, as with the two-author case, the first time you cite the work, you have to make sure that you put the authors in the correct order. Second, the next time—and all other times—you cite the work, you will usually not list all the authors. Instead of listing all the authors' surnames again, you will probably list only the first author's surname followed by "et al." (for details and examples, see 4.6.4). If the work has six authors, the first time—and every time—you cite the work, you will probably list only the primary author's last name followed by "et al." (for details and examples, see 4.5.4).

Note that the author's last name is the only information about the author that you should include in your citation. The citation should not include the author's title (e.g., Dr., Professor), the author's first name, the author's affiliation (e.g., Harvard), or any other author information that is irrelevant to evaluating the source (e.g., the author's hometown).

Citing the Publication Date: The Year Usually Works. Providing the publication date is usually straightforward: Just write down the year the source was published. The rule that providing the publication date involves just writing down the year the source was published has five exceptions. First, as we discussed in the previous section (4.3.3), you put the precise date for personal communication citations (e.g., October 15, 2012). Second, if the original source is dated differently from its translation, you separate the original year from the translation year with a slash (e.g., Kant, 1781/trans. 1965).

Third, if the article has not yet been published, you put "in press" (e.g., Jones, in press) for the date. Fourth, if the work has no documented publication date, you put "n.d." (no date) for the date (e.g., Garcia, n.d.). Fifth, if you have two or more citations from the same author published in the same year, you add an "a" after the year (e.g., Kakizaki, 1950a) for citations referring to the author's first reference list entry for that year and a "b" after the year (e.g., Kakizaki, 1950b) for citations referring to the author's second reference list entry for that year (for detailed directions, see 4.6.2).

4.4.2 General Strategies for Formatting Author and Date Information: Use Only Name Citations and Parenthetical Citations

As you have seen, your citation will provide two pieces of information about the source: its author(s) and its date. To format that information, you can choose between two types of citations: *name citations* and *parenthetical citations*.

If you use a *name citation*, you will probably make the last name(s) of the author(s) the subject of the sentence. Right after the author's name (or, if the source has more than one author, the authors' names), put—in parentheses—the year the source was published. Thus, you might write, "Jones (2011) noted that the studies failing to find a significant effect had insufficient power." If you wanted to use a name citation without making the author(s) the subject of the sentence, you might write, "According to Jones (2011), the studies failing to find a significant effect had insufficient power."

In a *parenthetical citation*, you provide the same information as a name citation: The difference is that both the author information and publication year are in parentheses. Thus, you might write, "The studies failing to find a significant effect had insufficient power (Jones, 2011)."

In your paper, you should use both name and parenthetical citations for two reasons. First, varying your citation type creates variety in your sentence structure, thereby making your paper more interesting to read. Second, varying your citation type is often necessary because the two citation types accomplish different goals. Consequently, as you will see as you read the rest of this section, a citation type that works well with one citation may be awkward with another citation.

Use a name citation when you are going to paraphrase extensively, such as when you are introducing a study that is important to your paper. A sentence such as "Smith (2005) conducted an experiment on the problem of response bias in psychological tests" alerts the reader that the remainder of that paragraph may refer to Smith's experiment (e.g., readers will know that "She tested 20 people . . ." refers to what Smith did in her experiment).

You may also want to use a name citation when introducing a work by a well-known author. In such a case, a name citation would assist readers who are already familiar with the work of the person you are citing by providing them with a clue about what they are about to read. For example, if you write, "Piaget (1953) stated," sophisticated readers will anticipate the particular points of Piaget's theory that you are going to outline.

When using name citations, the authors' names must fit into the grammar of the sentence. Thus, if you have more than one author, verbs relating to what the authors did must be plural rather than singular. Examples of common errors are "Smith and Brown

(2012) *states*" or "Brown et al. (2012) *states*." The correct forms are "Smith and Brown (2012) state" and "Brown et al. (2012) state" (et al. means "and others"; for more on using "et al." in citations, see 4.5.3, 4.5.4, and 4.6.4).

Whereas name citations come before the information to which they refer, parenthetical citations come after the information to which they refer. A parenthetical citation is particularly useful when you want the reader to focus on the results of a study rather than on who performed the study. By putting the author's name last, you imply that the findings would hold regardless of who did the study. To illustrate, compare "According to White (1982), IQ and socioeconomic class are correlated" with "IQ and socioeconomic class are correlated (White, 1982)."

Parenthetical citations also make it easy to cite related studies. To see the superiority of parenthetical citations over name citations for describing related studies, suppose you had used name citations to describe the following studies:

> White (1982) did a meta-analysis in which he found academic achievement and socioeconomic class to be correlated. McLoyd (1998) confirmed this in another review. Finally, Malecki and Demaray (2006) uncovered the same relationship in a more recent review.

Using parenthetical citations allows you to convey the same information much more efficiently, as you can see from the following example:

> ✔ Many studies have found that academic achievement and socioeconomic class are correlated (e.g., Malecki & Demaray, 2006; McLoyd, 1998; White, 1982).[5]

Using parenthetical citations also allows you to show the reader how related studies fit together. In the next example, note how using parenthetical citations summarizes the common information, yet preserves the detail that the studies were conducted at different times:

> ✔ The positive relationship between academic achievement and socioeconomic status has been persistently found in studies over the last 30 years, such as prior to 1982 (White, 1982), between then and 1998 (McLoyd, 1998), and up to 2006 (Malecki & Demaray, 2006).

There is one serious limitation of parenthetical citations: Each one applies only to the clause or sentence to which it is appended. As a result, when you need to repeat a particular citation in the same paragraph, parenthetical citations can be awkward. To illustrate, consider the following passage:

> The phenomenon of blindsight can have three alternative explanations (Ptito, Fortin, & Ptito, 2001). First, light scattered from one part of the retina to an intact part could allow observers to detect a stimulus (Ptito et al., 2001). Second, detection could be accomplished by small areas of residual function (Ptito et al., 2001). Third, blindsight might simply represent a conservative response criterion for near-threshold vision (Ptito et al., 2001).

---

[5]Note that the citations are not in order by date. Instead, they are in alphabetical order according to the last name of each article's first author. To learn more about how to sequence a series of citations, see 4.6.

Unfortunately, some students, in trying to avoid the awkwardness of repeating the same parenthetical citation make a much more serious mistake: They commit plagiarism. To illustrate, consider the following passage:

✗ The phenomenon of blindsight can have three alternative explanations. First, light scattered from one part of the retina to an intact part could allow observers to detect a stimulus (Ptito, Fortin, & Ptito, 2001). Second, detection could be accomplished by small areas of residual function (Ptito et al., 2001). Third, blindsight might simply represent a conservative response criterion for near-threshold vision (Ptito et al., 2001).

A professor would want the student to provide a citation for the first sentence because it is a statement of fact that needs to be supported. Given the repeated citation of Ptito et al. (2001), the professor would suspect that the first sentence was plagiarized from that source.

Trying to avoid repeating the same parenthetical citation can lead to even more blatant citation problems. To illustrate, imagine that the student has not read Fendrich, Wessinger, and Gazzaniga (2001) but did see it cited in Ptito et al. (2001). Furthermore, imagine that, to minimize repeating Ptito et al., the student wrote the following passage:

✗ The phenomenon of blindsight can have three alternative explanations. First, light scattered from one part of the retina to an intact part could allow observers to detect a stimulus (Ptito, Fortin, & Ptito, 2001). Second, detection could be accomplished by small areas of residual function (Fendrich, Wessinger, & Gazzaniga, 2001). Third, blindsight might simply represent a conservative response criterion for near-threshold vision (Ptito et al., 2001).

As before, the first sentence needs a citation because it is a statement that needs to be supported. In addition, the third sentence has an inappropriate citation: The student is citing a source (Fendrich, Wessinger, & Gazzaniga, 2001) that the student has not read.

To avoid the plagiarism and awkwardness problems caused by repeating a particular parenthetical citation in the same paragraph, reorganize the paragraph to use a single name citation. By so rewriting the previous passages, you might write the following paragraph:

✓ Ptito, Fortin, and Ptito (2001) listed three alternative explanations for blindsight. First, light scattered from one part of the retina to an intact part could allow observers to detect a stimulus. Second, detection could be accomplished by small areas of residual function. Third, blindsight might simply represent a conservative response criterion for near-threshold vision.

4.5 Formatting Individual Citations: Principles and Examples

In section 4.4.1, we discussed what information you should put in your citation (usually, the last name(s) of the author(s) followed by the publication year). In section 4.4.2, we gave you some general information about how to format your citations. In the next sections, we will be more specific. We will start with a simple case:

a single-author study (see 4.5.1). Then, we will move to illustrate what to do in more complicated cases (e.g., no author, authors sharing the same last name, six or more authors). However, before you try to absorb all the specific rules of citations, realize that most of those rules boil down to one rule: A citation must be complete enough to allow the reader to find the reference in your reference list.

4.5.1 Work by One Author: Whether the Listed Author Is a Person, Organization, or "Anonymous"

If the listed author is an individual, just state the person's last name and the date. Thus, a name citation and a parenthetical citation would look like the following:

Crovitz (1972) found[6] . . .

. . . (Crovitz, 1972).

If the listed author is a university or other organization, the citation would look the same, except that the organization's name would replace the person's last name. Thus, a name and parenthetical citation would look like the following:

Clarion University (2011) . . .

. . . (Clarion University, 2011).

In the rare case that the author is officially listed as "Anonymous," your citation would look like the following:

Anonymous (2012). . .

. . . (Anonymous, 2012).

If no author is listed, see 4.5.8.

4.5.2 Work by Two Authors

Always include the first author's last name, the second author's last name, and the year the work was published—and include that information in that order. If you are using a name citation, use the word "and" to join the two names and use parentheses to separate the publication date from the names. If you are using a parenthetical citation, use an ampersand ("&") to join the two names and use a comma to separate the publication date from the names. Note that regardless of whether you use a name citation or a parenthetical citation, you should not put any commas between the two authors' names.

Spear and Ganz (1975) found . . .

. . . (Spear & Ganz, 1975).

---

[6]It does not matter whether the person's full name is Harry Crovitz, Harry Crovitz, Jr., or Harold Crovitz III: The last name is Crovitz, and the last name is the only name you put in the citation.

4.5.3 Work by Three, Four, or Five Authors

The first time you cite such a source, list all of the authors' last names. Unlike in the two-author case, separate the authors' names with commas. Thus, for a three-author source, put a comma between the first and second authors' names, a comma between the second and third authors' names, and a comma before the final "and" (for a name citation) or "&" (for a parenthetical citation). After the names, put the year the work was published. If you have a name citation, put the publication year in parentheses; if you have a parenthetical citation, put a comma and a space before the publication year.

The next time(s) you cite such a source, you will usually not mention all of the source's authors. Instead, usually state only the primary (first) author's last name followed by "et al." and the year.

> Spear, Chow, Masland, and Murphy (1972) discovered that . . . confirmed the well–established effect (Spear et al., 1972). [Note that there is no comma between "Spear" and "et al."] Also, Spear et al. (1972) commented that . . . have been found (Burton, Nagshineh, & Ruddock, 1977).

Sometimes, however, using the primary author's last name followed by "et al." would violate the rule that each citation should clearly point to one reference in your reference list. For example, citing "(Knapen et al., 2009)" at the end of the next paragraph was a mistake because readers cannot know which of the three Knapen references the writer intended to cite.

> ✗ Knapen, Paffen, Kanai, and van Ee (2007) initiated the study of the phenomenon when they found . . . In a related study, Knapen, van Ee, and Blake (2007) showed . . . In addition, Knapen, Kanai, Brascamp, van Boxtel, and van Ee (2007) found that . . . To reconcile these disparate findings, one could reinterpret the results of Knapen et al. (2007).

If citing the first author's name followed by "et al." and the publication year does not clearly point to a single reference in your reference list, add the second author's name to the citation. If it is still not clear which of your references is being cited, add the third author's name to your citation, and so on. In short, the rule is that you should include the minimum number of authors' names that avoids confusion, then add "et al." followed by the publication year. However, because "et al." means "and *others*," this rule has an exception: If, after listing the minimum number of authors' names, only one *other* author is left, do not use "et al." Instead, list all the authors. Thus, in the previous example, the last citation should not read, "Knapen, van Ee, et al. (2007)." Instead, it should read, "Knapen, van Ee, and Blake (2007)."

4.5.4 Work by Six or More Authors

Provide the first author's last name followed by "et al." and the date (e.g., Smith et al., 2011), unless that citation could lead readers to more than one reference in your reference list. To illustrate how an "et al." citation could lead to confusion, suppose you referenced four articles that all (a) had Smith as the lead author and (b) were published in 2011. In that case, "(Smith et al., 2011)" would not tell readers which of the four you meant. In such a case, provide the second author's last name as well (Smith, Thomas, et al., 2011). If that citation would still not point to one—and only one—source in your reference list, add the third author's last name (Smith, Thomas, Schadle, et al., 2011). In short, provide the minimum number of authors' last names that avoids confusion.

4.5.5 Work by Author Sharing Same Last Name as Another Cited Author

If two coauthors share the same last name, cite them as you would any other coauthors (e.g., "(Garcia & Garcia, 2012)"). If, however, two *first* authors share the same last name, use the initials for their first and middle names when you cite their work.

G. J. Burton, Nagshineh, and Ruddock (1977) found . . . H. E. Burton (1945) set out . . . R. F. Burton (1884) stated . . .

4.5.6 Work With No Listed Author

If the source has no identified author, use the source's title (or, if the title is long, just its first few words) in place of the author's last name (e.g., "Keep the Small Fish," 2011). To signal the reader that you are referring to the title of a source, capitalize the first letter of major words and either surround it with quotation marks (do this for the title of a web page, the title of an article, or the title of a book chapter) or italicize it (do this for any other work, such as the title of a book).

Citing a chapter

The chapter "Social Psychology" (2008) gave . . .

. . . the common definition ("Social Psychology," 2008).

Citing a book

The book *General Psychology* (2012) . . .

. . . the common definition (*General Psychology*, 2012).

Note that if an author is listed—even if listed as "Anonymous" or as an organization such as American Psychological Association—cite that work as you would a single author publication (to see how, see 4.5.1).

4.5.7 Works With Dating Problems: Not Published, Not Yet Published, No Publication Date, Multiple Publication Dates

For unpublished works that are personal communications (see 4.3.3), give the precise date.

J. M. Jolley (personal communication, March 29, 2012)

(J. M. Jolley, personal communication, March 29, 2012)

For works that have been accepted for publication but have not yet been published, substitute "in press" for the date.

Garcia (in press).

(Garcia, in press).

For works that have no documented publication date (like many documents on the Internet), use the abbreviation for no date—"n.d."

Garcia (n.d.)

(Garcia, n.d.)

For works that have two dates—a date for the original source and a date for the translation (or the newer version you used)—separate the original year from the version you used with a slash.

Kant (1781/trans. 1965)

(Kant, 1781/trans. 1965)

Watson (1929/1970)

(Watson, 1929/1970)

4.5.8 Works From Nontraditional Sources: Personal Communications and Secondary Sources

If others cannot retrieve your source (e.g., the source talked to you in person, the source sent you an e-mail, or the source is a website that no longer exists), use the personal communication citation format described in 4.3.3. If, on the other hand, you read about someone's work in a book or an article but did not read the original source, cite the source you did read by using the format described in 4.3.1.

4.6 Formatting Multiple Citations

Sometimes you will have more than one citation for a statement. In this section, we will show you how to format such citations.

4.6.1 More Than Two Works by Different Authors

For name citations, if there are two or more sources that support a statement, give them in any order that makes sense.

Crovitz (1972) discovered the phenomenon. Spear and Ganz (1975) conducted further research. Burton et al. (1977) showed it was related to other phenomena.

For parenthetical citations, if there are two or more sources that support a statement, put them in alphabetical order according to the primary author's last name and separate them with semicolons.

. . . this important phenomenon (Burton et al., 1977; Crovitz, 1964, 1972; Spear & Ganz, 1975).

For more about putting sources in alphabetical order, see 4.10.3.

4.6.2 More Than Two Works by the Same Author

Order multiple citations of the same author(s) from oldest to most recent. State the name of the author(s) once and use commas to separate these citations from each other.

Williams (2010, 2011) found . . .

Karau and Williams (1993, 1995) found . . .

. . . (Williams, 2010, 2011).

. . . (Karau & Williams, 1993, 1995).

However, if the names—or even the order of the names—in two citations differ from each other, you should use semicolons to separate those citations, as the following example illustrates.

Several studies (Karau & Williams, 1993, 1995; Williams, 2011; Williams & Karau, 1991) have found . . .

If you refer to two or more works by the same author(s) published in the same year, alphabetize the references on the first word of the title (e.g., if you cited several articles that Williams published in 2007, the one titled "Androgens in action" would come before the one titled "Zebras in zoos"). Once you have ordered those references, put an "a" after the year for the first reference (e.g., Williams, 2007a), a "b" after the year for the second (e.g., Williams, 2007b), and so on until each citation is distinct.

Williams (2007a) found that . . . Williams (2007b) confirmed his finding. . . . a well-established finding (Williams, 2007a, 2007b).

4.6.3 Citing the Same Work by the Same Author More Than Once

If you are using a name citation for an article more than once in the same paragraph, you can usually omit the year the second time you mention the article.

First time: Williams (2011)

Second time: Williams

However, if leaving off the date would prevent readers from knowing which article you meant (e.g., you had a Williams [2008] and a Williams [2009]), cite the year every time you cite the article.

4.6.4 Citing the Same Work by the Same Authors More Than Once

If you are citing a source that has three, four, or five authors, you usually will include all the authors only the first time you cite the source. Thereafter, you can just cite the first author followed by "et al." and the date.

Name citation:

First time: Jamieson, Harkins, and Williams (2010)

Second time: Jamieson et al. (2010)

Parenthetical citation:

First time: (Jamieson, Harkins, & Williams, 2010)

Second time: (Jamieson et al., 2010)

However, if using the et al. citation would lead to more than one reference (e.g., if "Jamieson et al., 2010" could refer not only to Jamieson, Harkins, and Williams, 2010 but also to Jamieson, Garcia, and Smith, 2010), do not use "et al." For more on et al. citations, see 4.5.3.

4.7 Paraphrasing

Whether you are summarizing (condensing), paraphrasing (restating in your own words), or quoting what a source said, you need to cite that source because you are borrowing ideas from that source. Usually, when you borrow ideas from a source, you should show that you understand those ideas, and so you should use your own words rather than the source's words. Therefore, you should paraphrase more than you quote.

Unfortunately, many students who intend to paraphrase unintentionally plagiarize because they make one of the following three errors. First, some students mistakenly believe that they do not have to cite a source that they do not quote. Do not risk your academic career by making that mistake. Second, if, as they take notes, students do not put quotation marks around material they copied, they may forget that they copied that material. Third, some students mistakenly believe that anything other than an exact quote is a paraphrase. They believe that replacing a few words with synonyms counts as a paraphrase or that deleting or moving a few words around counts as a paraphrase. They are wrong: A paraphrase must be in your own words.

To put a passage in your own words, you must first understand the passage. Therefore, before paraphrasing a sentence or passage, read it carefully. Next, put away the passage and try writing a paraphrase in your own words. Then, go back and compare what you have written with the original. The only similarity between the passages should be the ideas. If your paraphrase looks or sounds similar to the original, you cannot turn in that paraphrase without being guilty of plagiarism (for more on plagiarism, see 1.2.4). Therefore, try again to paraphrase the passage. To prepare for your second try, start by studying the passage again to be sure you understand it. Then, wait until the next day to write your paraphrase. Waiting gives you a chance to forget the original passage's wording (Clarion University of Pennsylvania, n.d.).[7] If your paraphrase still resembles the original, consider quoting the original.

4.8 Quoting

If you are quoting a source, you will usually need to provide not only the author of the source but also the page number of the quotation. The reason you put the page number (for websites, the paragraph number or heading; for the Bible, chapter and verse) is so that the reader can find your quotation. Otherwise, you might quote three words from a book, and the reader would have to search that entire book to find those three words.

How you format the author and page number will depend on the length of your quotation. If it is fewer than 40 words, you will use an *embedded quotation*— you will embed the quotation within your own words but identify it as a quotation by using quotation marks. If it is longer than 39 words, you will use a *block quotation*—you will separate the quotation from your own words by making it an indented block of text. As we mentioned in Chapter 1, for every 1,000 words (four pages) in your paper, you should have no more than 50 quoted words. Therefore, if you do quote, try to use short, embedded quotations.

4.8.1 Embedded Quotations

If you use embedded quotations, the following advice will help you format them correctly. Indeed, the following two rules will help you format most quotations. First, provide a normal citation in the appropriate place and enclose the quotation in double quotation marks. Second, provide the original page number(s) from which the quotation comes. Those page numbers should be put at the end of the quotation and should be enclosed in parentheses.

> Jones (1984) argued that both "may follow Morgan's canons" (p. 232).

If you have an Internet source for which you cannot identify the page numbers, count how many paragraphs it comes after a major heading. Then, to help the reader locate the quotation, give the heading and the number of paragraphs (abbreviated "para.") that the quotation follows the heading. Thus, if you were quoting from the third paragraph of the results section, your citation might be as follows:

> (Merton, 2003, Results section, para. 3)

- Copy the original spelling, punctuation, and wording of the quotation, even if it is incorrect. After any error, put "[*sic*]" to emphasize that the error is not yours, but instead was present in the original.

> Jones (2004) argued that both "may follow Morgans [*sic*] canons" (p. 232).

---

[7]This citation is unusual because the author is an organization (Clarion University) and the publication does not have a date ("n.d." means "no date").

- Use ellipses (three dots [. . .]) to indicate any omission of material from within the original quotation. Add the usual end-of-sentence mark (e.g., period, question mark) to the end of an ellipsis if the quotation resumes on the following sentence.

  Jones (1984) argued that "lower-level judgments,. . . . may follow Morgans [*sic*] canons" (p. 232).

- Use single quotation marks to indicate quotation marks within the quotation.

  Jones (1984) applied "the term 'perception,' . . . to aesthetic judgments" (p. 232).

- Use brackets [thus] to indicate any material you have inserted into the quotation to make it fit into the sense of your text.

  Jones (1984) applied "the term 'perception,' to [both] aesthetic judgments, . . . [and] to lower-level judgments, . . . [arguing that both] may follow Morgans [*sic*] canons" (p. 232).

- The first letter of a quotation may be capitalized if what follows forms a complete sentence of its own.
- To highlight particular words in a quotation that are important for your argument, place them in italics. Follow the italicized words with "[italics added]."
- If a period is next to the closing (right) quotation mark, the period should be inside the quotation mark—even if the period has nothing to do with the quotation.
- If a comma is next to the right (closing) quotation mark, the comma should be inside the quotation mark—even if the comma has nothing to do with the quotation.
- If the quotation itself ends with a question mark or exclamation mark, enclose the question mark or exclamation point within the quotation marks. If, on the other hand, the sentence—rather than the quotation—contains the question mark or exclamation point, put the question mark or exclamation point outside of the quotation marks.

To understand these rules, study the following examples:

✔ "The term 'perception,' *when applied to aesthetic judgments* [italics added], must be distinguished from the term applied to lower-level judgments" (Jones, 1984, p. 232).

✔ Jones (1984) applied "the term 'perception,' . . . to [both] aesthetic judgments, . . . [and] to lower-level judgments, . . . [arguing that both] may follow Morgans [*sic*] canons" (p. 232).

4.8.2 Block Quotations

If your quotation has more than 39 words, use a block quotation. To format block quotations, use most of the same principles you would use if you had an embedded quotation. The difference is that instead of using quotation marks to identify the material you are quoting, you will use indentation. Specifically, indent all lines of the first paragraph of the quotation by five spaces from the left margin so that the first paragraph of the quotation forms a block of text (see Exhibit 4.3).

If your quotation is longer than a paragraph, signal the start of each subsequent paragraph by indenting the first line of that paragraph by five more spaces than the lines immediately above and below it. Thus, if you were quoting three consecutive paragraphs, you should start every line of the quotation five spaces from the left margin except for the first line of the second paragraph and the first line of the third paragraph, both of which you should start 10 spaces from the left margin.

End each block quotation by citing the quotation's source. Specifically, after the final period of a blocked quotation, enclose the last name(s) of the author(s), the publication year, and page number(s) of the quote in parentheses, as we have done in Exhibit 4.3.

4.9 Deciding What to Reference

You cited sources in text to achieve three goals: (a) to show that you read a wide range of recent, reliable sources; (b) to avoid plagiarism (for more about avoiding plagiarism, see Box 4.1); and (c) to lead readers to the reference in your reference list. To accomplish this third goal, your reference list must include all the retrievable sources (except for major classical works such as the Bible or Homer's Odyssey) that you cited in text.

You have a reference list for only one reason: to help the reader *retrieve* the sources that you cited ***and*** read. Therefore, you must exclude from your reference list any source that you did not cite in text—even if you read that source. In addition, as you will see in the next sections, you must exclude two types of cited sources from your reference list: (a) sources that readers cannot retrieve and (b) sources that you did not read but instead only read about in another source.

4.9.1 Cite but Do Not Reference Communications That Cannot Be Retrieved

Personal communications, such as conversations, letters, lectures, and e-mails, do not appear in the reference list because there is no easy way to allow a reader to obtain

EXHIBIT **4.3** An Example of a Section of a Paper That Contains a Block Quotation

---

When astronomers try to explain visual perception, their explanations can be confusing, as the following quotation illustrates.

> Mach bands are present because cones do not operate independently. One cone "knows" what its neighbor is seeing and responds both to the amount of light falling on it and the adjacent receptors. At the high contrast bright boundary . . . a bright stripe [is visible] where the image becomes dark [and vice versa]. (Lynch & Livingston, 1995, p. 225)

This explanation is confusing because cones neither see nor know what other cones are doing. . .

---

a copy. Messages posted to newsgroups, discussion groups, and electronic mailing lists are sometimes considered personal communications. If such messages cannot be retrieved, do not put them in your reference list. However, if you are reasonably confident that the reader will be able to access a particular message you cited, you may put it in your reference list (to see how to reference messages posted to newsgroups, discussion groups, and electronic mailing lists, go to our website).

4.9.2 Reference Secondary Sources You Read but Not Original Sources That You Only Read About

You reference only sources you actually cited and read. Therefore, if, rather than reading the original work, you read about the work in a secondary source, reference only the secondary source. You will mention the original work when you cite it in your paper (see 4.3.1), but you will not put the original work in your reference list.

As we stated earlier, you should try to read the original work whenever possible. Usually, your professor will expect your paper to be based on journal articles you

BOX 4.1 Avoiding Plagiarism: A Six-Step Program

1. When you first select a source, write down its title and APA-style reference.
2. Next, read the source without taking notes. (Try to think about what you are reading before you write.)
3. Once you have read the source, read it again and write down relevant information. However,
    a. When you write something down, try to put it in your own words. If you cannot put it in your own words, chances are you do not understand it. If you do not understand it, you should not use the information.
    b. Anytime you write down more than two consecutive words that match the source, put those words in quotation marks.
    c. For each thing that you write down, write down the page number from the source where you found it.
4. Remember to cite a source every time you incorporate an idea from it into your paper. If you have any doubts about whether to cite a source, cite it.
5. "Use name citations . . . when you are going to paraphrase extensively" (O'Shea et al., p. 73). Otherwise, you must put parenthetical citations at the end of every sentence of your paraphrase.
6. Once you have a draft of your paper, compare that draft to your sources. Ask yourself whether the authors of your sources could, if they read your paper, make the case that, at least in one place in your paper, (a) you used their words without acknowledging that you were quoting them, (b) you used their ideas without acknowledging that those ideas were theirs, or (c) you paraphrased them so closely that you were essentially quoting them. If the authors could possibly make such a case, add quotation marks, add citations, or rewrite sections to give your sources proper credit.

read—not on journal articles you read about in secondary sources such as magazines, newspapers, blogs, encyclopedias, or textbooks. If you must cite a secondary source or two, try to confine those citations to the first paragraph of your Introduction.

4.10 Formatting References

In the next few sections, you will learn how to format the major types of references. We did not provide you with every type of reference for two reasons. First, because at least 75% of your references should be journal articles, we focus on teaching you how to format journal articles. Second, we could not provide an example of every type of reference: The *Publication Manual* lists 97 different reference types—and warns that it has not included every reference type. Therefore, you may run into a reference that is outside the guidelines we list. In that case, do not panic. Your professor will probably not penalize you for mistakes in referencing some obscure reference type. Most teachers are delighted when students can reference journal articles correctly. We would be shocked if your professor penalized you for having a comma out of place in a reference to an anonymous, reprinted article in a United Nations technical report. However, if you are extremely concerned about perfectly formatting the reference for an unconventional source, see our website.

4.10.1 Starting the Reference Page

You can begin your list of references by centering the heading "References" on the top of a new page. However, realize that you will probably not be able to complete your reference list unless you have the following four pieces of information for each source:

1. who the author(s) is (are),
2. what the title of the work is,
3. when the work was published or presented, and
4. where the work was published or presented.

Furthermore, realize that the type of information you provide regarding where the work was published or presented depends on the type of source.

- **Book.** (a) Include the name of the publisher and (b) where it was published (the name of the city and either the abbreviation for the state [if the city is in the U.S.] or the name of the country [if the city is not in the U.S.]).
- **Journal article.** Include the name of the journal, the volume number of that journal, the page numbers, and the digital object identifier (DOI). The DOI is a long string of numbers (and possibly letters) that usually begins with "10." To find the DOI, just look for a long number that begins with "10" on your article's first page. If you do not have the first page of the article, you can access the article's DOI by going to the Chapter 4 section of this book's website.

- **Conference presentation.** Include the name of the conference and the name of the place (for U.S. cities, the city name and the postal abbreviation for the state; for other cities, the city name and country) where the conference was held.
- **Internet source.** Include the uniform resource locator (URL) or, if available, the DOI.[8]

4.10.2 General Tips for Formatting Individual References

Do not indent the first line of each reference. Instead, start the first line of each reference at the left margin. Subsequent lines for that reference should be indented five spaces. Thus, you will be formatting each reference in a way that is opposite of how you would format a paragraph. To format references this way, use your word processor's "hanging indent" feature.[9] If your reference has a single author, the beginning of your reference will probably adhere to the following format:

1. Author's last name, comma, *one space,* first initial, period, *one space,* second initial, period, *one space*

   Example: Fehr, B. F.
2. Date in parentheses followed by a period and *one space*

   Example: (1999).
3. Work's title followed by a period.

   Example: Laypeople's conceptions of commitment.

Note that the work's title is italicized only when the source is a book. Thus, because "Laypeople's conceptions of commitment" is not italicized, you know it is not a book title.

After providing the author's name ("who"), the publication date ("when"), and work's title ("what"), you need to provide the publication data ("where").

---

[8]In this case, "object" just means "anything," "digital object" means anything that has been digitized (put in electronic format) and put on the web, and "digital object identifier" is a number that identifies (allows us to locate) any digitized material that is registered with the DOI organization.

You will usually find the DOI on the first page. Often, on the top, right corner, just below the line that says "Copyright __ by . . .," there will be a second line that says, among other things, "DOI:" followed by the DOI itself (e.g., 10.1037/0022-3514.92.1.97). If the document's object identifier is not on the top of the first page, it may be on the side of the first page. Specifically, slightly below the row for title, the row for authors, and the row for the publisher, there may be a row labeled "Digital Object Identifier." If you still cannot find the DOI, our website will be able to help you—provided the document has a digital object identifier. For more about DOIs, see 4.10.2.

[9]Unless you like being frustrated, do *not* make hanging indents by inserting returns at the end of each line and tabs at the beginning of most lines. Instead, after ensuring that each reference is a single paragraph, free of returns and tabs, highlight your references and choose "hanging indent" from your word processor's paragraph formatting tool. For more help on getting your word processor to make hanging indents, go to http://www.writingforpsychology.com.

- For a book (see 4.10.8), stating the "where" may be as simple as stating the name of the city and country where the publisher is located followed by a colon, a space, the publisher's name, and a period (e.g., "London, England: Penguin Books.").
- For a book chapter (see 4.10.9), stating the publication data is more involved than a book. You must state the editors' names, italicize the book's title, and specify on what pages in the book the chapter can be found. Then, you provide the publication data for the book: the publisher's city, state, and name (e.g., "In A. Wertheim, W. Wagenaar, & H. L. Leibowitz (Eds.), *Tutorials in motion perception* (pp. 231–260). New York, NY: Plenum Press.").

For a journal article (see 4.10.10), the publication information consists of two parts. The first part tells readers in which journal, in which numbered volume of that journal, and on which page numbers in that volume the article appears. The second part is the article's doi, a number that identifies and allows people to locate any document that has been put in digital format and that has been registered with the doi organization. Specifically, a source's doi is a long string of numbers (and possibly letters) that begins with "10." (e.g., 10.1037/0022-3514.92.1.97) and acts as a permanent URL to the source. For recent articles, you will find the doi on the article's first page, often, in the top, right corner, just below the line that says "Copyright ____ by . . .." If you cannot find the doi, our website will be able to help you.

To format the publication information, put the title of the journal in italics, followed by a comma and a space; then, put the volume number in italics, followed by a comma and a space; and then type the number of the page on which the article starts, followed by an en dash, followed by the number of the page on which the article ends, and followed by a period (e.g., "*Journal of Personality and Social Psychology, 76*, 90–103."). Finally, if the article has a DOI, you just add "doi:" followed by the doi number (e.g., doi:10.1037//0022-3514.76.1.90). Note two things about formatting the DOI information: (a) "doi" is not capitalized and (b) the doi does not end with a period.

- For an Internet source (see 4.10.12), you will probably end your reference with information that will help the reader retrieve the source from cyberspace. If you read a published article, the source location will probably be the source's doi (see the previous bullet for information about DOIs). If the article does not have a doi, you may use the name of the database you retrieved it from (e.g., Retrieved from PsycARTICLES database). If you retrieved the material from a website, you can use the URL of the document (e.g., Retrieved from http://faculty.washington.edu/agg/pdf/Gwald_JEPHPP_2004.pdf) or the URL of the website's home page (e.g., Retrieved from http://faculty.washington.edu/agg/index.htm). For more on referencing sources located from the Internet, see 4.10.12.

4.10.3 Put Your References in Alphabetical Order and Follow These Rules to Break Ties

References must be in alphabetical order according to the first author's last name. Thus, Alpha, Z. would come before Beta, A.

With compound names (e.g., von Helmholtz, van der Zwan), check the author's own reference list to see where the author's name appears (in van der Zwan's case, it is with the Vs). If you cannot find the author's name in the author's own reference list, alphabetize on the first capitalized part of the name. Put the uncapitalized parts of the name after the initials (e.g., Helmholtz, H. L. von).

If different authors have the same last name, break the tie by looking at initials. Thus, Burton, H. E. (1945) would come before Burton, R. F. (1884). For references with the same first author, alphabetize on the second author. Thus, Wenderoth, P., Johnstone, S., & van der Zwan, R. (1989) comes before Wenderoth, P., & van der Zwan, R. (1989), and Williams K. D. (2010) would come before Williams, K. D., & Karau, S. J. (1991).

For references with the same author(s), put the oldest references first. Thus, Lehmkuhle, R. T., & Fox, S. L. (1975) comes before Lehmkuhle, R. T., & Fox, S. L. (1976).

For references with the same author(s) and year, alphabetize on the first word of the title (ignoring "a" and "the") and distinguish references by single, lowercase letters immediately after the year. For example, suppose you cited two articles published by Kramer in 2012: "The alpha army ants" and "A zebra zygote." The article titled "The alpha army ants" article would be listed first and would begin "Kramer, J. (2012a)." The article titled "A zebra zygote" would be listed second and would begin "Kramer, J. (2012b)."

Examples.

Burton, G. J., Nagshineh, S., & Ruddock, K. H. (1977). Processing by the human visual system of the light and dark components of the retinal image. *Biological Cybernetics*, 27, 189–197. doi:10.1007/BF00344140

Burton, H. E. (1945). The optics of Euclid. *Journal of the Optical Society of America, 35,* 357–372. doi:10.1364/JOSA.35.000357

Burton, R. F. (1884). *The book of the sword.* London, England: Chatto & Windus.

Crovitz, H. F. (1972). Transient binasal hemianopia in a pair of plastic soupspoons. *Psychonomic Science*, 28, 234.

Helmholtz, H. L. von (1962). *Handbook of physiological optics* (J. P. C. Southall, Trans.). New York, NY: Dover. (Original work published 1910)

Kakizaki, S. (1950a). The effects of preceding conditions upon binocular rivalry. *Japanese Journal of Psychology, 20,* 124–132.

Kakizaki, S. (1950b). Preceding conditions and binocular rivalry. *Japanese Journal of Psychology, 20,* 511–517.

Knapen, T., Kanai, R., Brascamp, J., van Boxtel, J., & van Ee, R. (2007). Distance in feature space determines exclusivity in visual rivalry. *Vision Research, 47,* 3269-3275. doi:10.1016/j.visres.2007.09.005

Knapen, T., Paffen, C., Kanai, R., & van Ee, R. (2007). Stimulus flicker alters interocular grouping during binocular rivalry. *Vision Research, 47,* 1-7 doi: 10.1016/j visres.2006.09.007

Knapen, T., van Ee, R., & Blake, R. (2007). Stimulus motion propels traveling waves in binocular rivalry. *PLoS ONE,* 2(8), e739. doi: 10.1371/journal.pone.0000739

Malecki, C. K., & Demaray, M. K. (2006). Social support as a buffer in the relationship between socioeconomic status and academic performance. *School Psychology Quarterly, 21,* 375-395. doi:10.1037/h0084129

McLoyd, V. C. (1998). Socioeconomic disadvantage and child development. *American Psychologist, 53,* 185-204. doi: 10.1037/0003-066X.53.2.185

Piaget, J. (1953). *The origin of intelligence in the child.* New York, NY: Routledge & Kegan Paul.

Ptito, A., Fortin, A., & Ptito, M. (2001). 'Seeing' in the blind hemifield following hemispherectomy. *Progress in Brain Research, 134,* 367–378. doi:10.1016/S0079-6123(01)34024-4

Spear, P. D., Chow, K. L., Masland, R. H., & Murphy, E. H. (1972). Ontogenesis of receptive field characteristics of superior colliculus neurons in the rabbit. *Brain Research, 45,* 67–86. doi:10.1016/0006-8993(72)90216-8

Spear, P. D., & Ganz, L. (1975). Effects of visual cortical lesions following recovery from monocular deprivation in the cat. *Experimental Brain Research, 23,* 181–201. doi:10.1007/BF00235460

van der Zwan, R., Wenderoth, P., & Alais, D. (1993). Reduction of a pattern-induced motion aftereffect by binocular rivalry suggests the involvement of extrastriate mechanisms. *Visual Neuroscience, 10,* 703–709.

Wenderoth, P., Johnstone, S., & van der Zwan, R. (1989). Two dimensional tilt illusions induced by orthogonal plaid patterns: Effects of plaid motion, orientation, spatial separation, and spatial frequency. *Perception, 18,* 25–38. doi:10.1068/p180025

Wenderoth, P., & van der Zwan, R. (1989). The effects of exposure duration and surrounding frames on direct and indirect tilt aftereffects and illusions. *Perception and Psychophysics, 46,* 338–344. doi:10.3758/BF03204987

Wenderoth, P., van der Zwan, R., & Johnstone, S. (1989). Orientation illusions induced by briefly flashed plaids. *Perception, 18,* 715–728. doi:10.1068/p180715

White, K. R. (1982). The relation between socioeconomic status and academic achievement. *Psychological Bulletin, 91,* 461-481. doi:10.1037/0033-2909.91.3.461

4.10.4 Formatting the First Part of the Reference: The Author Names

Invert authors' names (i.e., put the last name first, then the first and middle initials). Separate last names from first initials by putting a comma and a space after last names. Separate first initials from second initials by putting a period and a space after first initials. If a last name or a name suffix (e.g., "Jr." or "III") follows a second initial, put a period, a comma, and space after the second initial; if the publication date follows a second initial, put a period and a space after the second initial.

If your source has more than one—but fewer than seven—authors, (a) separate all the author names with commas and (b) separate the final name from the rest with both a comma and an ampersand (e.g., Burton, G. J., Nagshineh, S., & Ruddock, K. H.). If your source has more than six listed authors, use only the first six authors' names: Replace the other authors' names with "et al." If, on the other hand, your source does not list anything—not an organization name, not even "Anonymous"—as the author, put the source's title in the author position.

Examples.

Benjamin, L. T., Jr. (2008). A history of teaching machines. *American Psychologist, 43,* 703–712. doi:10.1037//0003-066X.43.9.703

Crovitz, H. F. (1972). Transient binasal hemianopia in a pair of plastic soupspoons. *Psychonomic Science, 28,* 234.

High-handed professor's comments called hot error. (2005, August 16). *USA Today,* p. 2c.

Social psychology. (1999). In *The new encyclopaedia Britannica* (Vol. 27, pp. 802–803). Chicago, IL: Encyclopaedia Britannica.

4.10.5 Formatting the Second Part of the Reference: The Publication Date

After the name(s) of the author(s), put the reference's publication date in parentheses followed by a period [e.g., "Williams, K. D. (2011)."]. For journals, the publication date is the year the journal was published. For books, the publication date is the most recent copyright year (you can usually find the copyright year on the back of the title page). If you used an English translation of a book, put the publication year of the book you used after the author information [e.g., "Kant, I. (1965)."] just as you would for an ordinary book, but also append "(Original work published [publication year] [date])" to the end of the reference.

For some sources, you will provide a more specific publication date than just the year. For example, with a daily newspaper article, knowing what year it was published would not be nearly as helpful as providing the date it was published. Therefore, for daily and weekly publications, enclose the year of publication, a comma, and the month and day of publication in parentheses, followed by a period. Thus, a reference for a newspaper article, a magazine article, or even an Internet magazine article might start as follows: Homichl, J. (2008, August 6). Similarly, you may provide the month or season (Winter) of the publication of a newsletter. Finally, if your source is a paper or a poster presented at a conference, always follow the year of the conference with a comma and the month the conference was held (e.g., "2011, August").

Thus far, we have discussed cases in which you can and do provide a more specific publication date than just the year the source was published. However, sometimes, you will not even know what year the source will be published. If the source has been published but there is no recognized publication date, put "n.d." in place of the date. If the source has been accepted for publication, but is not yet published (the delay between article acceptance and publication is often more than a year), use "in press" in place of the date.

Examples.

Honomichl, J. (2008, August 6). Answering machines threaten survey research. *Marketing News,* p.11.

Kant, I. (1965). *Critique of pure reason* (N. K. Smith, Trans.). New York, NY: St. Martin's. (Original work published 1781)

Neisser, U. (1984, August). *Ecological movement in cognitive psychology.* Invited address at the annual meeting of the American Psychological Association, Toronto, Canada.

Williams, K. D. (in press). Causes and effects of ostracism. *Personality and Social Psychology Review.*

4.10.6 Formatting the Third Part of the Reference: The Title

Readers expect that the title you list in your reference is the title of the original work. They may even search for that work by title. Therefore, except for capitalization and font style, type the title of the reference exactly as it appears in the original.

Capitalize only the first letter of the titles and the first letter of the subtitles of books, journal articles, and book chapters (if a work has a subtitle, the subtitle is the part of the title that follows a colon or question mark). Italicize book titles as well as book subtitles. Do not italicize titles or subtitles of articles, book chapters, or papers. End the title section of each reference with a period.

4.10.7 Abbreviations

As you will see in 4.10.8, for books published in the United States, use the two-letter U.S. Postal Service's abbreviation for that state instead of spelling out the entire state name. To learn about other abbreviations that you should use in your reference list, see Table 4.8.

4.10.8 Referencing Books

Usually, less than one-fourth of your references will be books; most of your references will be journal articles. Usually, books will be the shortest and easiest sources to reference. Like most references, book references start with the author's name (inverted and abbreviated, e.g., "Smith, M. T."), then—in parentheses—the year the work was published, followed by a period, like this:

Smith, M. T. (2009).

Next comes the book's title. Note that you italicize the book's title and subtitle. As a general rule, the first letter of the first word of the book title is the only letter capitalized. The two exceptions to this rule are that you capitalize (a) the first letter of the first word of a subtitle (if the title contains a colon, the first word of the subtitle will usually be the first word after that colon) and (b) the first letter of words that are capitalized in the dictionary, such as names of particular people (e.g., Skinner),

Table 4.8
Abbreviations Used in References

Abbreviation	Translation	Comments
c.	About	When a publication year is uncertain
chap.	Chapter	
1st, 2nd, etc.	first, second, etc.	Do not use periods or superscripts (e.g., do not write "2nd." or "2nd"). Use with "ed." (see next entry).
ed.	edition	To indicate the fifth edition of a book, write "(5th ed.)" after the book's title.
Ed.(s.).	editor(s)	If not capitalized, it is the abbreviation for edition.
n.d.	no date	
p.	page	For one-page newspaper articles; do not use for referencing journal articles.
pp.	pages	For book chapters; do not use for journal articles.
Rev.	revised	Putting "(Rev. ed.)" after a book's title means the book you read was a revised edition.
Trans.	translator(s)	
Vol.	volume	Use with books; do not use with journals.
Vols.	volumes	Use with books; do not use with journals.
–	to	As in "pp. 22–33"

countries (e.g., France), organizations (e.g., American Psychological Association), and ethnic groups (e.g., Asian Americans).

Usually, you will put a period right after you type the book's title unless the book has been through several editions or translated. If the book has been through multiple editions or has been translated, put—in parentheses—a nonitalicized phrase that tells the reader which edition of the book you are using or who translated the book. In other words, if the title alone would not necessarily lead the reader to the right source (e.g., the book is a revised edition, a third edition, a translation, the second volume), you need to add information after the title that will help the reader locate the right source. Abbreviate that information and put it in parentheses, in normal, nonitalicized font (e.g., "(Rev. ed.)," "(3rd ed.)," "(Trans.)," "(Vol. 2)").

Next, put the place the book was published. If that place is a city in the United States, follow the city name with the two-letter U.S. Postal Service's abbreviation for the state rather than typing out the entire state name (e.g., "PA" instead of "Pennsylvania"). Note that the postal abbreviation is capitalized and does not contain any periods. If the city where the book was published is not in the United States, put the city name followed by the country name.

Add a colon after the publication location. After that colon, put a space and the name of the publisher (e.g., "Pacific Grove, CA: Wadsworth."). In listing the publisher's name, keep it short by omitting the words or abbreviations for "Company" or "Incorporated." Put a period after the publisher's name.

Normally, your reference will end at that period. However, there may be cases in which the publication year of the book you read is quite a bit later than the year the book was originally published. For example, a book may be reprinted or translated into English decades after it was first published. In such cases, the publication date may make it seem like a person who has been dead for years has just written a book. Without an explanation, such a publication date might confuse the reader. Therefore, after the ending period, add a parenthetical explanation such as "(Original work published 1871)" at the end of the reference. As you can see from the following model and examples, you should not end this explanation with a period.

General form.

Author, I. N. (year). Book title italicized (information about specific edition—if needed). Place of publication: Publisher. (Explanatory material—if needed)

Examples.

Alhazen, I. (1989). *The optics of Ibn Al-Haytham: Books I–III: On direct vision* (A. I. Sabra, Trans.). London, England: The Warburg Institute. (Original work published c. 1024)

Burton, R. F. (1884). *The book of the sword.* London, England: Chatto & Windus.

Helmholtz, H. L. von (1962). *Handbook of physiological optics* (3rd ed.) (J. P. C. Southall, Trans.). New York, NY: Dover. (Original work published 1910)

Strunk, W., Jr., & White, E. B. (2000). *The elements of style* (4th ed.). New York, NY: Longman.

4.10.9 Referencing Book Chapters

Referencing a specific book chapter is more complicated than referencing a book. As with a book reference, start with the author's last name followed by the author's first and middle initials. Then, in parentheses, put the year of publication. End this author and date section with a period.

After that period, provide the chapter title—but do not italicize it. Follow the chapter title with a period, a space, and the word "In." Thus, the first part of your reference could look like this:

Leibowitz, H. W., Post, R. B., Brandt, T., & Dichgans, J. (1982). Implications of recent developments in dynamic spatial orientation and visual resolution for vehicle guidance. In

Then, if the book is an edited volume containing chapters written by different authors, tell the reader who edited the book. Specifically, provide the name(s) of the editor(s) followed by either "(Ed.),"—if there is only one editor—or "(Eds.),"—if there is more than one editor. At this point, the first part of our sample reference looks like this:

Leibowitz, H. W., Post, R. B., Brandt, T., & Dichgans, J. (1982). Implications of recent developments in dynamic spatial orientation and visual resolution for vehicle guidance. In A. Wertheim, W. Wagenaar, & H. L. Leibowitz (Eds.), [publication information follows; see later in this section for the complete reference]

Note three points about our (incomplete) sample reference. First, the names of the chapter's authors—not the names of the book's editors—come first. Second, unlike the authors' names, editors' names are not inverted. Thus, it is "A. Wertheim, W. Wagenaar, & H. L. Leibowitz"—not "Wertheim, A., Wagenaar, W., & Leibowitz, H. L." Third, the editors' names are followed by "(Eds.)" and a comma. Noting these three points will help you avoid three common mistakes students make in formatting the editor information: (a) putting the editor's name where the author's name should be, (b) inverting the editor's name, and (c) not putting "(Ed.)," after the editor's name.

After telling the reader who edited the book, tell the reader what the book is. Specifically, put the book title in italics. Now that the reader knows in which book to look for the chapter, tell the reader where—on what pages—of that book to look for the chapter. Abbreviate this page number information and put it in parentheses. Specifically, type a left (opening) parenthesis, then "pp." followed by the number of the page in the book on which the chapter starts, an en dash, the page number on which the chapter ends, followed by a right (closing) parenthesis and a period. For example, you might type: (pp. 56–92).

Finally, add the publication information. When adding the publication information, use the same format you would if you were referencing an entire book. Specifically, put the place of publication followed by a colon and a space, followed by the name of the publisher, followed by a period (e.g., "New York, NY: Plenum Press.").

General form of an edited book in which different individuals authored different chapters.

Author, I. N. (year). Chapter title. In A. N. Editor (Ed.), *Book title italicized* (information about specific edition, if available) (pp. start page–finish page). Place of publication: Publisher.

Example of an edited book in which different individuals authored different chapters.

Leibowitz, H. W., Post, R. B., Brandt, T., & Dichgans, J. (1982). Implications of recent developments in dynamic spatial orientation and visual resolution for vehicle guidance. In A. Wertheim, W. Wagenaar, & H. L. Leibowitz (Eds.), *Tutorials in motion perception* (pp. 231–260). New York, NY: Plenum Press.

If the book is not an edited volume (the same authors wrote all the chapters), you would probably cite the book rather than the chapter. However, if you want to cite the particular chapter, use the following format:

General form.

Author, I. N. (year). Chapter title. In *Book title italicized* (information about specific edition, if relevant) (pp. start page–finish page). Place of publication: Publisher.

Example.

Strunk, W., Jr., & White, E. B. (1979). Elementary principles of composition. In *The elements of style* (3rd ed., pp. 15–33). New York, NY: Macmillan.

4.10.10 Referencing Journal Articles

As we mentioned earlier, most of your references should be to journal articles. Fortunately, the general form is simple and applies to most journal articles.

General form.

Author, I. N. (year). Article title. *Journal Title Italicized and Capitalized, volume number italicized* (issue number only in the extremely rare event that each issue begins with page 1), start page–finish page. doi:10.xxxxxxxxx

Examples.

Fehr, B. F. (1999). Laypeople's conceptions of commitment. *Journal of Personality and Social Psychology, 76,* 90–103. doi:10.1037//0022-3514.76.1.90

Knapen, T., Kanai, R., Brascamp, J., van Boxtel, J., & van Ee, R. (2007). Distance in feature space determines exclusivity in visual rivalry. *Vision Research, 47,* 3269-3275. doi: 10.1016/j.visres.2007.09.005

Spear, P. D., & Ganz, L. (1975). Effects of visual cortical lesions following recovery from monocular deprivation in the cat. *Experimental Brain Research, 23,* 181–201. doi:10.1007/BF00235460

To reiterate, the following is the general format for references to articles:

1. Author's last name, comma, *space*, first initial, period, *space*, second initial, period, and either a *space* (if no other names follow) or a comma and a space (if other names follow)

   Example: Fehr, B. F.
2. Date in parentheses followed by a period and a space

   Example: (1999).
3. Title of article followed by a period and a space

   Example: Laypeople's conceptions of commitment.

4. Title of journal followed by a comma (note that the entire title is italicized but that only the first letters of major words are capitalized) and a space
   Example: *Journal of Personality and Social Psychology,*
5. Volume number (*italicized*) followed by a comma and a space
   Example: *76,*
6. First page of article followed by an en dash followed by the last page of the article followed by a period.
   Example: 90–103.
7. If the article has a DOI, type "doi:" and the DOI number.

In the text that follows, we tell you how to adapt this format to almost any source—even those with no known author and no known publication date.

Multiple authors and missing information about authors. Variations in how you present the information about the name(s) of author(s) come from four cases. First, when there is more than one author, (a) use a comma to separate one author's name from the next author's name and (b) use both a comma and an ampersand ("&") to join the last author's name to the list (e.g., Johnson, L. B., Smith, A. O., & Jones, E. F.). Second, if the original source does not provide an author's middle initial, do not include that author's middle initial, even if you know it from a different source. Third, if the article has more than six authors, list only the first six. After the sixth author, place a comma and "et al." Fourth, if no one—not even "Anonymous"—is listed as the author of the source, use the title of the article as the author.

When you do not have the publication year or when you need more than the publication year. Variations in the date come from three cases, most of which will not apply if you stick to published journal articles. First, magazines, newsletters, and newspapers often provide more detail than the year of publication. For example, Internet journals and newsletters may note the season (2012, Winter) or months (2008, September/October) that they come out, whereas newspapers and magazines may have the exact date (2008, August 26). Second, if the article is not yet published, the phrase "in press" is put in parentheses. Third, if the article has no date, such as some Internet sources, put "n.d." in parentheses rather than the date.

Other variations: Page numbers and issue numbers. Variations in the rest of the reference are rare, especially if you limit your sources to journal articles you find in your library. For example, if you are referencing a journal article, never refer to page numbers by using the word "page" or some abbreviation (e.g., "p.") for page. If, on the other hand, you are referencing newspapers, use "p." before the page number of an article that appears on a single page (e.g., "p. D4," "p. 5") and use "pp." before the page numbers of an article that appears on multiple pages (e.g., "pp. D4–D6," "pp. 1, 5").

Similarly, if you are referencing the print version of a journal article, you will probably never put the issue number in your reference. (The issue number is usually on the journal's cover page right after the volume number. Thus, if the cover says, "Volume 35 Number 1," the issue number is "1.") You would put the issue number in parentheses only if each issue in the journal begins on page 1. However, that never happens in APS and APA journals and rarely happens elsewhere.

Finally, if you were referencing a print journal, you would always have page numbers and volume numbers. However, if you were referencing an Internet source, you might not have page numbers or volume numbers.

4.10.11 Referencing Abstracts of Journal Articles

If you have searched sources such as *Psychological Abstracts*, you have access to journal articles' abstracts. If you want to cite one of these articles, you should find and read it. If, however, an abstract is all that is available (e.g., your library does not subscribe to the journal and you cannot obtain it from interlibrary loan), cite the abstract using the following format:

General form.

Author, I. N. (year). Article title. *Journal Title Italicized and Capitalized, volume number italicized* (issue number if each issue begins with page 1), start page–finish page. Abstract obtained from *name of source, year of source, publication year of source, volume number,* "Abstract No. [abstract number]," and period.

Example.

Lo, T. Y. (1925). Correlation of name and fame. *Chinese Journal of Psychology, 3,* 701. Abstract obtained from *Psychological Abstracts, 1927, 1,* Abstract No. 319.

Usually, if you have access to the entire article, you should read the entire article. You should not merely skim the abstract. However, if, for some reason, you access the entire article, but read only the abstract (e.g., your professor specifically stated that for a particular writing assignment reading abstracts was all that was required), cite the abstract just as you would the article except that you add "[Abstract]" right after the article's title. That is, cite the abstract using the following format:

General form.

Author, I. N. (year). Article title [Abstract]. *Journal Title Italicized and Capitalized, volume number italicized* (issue number if each issue begins with page 1), start page–finish page.

Example.

Spear, P. D., & Ganz, L. (1975). Effects of visual cortical lesions following recovery from monocular deprivation in the cat [Abstract]. *Experimental Brain Research, 23,* 181–201. doi:10.1007/BF00235460

4.10.12 Referencing Internet Sources

We have saved Internet referencing for last because it is not much different from referencing any other source. As with any reference, you start with the author's name and the publication date—if they are known. With web references, you are more likely to have references for which you do not know the source's (a) author or (b) publication date. Thus, with web resources, you are more likely to have to substitute (a) the work's title for the author's name or (b) the abbreviation "n.d." (meaning "no date") for the date. For example, if you used an online dictionary, your entry would resemble the following:

Reinforcement. (n.d.). In *Merriam-Webster's online dictionary* (11th *ed.*). Retrieved from http://www.m-w.com/dictionary/reinforcement

If you find a source online, try to find the final version. Otherwise, the source your readers find may be different from the one you read. If your source may be rewritten, you need to mention when you retrieved that source. Thus, if your professor allowed you to reference a wiki such as Wikipedia, your entry might look like the following:

Negative reinforcement. (n.d.) In Wikipedia. Retrieved February 15, 2011 from http://en.wikipedia.org/wiki/Negative_reinforcement

- Do not include an author because the authors of a wiki entry are constantly changing. Instead of the author names, use the title.
- Put (n.d.) because the posted content of a wiki is the result of several authors writing and editing at various points in time.
- Include retrieval date because content may change.
- Do not put a period after the URL.
- To see how to reference an online encyclopedia other than Wikipedia, see our website.

If you stick to books and journals, referencing Internet sources is relatively easy—as you will soon see. The main challenge to referencing Internet sources is that there are so many types: press releases, PowerPoint® slides, audio files, video files, brochures, fact sheets, software, interview transcripts, data files, and many others. The general rule for handling this wide variety of sources is just to put the type of resource in brackets (e.g., [Brochure]) right after the title of the resource. For specific instructions about referencing a variety of Internet sources, see the Chapter 4 section of our website.

Books. To reference Internet books, begin by putting the author, year, and title—just as you would for a printed book. Then, add "Retrieved from" followed by the URL or database from which you accessed the book.

Book existing only as an Internet document.

General form.

Author, I. N. (year). *E-title italicized.* Retrieved from URL (if it is not possible to avoid an unnecessary line break in the pathname, start the URL on a new line)

Example.

American Psychological Association. (2007). *APA style guide to electronic references.* Retrieved from http://books.apa.org/books.cfm?id=4210509

If the book is an electronic version of a print book, begin by putting the author, year, and title—just as you would for a printed book. Then, if the book has a doi, type "doi:" and the doi number. If the book does not have a doi, put "Retrieved from" followed by the URL that the reader could use to order or download the book. **Electronic version of a printed book.**

For books with a DOI:

General form.

Author, I. N. (year). *Book title italicized (information* about specific edition—if needed). doi:10.xxxxxxxxxxx

Example.

Petry, N. M. (2005). Pathological gambling: Etiology, comorbidity, and treatment. doi:10.1037/10894-000

For books without DOIs:

General form.

Author, I. N. (year). *Book title italicized* (information about specific edition—if needed). Retrieved from (URL or database)

Example.

Munsterberg, H. (1913). *Psychology and industrial efficiency.* Retrieved from http://psychclassics.yorku.ca/Munster/Industrial/

Electronic version of a book chapter from a printed book when the book is an edited volume.

General form.

Author, I. N. (year). Chapter title. In A. N. Editor (Ed.), *Book title italicized* (information about specific edition—if necessary) (pp. start page–finish page). doi:DOI number

Example.

Reddy, P., & Lantz, C. (2010). Myths, maths, and madness: Misconceptions around psychology. In D. Upton & A. Trapp (Eds.), *Teaching psychology in higher education* (pp. 54-81). doi:10.1002/9781444320732.ch3

- The only difference between referencing an electronic version and referencing a print version is that you replace the publisher's name and location with the DOI or the URL.
- If the book has authors instead of editors, the format is even simpler:

General form.

Author, I. N. (year). Chapter title. In *Book title italicized* (information about specific edition—if necessary) (pp. start page-finish page). doi:DOI number

Example.

Pope, K. S., & Vasquez, J. T. (2005). Using computers and the Internet. In *How to survive and thrive as a therapist: Information, ideas, and resources for psychologists in practice* (pp. 77-85). doi:10.1037/11088-010

Book chapters from an edited book that exists only on the Internet.

General form.

Author, I. N. ([insert year]). Title of e-chapter. In A. N. Editor (Ed.) *E-title italicized.* Retrieved from [*insert* URL]

Example.

Dennett, D. C. (2004). Consciousness in human and robot minds. In S. Harnad (Ed.), *CogPrint: Cognitive sciences eprint archive.* Retrieved from http://cogprints.soton.ac.uk/archives/comp/papers/199803/199803001/doc.html/concrobt.htm

Journal articles. Referencing a journal article you retrieved online is usually the same as referencing a journal article you read. The only difference is that you may need to add information so that the reader can find the article in cyberspace. However, if the reference is a scholarly article, the information that will allow the reader to track down the reference to a scholarly article is the DOI—and you include the DOI when you cite a published journal article. (The DOI is a long string of numbers—and possibly letters—that begins with "10." and acts as a permanent URL to the source.) The advantage of finding the article online is that you can cut and paste the DOI instead of having to transcribe it. If the article has a DOI, you just add "doi:" and the DOI to the end of your reference (see the example that follows). If your article does not have a DOI, use the URL—as in the second example that follows.

General form for referencing a journal article you obtained online when that article has a DOI.

Author, I. N. (year). Article title. *Electronic Journal Title Italicized and Capitalized, volume number italicized,* issue number in parentheses only if all issues start on page 1, page numbers. doi:doi number

Example.

Sweeny, K. (2007). Being the best bearer of bad tidings. *Review of General Psychology,* 11, 235–257. doi:10.1037/1089–2680.11.3.235

- Do not put a retrieval date when you have retrieved the final (sometimes called "archival") version of an article. Usually, articles with DOIs are final versions.
- If each issue starts on page 1, include the journal issue number by putting it in parentheses: Do not italicize it.
- "doi" is in all lowercase letters: It is not capitalized.
- Do not put a period at the end of the reference because readers might think the period was part of the DOI.

General form for referencing a journal article you obtained online when that article does not have a DOI.

Author, I. N. (year). Article title. *Journal Title Italicized and Capitalized, volume number italicized,* page numbers. Retrieved from URL

Example.

Schmitt, D. P., & Schackelford, T. D. (2008). Big five traits related to short-term mating: From personality to promiscuity across 46 nations. *Evolutionary Psychology, 6,* 246–282. Retrieved from http://www.epjournal.net/filestore/ep06246282.pdf

- If you have retrieved the final version of an article, do not put the date you retrieved the article. If you believe the version you read might be revised, insert the retrieval date between "Retrieved" and "from" (e.g., "Retrieved September 10, 2012 from . . .").
- If each issue starts on page 1, include the journal issue number.
- Do not italicize the journal issue number.
- Do not put a period at the end of the reference because readers might think the period was part of the URL.
- Do not underline the URL.[10]
- The full URL is included because anyone can get the article using that URL. If, however, only people who had subscriptions to the source could see the article, the reference would not include the full URL. Instead, it would include the URL to the journal's home page.

Journal article abstracts. If you try to retrieve an article from the Internet, you may be able to retrieve only the article's abstract. If you want to cite that article, you should find and read it. If, however, you can access only the abstract (e.g., your library does not subscribe to the journal and you cannot obtain it from interlibrary loan)—or you access the article but read only the abstract, cite the abstract using the following format:

General form.

Author, I. N. (year). Article title. *Journal Title Italicized and Capitalized, volume number italicized,* start page–finish page. Abstract retrieved from URL, DOI, or name of source.

- If the source is a URL or DOI, there is no period at the end of the reference. If the source is a database, there is a period.

Examples.

Greenwald, A. G., & Farnham, S. D. (2000). Using the Implicit Association Test to measure self-esteem and self-concept. *Journal of Personality and Social Psychology, 79,* 1022–1038. Abstract retrieved from PsycINFO database.

[10]Although the URL should not be underlined, your word-processing software may automatically underline it. To learn how to turn off that feature, see our website (http://www.writingforpsychology.com) or see 7.1.2.

Greenwald, A. G., & Farnham, S. D. (2000). Using the Implicit Association Test to measure self-esteem and self-concept. *Journal of Personality and Social Psychology, 79,* 1022–1038. Abstract retrieved from PubMed database.

Greenwald, A. G., & Farnham, S. D. (2000). Using the Implicit Association Test to measure self-esteem and self-concept. *Journal of Personality and Social Psychology, 79,* 1022–1038. Abstract retrieved from http://faculty.washington.edu/agg/bytopic.htm

Sweeny, K. (2007). Being the best bearer of bad tidings. *Review of General Psychology, 11,* 235–257. Abstract retrieved from doi: 10.1037/1089–2680.11.3.235

Schmitt, D. P. (2008). Big five traits related to short-term mating: From personality to promiscuity across 46 nations. *Evolutionary Psychology,* 6, 246–282. Abstract retrieved from http://www.epjournal.net/filestore/ep06246282.pdf

4.11 Checklists

4.11.1 Academic Honesty Checklist

☐ I cited any source from which I got ideas—even if I did not directly quote that source.
- When I summarized or paraphrased from a source, I cited that source.
- If I had any paragraph without a citation (a) in any section of my term paper or (b) in the Introduction or Discussion sections of my research proposal or report, I went back to my notes to make sure that I had not left out a citation.
- I double-checked my notes and my sources to make sure that I neither had inadvertently quoted someone nor had a paraphrase that looked similar to the source quotation.
- If I had any doubt about whether to cite a source, I cited it.
- If I took words from a source, I made it clear that I was quoting that source.
- If I got ideas or quotes from an informal source, I cited that source as a personal communication (see 4.3.3).

☐ If a source was not the original report of a study, I admitted it.
- If I read a secondary source instead of the original article, I made it clear that I had read only the secondary source by correctly citing (4.3.1) and referencing (4.9.2) only that secondary source.

— If I read a theoretical or review article, I made it clear that the article was not an empirical article. In other words, for review articles, I wrote "(for a review, see Smith, 2011)" and for theoretical articles, I wrote "Smith (2011) argued" rather than "Smith found."

— If I read only the abstract, I made it clear that I did not read the entire article (4.10.11).

4.11.2 Formatting Citations Checklist

- ☐ When citing sources, I did not use footnotes; mention article or journal titles; or mention authors' first names, professional titles (e.g., "Dr."), or professional affiliations (e.g., "Harvard University Professor").
- ☐ If I used a name citation, I put only the date in parentheses (e.g., "Jolley and Mitchell (2013) argued that . . .").
- ☐ If I used a parenthetical citation, I put the authors' names and the date in parentheses, and I separated the last author's name from the date with a comma: "Some have argued that . . . (Jolley & Mitchell, 2013)."
- ☐ If I used a name citation for a multiple-author source, I used "and" to connect the next-to-last author's name to the last author's name; however, if I used a parenthetical citation for a multiple-author citation, I used "&" to connect the next-to-last author's name to the last author's name.
- ☐ If I cited several articles within one set of parentheses, I listed the articles in alphabetical order, and I separated the articles from each other with semicolons: (Brickner, 2000; Jolley, 2007; Mitchell, 2013; Ostrom, 1985; Pusateri, 2012; Williams, 2002).
- ☐ If the paper had more than six authors, I listed only the first author's last name followed immediately (with no comma) by "et al." (e.g., Glick et al., 2011).
- ☐ If I discussed a paper with three to five authors, I mentioned all the authors' last names the first time—and only the first time—I cited that paper.
- ☐ If I discussed a paper with three to five authors and had already cited the paper, I used the first author's last name, followed immediately (with no comma) by "et al." (e.g., First et al., 2011).
- ☐ I checked all my citations that used the phrase "et al." to make sure that I had (a) correctly used such citations and (b) correctly punctuated such citations.
- ☐ I listed all authors' names the first time I introduced a paper with fewer than six authors.
- ☐ I never used "et al." with a two-author paper.
- ☐ I correctly punctuated my "et al." citations: I never put a period after "et" (e.g., I wrote "et al." instead of "et. al."), and I never put a comma

between the first author's last name and "et al." (e.g., I wrote "First et al."—not "First, et al.").

☐ I listed the page number of the source from which I got the quotation. (If there was no page number, as in a website, I consulted 4.8.)

☐ I used the short quote format for quotations under 40 words (see 4.8.1), but used the block quote format for quotations of 40 or more words (see 4.8.2). If the source had a DOI, my reference for that source ended with "doi:" followed by the source's DOI.

4.11.3 Finding and Using Sources Checklist

☐ My citations are from journal articles describing actual research studies rather than from secondary sources such as textbooks, magazines, and newspapers.

☐ If my professor required the paper to have a certain number of sources, I met that requirement. For example, if my professor required a minimum of five sources, I cited at least five empirical articles published in refereed journals.

☐ Rather than quoting, I paraphrased, summarized, interpreted, and critiqued. As a result, I limited quotations to fewer than 50 words for every 1,000 of my own.

☐ I paraphrased and summarized empirical research reports in a way that makes it clear that (a) I read them rather than skimmed their abstracts and (b) I understood them.

☐ I showed, through my paraphrases and summaries of those articles, how the different articles fit together—and how they related to the main point of my paper.

☐ I commented on weaknesses I found in published research. If I had trouble finding weaknesses, I consulted Chapter 5.

4.11.4 Reference Page Checklist

☐ My reference section starts on a separate page. The centered heading "References" is at the top of that page in plain (not boldfaced) 12-point type.

☐ Everything is double-spaced.

☐ The first line of each reference is not indented. Instead, it begins at the left margin.

☐ When a reference takes up more than one line, I indented those additional lines five spaces by using my word processor's hanging indent feature.

☐ My references are listed in alphabetical order (according to the last name of the first author).

- ☐ Each reference begins with the authors' last names and initials, followed by the year of publication (in parentheses), and then a period.
- ☐ Every reference ends with a period—except for (a) those ending with either a URL or DOI and (b) those ending with a parenthetical explanation about the work's original source.
- ☐ I put one space after each comma.
- ☐ I put one space after each period except that I left no spaces after a period when it (a) came right before a comma or (b) came after the "n" in the abbreviation ("n.d.").
- ☐ If a source had more than one author, I separated authors' names with commas.
- ☐ I italicized only book titles, names of journals, and the volume numbers—not issue numbers—of journal articles.
- ☐ I capitalized only the following parts of article and book titles: the first word of the title, the first word following a colon, and proper nouns (for more information on proper nouns, see 6.1.1).
- ☐ I capitalized the first letter of words in journal titles—except for words with fewer than four letters that were either (a) prepositions (e.g., "of") or (b) conjunctions (e.g., "and").
- ☐ When citing journal articles, I avoided both the word "pages" and the abbreviation "pp."
- ☐ When citing journal articles, I avoided both the word "volume" and the abbreviation "vol."
- ☐ If a book was published in the United States, I abbreviated, rather than wrote out, the name of the state. I used the same state abbreviations (e.g., "PA" for Pennsylvania) that the U.S. Postal Service uses. I remembered that these abbreviations are capitalized and do not contain periods.
- ☐ I made sure that all URLs in my paper and in my reference section were in the same color (black), font size (12-point), and style (not underlined) as regular text. (I turned off the "auto-underline" feature of my word-processing software.)
- ☐ All the references in this section are also cited in my paper. If a reference was not cited, either I added a citation to that reference to the body of my paper or I deleted the reference.
- ☐ All the sources cited in my paper are also listed in this section except for "personal communication" citations (see 4.3.3), original works that I did not read but instead learned about through a secondary source (see 4.3.1), and classical works (e.g., the Bible).

4.12 Summary

1. You need to find good sources to write a good paper. Good sources will usually be research articles published in scientific journals. To emphasize how important sources are, some professors will judge your paper from its reference list, because that list will tell them whether your paper is based on a fair sample of solid, current information.
2. It is vital to cite and to reference your sources correctly.
3. One source may give you leads to other sources (see 4.1.2).
4. Computerized databases can help you find sources. If you have trouble finding enough sources, consult Table 4.2.
5. When you find a source, read it, reread it, and take notes on it. Taking notes is different from copying: Your notes should include an APA-style reference to the source, your critical comments on the source, and quotation marks around any words you are copying from the source.
6. When you get an idea from a source, you must cite that source. When you paraphrase from a source, you must cite that source. When you quote a source, you must cite that source. When you are not sure about whether you should cite a source, cite that source.
7. When you quote a source, not only must you cite it, but you must also indicate (a) that you are quoting and (b) the page you are quoting. For short quotations (fewer than 40 words), you use quotation marks to indicate that you are quoting; for long quotations, you use a different strategy: blocked quotations (see 4.8.2).
8. Use a personal communication citation (4.3.3) to give credit for ideas that you acquired through informal sources. Do not put these personal communications in your reference list.
9. When citing, do not provide any information about the authors except for their last names—unless you have more than one author with the same last name (in that case, see 4.5.5). Never mention authors' first names, titles, or professional affiliations.
10. Each of your citations—except personal communication citations and citations of classical works—should point to one specific entry in your reference list.
11. There are two types of citations: name citations and parenthetical citations. Use a name citation when you are going to paraphrase extensively from a single source. Use parenthetical citations to show the reader how related studies fit together. Do not use footnotes to cite sources.
12. When using a name citation, put the date in parentheses. When using a name citation for a paper with two authors, connect the last names with the word "and." When using a name citation for a paper with three to five authors, use a comma between all the authors' names and add the word "and" before the last author's name.

13. When using a parenthetical citation for a paper with two authors, connect the last names with the symbol "&" and separate the last name from the date with a comma (e.g., "Mitchell & Jolley, 2013"). When using a parenthetical citation for a paper with three to five authors, use a comma between all the authors' names and add the symbol "&" before the last author's name (e.g., "Mitchell, Jolley, & O'Shea, 2013").
14. When citing several articles within one set of parentheses, (a) put the articles in alphabetical order according to primary authors' last names and (b) separate the articles by different authors from each other with semicolons.
15. When citing a source with six or more authors, provide only the primary (first) author's last name followed immediately (with no comma) by "et al." (e.g., "Glick et al., 2004").
16. When citing a source with three to five authors that was cited earlier in the paper, use the primary author's last name, followed immediately (with no comma) by "et al.," and the publication year (e.g., "Mitchell et al., 2013").
17. The Reference section starts on a separate page titled "References."
18. All the sources listed in the references should be (a) cited in the paper and (b) put in alphabetical order according to the last name of the primary author (see 4.10.3).
19. The first line of a reference starts at the left margin. The rest of the reference is indented five spaces.
20. If your source as an official author, publication year, and DOI, your reference should contain that information.
21. In the past, one problem with Internet references was that URLs changed. To address that problem, almost any recent journal article you find has a DOI: a long string of characters that provides a permanent link to the article. Usually, you can find the DOI on the first page of the article. Sometimes, the number will be preceded with "DOI:"—but not always. If, you cannot find "DOI:" on the first page, look for a long string of numbers (and possibly letters) starting with "10." That number will probably be the DOI.
22. Each reference begins with the authors' last names and initials, followed by the year of publication (in parentheses), and then a period. Separate last names from initials with a comma. Separate initials with a space. Separate different authors' names with a comma. For two or more authors, separate the final name from the rest with a comma followed by an ampersand (e.g., "Burton, G. J., Nagshineh, S., & Ruddock, K. H.").
23. The following are examples of a reference for a paper book and for an electronic version of the same book.

Paper version.

Strunk, W., Jr., & White, E. B. (1918). *The elements of style* (1st ed.). Geneva, NY: W. P. Humphrey.

Internet version.

Strunk, W., Jr., & White, E. B. (1918). *The elements of style* (1st ed.). Retrieved from http://www.bartleby.com/141/

24. The following are examples of a reference for a chapter from an edited paper book (for more on referencing chapters from printed books, see 4.10.9) and for an electronic version of the same chapter (for more on referencing book chapters you read online, see 4.10.12):

Paper version.

Alderdice, J. L. (2010). On the psychology of religious fundamentalism. In P. J. Verhagen, H. M. van Praag, Herman M., J. J. López-Ibor, Jr., J. L. Cox, & D. Moussaoui (Eds.). *Religion and psychiatry: beyond boundaries* (pp. 305-317). Chichester, England: Wiley-Blackwell.

Internet version.

Alderdice, J. L. (2010). On the psychology of religious fundamentalism. In P. J. Verhagen, H. M. van Praag, Herman M., J. J. López-Ibor, Jr., J. L. Cox, & D. Moussaoui (Eds.). *Religion and psychiatry: beyond boundaries* (pp. 305-317). doi:10.1002/9780470682203.ch17

25. If you read the print version of a journal article that does not have a DOI, reference it by using the following format (for more on referencing print versions of journal articles, see 4.10.10):

Crovitz, H. F. (1972). Transient binasal hemianopia in a pair of plastic soupspoons. *Psychonomic Science, 28,* 234.

26. If you are referencing an article that has a DOI, include that DOI in your reference—regardless of whether you read the article in a paper journal or online. Thus, what follows is an example of a reference for a journal article that has a DOI—and the format would be the same whether you read a paper copy or an online copy:

Sweeny, K. (2007). Being the best bearer of bad tidings. *Review of General Psychology, 11,* 235–257. doi:10.1037/1089–2680.11.3.235

Making Your Case: A Guide to Skeptical Reading and Logical Writing

When you read articles that you may use in your paper, you want to know when authors are making arguments that do not logically follow from their earlier statements, and you want to know when authors are making claims that do not follow from the evidence. When your professor reads your paper, you do not want your professor to write any of the following comments on your paper: "illogical," "not true," "not fair," "does not follow," "not necessarily," "unsupported assertion," "the evidence does not support that claim," or "that is only one interpretation." Instead, you want your professor to recognize that you have accomplished two competing tasks: (a) making a strong case in support of your claims and (b) acknowledging the case against your claims. In this chapter, we will help you refine two abilities that will enable you to defend your claims fairly and forcefully: the ability to evaluate arguments and the ability to interpret evidence.

To make a strong argument, you must convince your readers (a) that your argument follows logically from the *premises*—statements, assumptions, and beliefs—on which it is based and (b) that those premises are probably true. To show that your premises are true, you will back up your claims with evidence—and your evidence will usually be a citation of someone else's work. If you do not cite evidence to support a claim, your professor may write "unsupported assertion" or "evidence?" next to your claim.

To show that your conclusion follows logically from your premises, you must state your premises and, like a district attorney making an opening statement, you must carefully lay out your reasoning. To show all your steps—and to prevent your professor from writing "non sequitur" (does not follow) or "quite a leap" next to your conclusion—you may wish to outline your argument.

Scrutinizing an outline of your argument—or better yet, having a friend who disagrees with your conclusion scrutinize that outline—is a simple way to try to determine whether you have succeeded in both (a) providing evidence for your premises and (b) showing that your conclusion logically follows from those premises. To use more sophisticated strategies, you need to know whether your argument is deductive or inductive.

5.1 Deductive Arguments

When you make a deductive argument, you usually start with a rule, a *premise*, (P1) that implies or includes an absolute term (e.g., "all," "every," "always"). Next, you state a second premise (P2) in which you apply that general rule to a specific case. Then you draw a *conclusion* (C1). For example, in Ann's term paper (2.11), she suggested that some researchers had used the following deductive argument:

P1. All functions that depend on biological processes will decline with age.
P2. Intelligence is a function that depends on biological processes.
C1. Intelligence is a function that will decline with age.

In the Introduction of a research paper, you might use a general rule (e.g., a theory) to generate a specific prediction. For example, you might make the following deductive argument:

P1. According to terror management theory, reminding participants that they will die will result in making participants more committed to their worldviews.
P2. This study will involve reminding participants that they will die.
C1. According to terror management theory, this study will result in making participants more committed to their worldviews.

As you can see, making a deductive argument can boil down to using this simple, three-step formula, called a *syllogism*:

P1. Every A is a C.
P2. B is an A.
C1. B, like A, is a C.

Unfortunately, students commonly make three mistakes when trying to insert deductive arguments into their papers.

The first involves stating an untrue premise, such as stating a myth (e.g., "people use only 10% of their brains"), overstating the incidence of a phenomenon (e.g., "everyone believes in God"), or stating that a theory makes a certain claim when the theory does not make that claim. If you insert this first type of unsound deductive argument into your paper, your professor may write "citation?" or "No!" next to your questionable premise.

The second common type of unsound deductive argument involves leaving out a premise. For example, consider the following syllogism:

P1. If people had more positive attitudes toward children, they would bond with children more closely.

P2. If people bonded with children more closely, child abuse would be reduced.

C1. Therefore, if people had more positive attitudes toward children, child abuse would be reduced.

The preceding syllogism is logically valid. However, suppose you wrote the following incomplete syllogism:

P1. "If people had more positive attitudes toward children, people would bond with children more closely.

C1. Therefore, if people had more positive attitudes toward children, child abuse would be reduced."

Because you left out the second premise—that bonding with children more closely would reduce child abuse—your statement is not logically valid. Consequently, your professor might respond to your statement by writing "does not follow," "not necessarily," or "non sequitur."

The third common type of unsound deductive argument involves starting with "If A, then B" but concluding the reverse: "B, therefore A." For example, some students start arguing, "If Theory A is correct, B will occur," but end up arguing, "B occurs, so Theory A is correct." Although the two arguments may seem similar, they are different. To illustrate, assume that we find a group for which the following is always true: "If they see a puppy (A), they smile (B)." Then, if we know they see a puppy (A), we can conclude that they are smiling (B). However, if we see them smile, we cannot conclude that they have seen a puppy because they may be smiling for some other reason, such as seeing a kitten, accepting a marriage proposal, or reading this book.

When constructing your own argument or when reconstructing someone else's, write out the argument, preceding premises with the word "If," separating each premise with the word "and," and preceding the conclusion with the word "then." Writing out the argument makes it less likely that you will start with "If A, then B" but end up with "B, then A." Adding "If" to the premises alerts you to the possibility that any of the premises could be wrong. Adding "and" reminds you that all your premises must be correct to make a valid argument. Careful reading of the literature on a topic will be required to convince yourself, and careful reporting of that literature will be required to convince your reader, that all your premises are correct.

Writing out your arguments can help you write research reports if, as is often the case, you can think of your hypothesis as the conclusion of a deductive argument. For example, if you hypothesized that handedness will show an acquisition curve, you might summarize your argument as follows:

If	a. all learning phenomena show acquisition curves.
And if	b. handedness is a learning phenomenon,
Then	c. handedness will show an acquisition curve.

You will find that making such an outline of your argument will make it easier to write the Introduction of your paper. You will know to (a) state your premises, (b) defend your premises, and, finally, (c) explain how your premises lead to the conclusion that your hypothesis is correct.

When you write the Discussion section, you will again find it useful to think of your hypothesis as the conclusion of a deductive argument. For example, suppose your study shows that your hypothesis—your argument's conclusion—is false. In that case, not only would your conclusion be false, but at least one of your premises would be false as well (assuming your logic was valid). Thus, in your Discussion, you might make the case that your results not only call into question the conclusion (the hypothesis that handedness shows an acquisition curve) but also call into question the premise that led to that conclusion (that handedness is learned). Similarly, if one of your premises were a theory's core premise, you would not only argue that your results disprove your hypothesis, but you would also argue that they challenge the validity of that theory.

5.2 Inductive Arguments: Making Relatively Careful Generalizations

When you make a deductive argument, (a) you are usually applying a general rule to a specific case (e.g., how a theory applies to a particular situation) and (b) your premises are couched in absolute (e.g., "all," "every," "always") terms. When you make an inductive argument, on the other hand, (a) you are usually forming a general rule from observing some specific cases (e.g., determining what most people believe from a poll of a few people) and (b) at least one of your premises is couched in relative (e.g., "some," "most," "usually") terms. If you make an inductive argument from a sample, you can take two steps to increase the chances that your conclusion will be correct.

First, accurately represent what happened in the sample of cases. Do not understate or overstate how often something occurred. For example, if you have evidence that some people in a sample had been sexually abused, write that, rather than writing, "most people in the sample had been sexually abused."

Second, use a sample that should accurately represent what happened in the larger group. Do not use your personal experiences to estimate the frequency of abuse, because your experiences probably are not representative. Instead, use a large, random sample because such samples probably are representative.

Even when you accurately represent what happened in a large, random sample, your generalizations from this sample may be wrong for at least three reasons.

1. Even large, random samples do not reflect their populations perfectly. Thus, a rule or pattern that fits your data may not fit the larger group.
2. Even if your rule fits your data, a different rule also might fit your data—and the larger group's data—better: As the existence of competing theories and explanations shows, more than one rule can fit the same data. (One consequence of there being so many alternative explanations for events is that you will usually have to argue that your explanation for an event is better than competing explanations. To argue for your explanation, you will often have to argue that your explanation involves fewer assumptions, involves fewer principles, or is more consistent with other findings than the competing explanations are.)
3. Even if your rule was the best fit for both your data and for the larger group's data, the rule may no longer apply because people and patterns change.

To illustrate that you may not find out until too late that a rule that fits the existing data is incorrect, consider the classic story of the "inductive turkey." Every morning, the farmer feeds the turkey. The turkey induces that this kind treatment will always be the case. On Thanksgiving morning, however, the turkey finds that inductive reasoning has a fatal flaw.

Like the turkey, science uses inductive reasoning. Thus, like the turkey, science can come to incorrect conclusions. Therefore, in your psychology papers, do not write, "science has proven" or any similar phrase.

Although science cannot overcome all the limits of induction, the best scientific practices avoid four common problems with informal attempts to use induction. Therefore, when judging the quality of a conclusion that is based on evidence, you should ask four questions.

First, ask whether the individual scores are accurate and unbiased. If the scores are based on a measure that was objectively scored (e.g., a multiple-choice test or a reaction time test), you could assume that scoring did not bias the results. However, you should still look for evidence that the measure is a valid (accurate) measure of the variable it is supposed to be measuring. If the researcher used observers, ask whether the researcher trained the observers, whether the researcher checked to see whether independent observers gave the same participant the same score, and whether the researcher made observers unaware of which treatment the participant they were observing had received. If the researcher used a questionnaire or other instrument that had participants report on themselves, ask whether participants knew which condition they were in and ask whether these self-reports can be trusted.

Second, ask whether the sample of observations is as representative and unbiased as possible. Specifically, ask whether the researchers had clearly defined a population, taken a large random sample from that population, and had gotten most of the people they sampled to participate.

Third, ask whether the conclusions drawn from the sample were accurate and unbiased. Because people's biases may cause them to see a pattern in the sample that does not exist and because people's ignorance of how chance works may cause them to mistake a coincidence for a reliable pattern, ask whether the conclusions were based on results that reached conventional levels of statistical significance. If a conclusion is not supported by sound statistical evidence, the authors may have made a hasty generalization.

Fourth, ask whether the authors' explanation for the evidence could be replaced by a better explanation. If the authors did not look for evidence to disprove their explanation or did not think about other explanations that could account for their findings, you should do that work.

5.3 Argument by Analogy

Some philosophers consider argument by analogy—arguing that what is true for one thing is true for another similar thing—to be a form of inductive reasoning. Like inductive reasoning, argument by analogy can lead to brilliant insights as well as to incorrect conclusions.

You will see at least two forms of argument by analogy. In one form, people argue that (a) X and Y are similar because they are known to share certain properties (e.g., humans and nonhuman animals have brains and learn), (b) X has certain property (e.g., humans have abstract thought), and (c) because Y is similar to X, Y also has this property (e.g., nonhuman animals have abstract thought).

In another form of argument by analogy, people argue that because Y (e.g., handedness) has several characteristics of X (learned behavior), Y is an X. For example, they may argue that handedness is a learned behavior because it shares several characteristics of learned behavior: It takes time to develop, it may be exhibited in one situation but not in another, and it exhibits spontaneous recovery. The more similarities people find between Y and X, the better their case that Y probably belongs to the X category. However, they can never prove that Y is a member of the X category (e.g., ants have many similarities to humans, but ants are not humans). Thus, it is often more productive to search for differences between two categories that may cause them to act differently. For example, by looking for possible effects of one difference between humans and computers—that humans have bodies—researchers have found that, unlike computers, people process information differently when sitting down than when standing up, when exercising than when at rest, when holding a warm beverage than when holding a cold beverage, and when smiling than when frowning (Kahneman, 2011).

In conclusion, arguments by analogy can lead to interesting insights (e.g., modern cognitive psychology has benefited from comparing human memory to computer memory) and useful applications (e.g., research on nonhuman animals has been successfully applied to humans). However, being like something is different from being identical to something. Consequently, arguments by analogy may lead to false conclusions (e.g., the conclusion that nonhuman animals have abstract thought is probably false).

5.4 Overview of Problems in Making Arguments

As we have pointed out, your paper must make at least one argument. In the next sections, we will show you what errors to avoid in making arguments. Note that you should try to catch these errors both when reading your own paper as well as when reading other people's works. As you will see, these errors in making arguments can be broken down into three types: (a) failing to base an argument on evidence, (b) failing to be fair, and (c) failing to consider alternative explanations for the evidence.

5.5 Appeals to Emotion, Faith, or Authority

To make your case, use objective evidence and logical reasoning. Do not substitute appeals to emotion, faith, or authority for logical reasoning.

5.5.1 Appeals to Emotion

Appeals to emotion ask the reader to suspend objectivity—a key element of science—and to experience pity, fear, or some other emotion instead (Zechmeister & Johnson, 1992). In a paper arguing for the accuracy of recovered memories, a student might try to evoke pity by writing, "The distress shown by clients as they retrieve these painful memories compels us to believe that the memories are real." Alternatively, a student might try to evoke the fear of being considered insensitive by writing, "Only someone devoid of human feelings could doubt clients as they recall these painful memories."

To make appeal-to-emotion arguments, students commonly ask rhetorical questions. For example, suppose a student posed the following question: "Who could doubt such clients' experiences?" The question is rhetorical because the writer is convinced that the reader will be forced to answer, "Nobody could." Rhetorical questions are out of place in scientific discourse; avoid them.

5.5.2 Appeals to Faith

Like appeals to emotion, appeals to faith set aside objectivity. Imagine a writer asserting that there are fairies at the bottom of the garden, but that the fairies will reveal themselves only to those who believe in them. Further, the writer adds, the fairies will refuse to give any evidence of themselves. Such an appeal to faith would probably be ineffective. Unfortunately, however, if, instead of appealing to faith in fairies, the writer appealed to faith in a particular religious, political, or theoretical position, the writer would sway some readers.

5.5.3 Appeals to Authority

An appeal to authority is made when a well-respected person's name is cited for a particular position. The assumption underlying appeal-to-authority arguments is that any position associated with someone so wonderful must be a correct position.

Do not rely on appeal-to-authority arguments. At best, arguments made by appeal to authority are weak. For example, it would be weak to write, "In his presidential address to the American Psychological Association (APA), Smith (2008) asserted that most repressed memories of childhood sexual abuse surfacing in therapy are examples of false memories." This citation of Smith is weak because there is nothing in it to allow the reader to evaluate Smith's opinion that therapist-elicited repressed memories are false memories. For example, there is no discussion of research demonstrating the falsehood of the memories. Consequently, the only reason to believe Smith's opinion rests on Smith's reputation as president of the APA.

5.6 Unfair Arguments

5.6.1 Ad Hominem Arguments

Whereas the writer making an appeal-to-authority argument implies that the reader should believe a position because a person with a good reputation believes in that position, a writer making an *ad hominem* argument implies that the reader should disbelieve a position because the person advocating the position has a poor reputation. Specifically, whenever a writer attacks the character of the person providing the evidence, the writer has made an ad hominem argument (the English translation of the Latin phrase "ad hominem" is "toward the person"). The assumption underlying ad hominem arguments is that any position associated with someone so disreputable cannot be a correct position. For example, let us say that Jones (2010) has shown that some therapists consistently elicit reports of childhood sexual abuse from clients randomly assigned to them. Ad hominem arguments would include claims that Jones used cocaine or that Jones was a fascist. Ad hominem arguments would not address the quality of Jones's research. In short, ad hominem arguments are unfair because you are "acting as though you knocked down your opponent's argument when, in fact, you only knocked down your opponent" (J. L. Phillips, personal communication, August 15, 2008).

5.6.2 Ignoring Contradictory Evidence

Another unfair way for a writer to favor one position at the expense of opposing positions is to ignore any contradictory evidence. For example, you could make a convincing argument that the world is flat if you ignored all the evidence that the world is round. Similarly, you could make a convincing case for the validity of recovered memories by accepting uncritically only papers in which the authors concluded that recovered memories were accurate.

Students are often guilty of not citing and discussing contradictory evidence. To avoid making this error, you must (a) read widely enough on a topic to be able to write about the evidence relating to both your position on an issue as well as to the opposing position and (b) be open-minded enough to be fair to the opposing position.

5.6.3 Straw Man Arguments

If you cannot be fair to the opposing position, you may create and attack a *straw man:*[1] a misrepresentation of the opposing position. By discrediting a weakened version of the opposing position (the straw man), writers make their own position appear stronger. For example, suppose a writer wants to argue that there have been no reliable demonstrations of repressed memories. The writer could construct a straw man by presenting a weak case for repressed memories. One way to create a weak case would be to build the case using only the most seriously flawed studies the writer could find. The writer would then proceed to demolish the straw man by listing all the methodological flaws.

The straw man argument is likely to surface when students are attacking a theory they do not like. To destroy the theory, they oversimplify it and misstate its premises. Then, the professor, like a referee calling a foul or a judge anticipating the objection from the theory's attorney, scolds the students for attacking a "straw man version" of the theory rather than the theory itself.

Although even some published writers make straw man arguments, resist the temptation to provide weakened and oversimplified versions of positions that disagree with your position. Instead, if you want to demolish an argument opposing yours, make sure you demolish the strongest possible version of that argument.

5.7 General Errors in Reasoning From Evidence

Thus far, we have discussed errors caused by ignoring the evidence, such as attacking a cartoon version of an opposing idea rather than the idea itself, attacking the person who proposed an opposing idea rather than the person's idea, and ignoring evidence that favors an opposing idea. That is, we have discussed errors resulting from passion overriding reason. In the next section, we will discuss errors in which the person looks at the evidence but errs by failing to consider alternative explanations for that evidence. Reading this section will help you evaluate other people's published papers as well as help you evaluate drafts of your own papers.

5.7.1 Inferring Causation From Correlation

If you conduct a correlational study or read a report of one, you often learn that two variables are related. Unfortunately, you may also jump to the conclusion that the research has also established that the two variables are causally related. That is, you may label one variable the "cause" and the other the "effect"—despite the fact that you cannot make cause-effect statements from correlational studies.

To understand why you cannot draw cause-effect conclusions from correlational studies, imagine reading about a correlational study that found a relationship between

---

[1]The original straw man was a soldier's uniform stuffed with straw that was propped on the battlements of a castle. It was designed to draw the arrows of enemy archers, leaving the real soldiers unharmed. Because the soldiers were always dressed as men, it is inaccurate, and possibly disrespectful to women, to use the term "straw person argument."

television watching and depression. Specifically, suppose that a survey found that people who watched more television were more likely to be depressed. You would be tempted to believe that television viewing caused some of those surveyed to become depressed. Yet to do so would be to commit the error of inferring causation from correlation. The reason we cannot infer causation from correlation is that there are numerous explanations for a correlation between two variables. For example, it may be that television watching, rather than being a cause of depression, may be an effect of depression: Perhaps depressed people watch more television because they are more likely to feel that they do not have the energy to do anything else. Alternatively, both television watching and depression may be side effects of some other factor: Perhaps people who lose their jobs are more likely to (a) become depressed and (b) have more time to watch television.

To make cause-effect statements, you cannot rely on surveys or other correlational studies. Instead, the only studies that allow causation to be inferred correctly are *experiments*,[2] most of which embody three principles:

1. At least two groups of individuals are formed by random assignment.[3]
2. Each group is treated identically except for the *manipulated variable:* the *independent variable.*[4] Sometimes, the experimental group receives a treatment that contains a moderate or a high amount of the manipulated variable, whereas another group, a *control* group, gets no treatment. Usually, however, if there is a control group, either that group will receive a treatment that contains a small amount of the manipulated variable or it will receive a *placebo treatment:* a fake treatment, such as a sugar pill in a drug study, that does not contain any of the manipulated variable.
3. A statistical test is used to see whether the groups' scores on the *measured variable* (also known as the *dependent variable*) are significantly (reliably) different from each other.

To see how you could do an experiment that incorporated these three principles, imagine that you want to determine whether watching violent television causes children to be aggressive. In that case, you might design the following experiment.

1. Randomly assign children to violent-television-viewing and nonviolent-television-viewing groups. Random assignment might involve flipping a coin for each child: A head means the child goes into the violent-television group, and a tail means the child goes into the nonviolent-television group.

---

[2]We will not discuss small-*n* research, quasi-experiments, or causal modeling because such techniques are beyond the scope of this book.

[3]We will not consider experiments in which people participate in more than a single experimental condition. Researchers using such within-subjects (repeated-measures) experiments can make cause-effect statements because they (a) manipulate the independent variable(s) and (b) control for order effects by randomizing or counterbalancing the order in which participants receive the treatments.

[4]Experiments can have more than one manipulated variable. However, for simplicity's sake, we will confine ourselves to the simple, single-factor experiment.

2. Treat the groups identically except that you show one group a violent television program and the other group a nonviolent program (the independent variable manipulation). All children then have an identical session of free play in which an observer counts the number of aggressive acts committed by each child. The number of aggressive acts represents the measured (dependent) variable.
3. Test whether there is a statistically significant (reliable) difference between the two groups' scores. If there is such a systematic difference in how the two groups behaved, one can conclude that the difference in the content of the two television programs caused the difference in aggressive behavior.

If any one of the three principles is violated, causation cannot be inferred. In the next section, we will show you why the first principle, random assignment, is crucial to making cause-effect statements.

If the researcher does not randomly assign participants to groups, the groups may be systematically different even before the treatment is introduced. For example, suppose the researcher decided to assign boys to see the violent program and girls to see the nonviolent program. In that case, skeptics could argue that the difference between the groups' behavior was due to gender rather than to the manipulation. Alternatively, suppose the researcher let all the children who wanted to go first watch the violent program and had the more hesitant children watch the nonviolent program. In that case, skeptics could argue that the difference between the groups' behavior was due to personality differences between the children in the groups (e.g., maybe assertive children are more aggressive than reserved children) rather than to the manipulation.

Another form of nonrandom assignment that creates groups that are systematically different before the manipulation is administered is *self-selection:* letting people choose their treatment condition. If the researcher in the television violence study we have been discussing were to let children self-select, the aggressive children might be more likely than less aggressive children to choose to watch the violent television program.

Although self-selection might seem far-fetched for the study we are considering, self-selection is a problem with much survey research. For example, suppose that a survey researcher questions children and finds that children who watch more hours of violent television are more aggressive than children who watch fewer hours of violent television (i.e., aggression and watching violent television are correlated). The researcher cannot conclude that watching violent television causes a child to be aggressive because of the problem of self-selection: Aggressive children may be more likely than less aggressive children to choose to watch violent television.[5]

Any study that uses self-selection is a correlational study and should not be used as the basis of a cause-effect conclusion. For example, in the 1960s, researchers found

[5]Note that it is self-selection—not the survey instrument itself—that prevents the survey researcher from making valid cause-effect statements. If a questionnaire is used as the dependent measure in an experiment, the experimenter can make a cause-effect statement. For example, in our television violence experiment, we could have used a questionnaire—rather than observation—to measure aggressiveness. In that case, we could still have made a cause-effect statement because, instead of using self-selection, we randomly assigned participants to receive different manipulations.

that people who smoked were more likely to have heart disease than people who did not smoke. However, that finding was not based on randomly assigning people to smoke. Smoking was not even a manipulated variable. Instead, the smoking and nonsmoking groups were formed by self-selection: People chose either to smoke or not to smoke. Thus, the finding that smokers had more heart disease than nonsmokers was a correlational finding. Such a correlational finding did not establish that smoking had any effect on heart disease. Indeed, in the 1960s, when researchers knew only that smokers were more prone to heart disease than nonsmokers, many reasonable people argued that both smoking and heart disease could be side effects of another variable (e.g., stress may cause people to have heart disease as well as cause people to smoke).

5.7.2 Making Something out of Nothing: Misinterpreting Null Results

The failure to consider alternative explanations for a correlational finding is one of the most common and one of the most serious reasoning errors that students make. The second most common and second most serious reasoning error is the failure to appreciate that there are two explanations for *null results:* results that do not establish that variables are related.

One explanation for null results is that the variables are unrelated. However, another explanation is that the variables are related, but the study failed to uncover the relationship. A study may fail to detect an existing relationship between variables for many reasons: using a treatment manipulation that was not strong enough to produce detectable differences between conditions, using a measure that was not sensitive enough to detect differences between conditions, or using a design (e.g., a between-subject design that tested only a few participants) that was not sensitive enough to detect differences between conditions.

In short, null results, like "not guilty" verdicts, are inconclusive. On the one hand, you cannot use null results to conclude that variables are related because they do not provide evidence beyond reasonable doubt that the variables are related. On the other hand, you cannot use null results to conclude that the variables are unrelated because, like a not guilty verdict, the failure to find a relationship may reflect a problem with the investigation rather than a lack of a relationship.

5.7.3 Adding Meaning to Significance: Misinterpreting Significant Results

If you observe a relationship between two variables in your study, you need to view that finding with caution. Sometimes, random error makes it appear that two variables are related when, in fact, the variables are not related. Therefore, you need to ask whether the pattern of results you observed is reliable: If you repeated the study, would you get similar results? The best and most direct evidence for reliability is replication: Others have repeated the study and obtained similar results.

For better or worse, the evidence that psychologists have typically used to evaluate the reliability of a single study is the evidence from statistical significance tests. Such tests answer the question: If the *null hypothesis*—the hypothesis that there is no relationship between the variables—is true, how likely are the study's results?[6]

To introduce the logic behind statistical tests by using a nonresearch example, suppose a person flips a coin and gets six heads in a row. Statistical tests can tell us that, if the coin is not biased (the null hypothesis that the coin is no more likely to get heads than tails is true), those results are unlikely. Specifically, statistics can tell you that the chances of those results are 1 in 64. Based on that information, you might decide that the coin is biased.[7]

To illustrate the logic of statistical tests in an experiment, suppose that the average aggression score of participants assigned to play a violent video game is 75, whereas the average aggression score of participants assigned to play a nonviolent game is 70. Although this 5-point difference might reflect a treatment effect, it could just be a coincidence. To rule out coincidence, psychologists have traditionally turned to statistical significance tests. Such tests can answer the question: "If the null hypothesis is true (the two video games used in the study produce equal amounts of aggression), how likely would it be to observe a difference between the groups of at least 5 points?" If the answer that significance tests give to that question is, "not very likely" (less than 5 in 100, also known as $p < .05$), psychologists will tend to reject the null hypothesis. In other words, psychologists have often decided that if statistics suggests that coincidence is an unlikely explanation for the observed relationship, the observed relationship reflects a real relationship rather than a coincidence. Historically, psychologists have indicated that such results are reliable by calling such results "statistically significant."

Note that statistically significant results are not necessarily significant in the sense of being big or important. Many statistically significant results that are based on huge samples are small and meaningless. Indeed, some argue that, with a large enough sample size, the relationship between any two variables (e.g., shoe size and IQ) would be statistically significant (Cohen, 1990). In short, if you want to estimate the size of an effect, you must do more than look at the results of a significance test.

---

[6]As Cohen (1994) points out, significance tests tell us how likely our results are (given the null hypothesis is true), but what we really want to know is how likely it is that the null hypothesis is true (given our results). To come closer to what we want to know, some researchers use the probability that the results will replicate: p_{rep}. A p_{rep} of .95 suggests that, if the study was repeated, the probability of getting the same pattern of results would be 95%.

[7]Your statistical analysis is telling you one thing (how likely it is to get these results if the coin is fair) when you really want to know something else (how likely it is that your coin is fair). That is, as with statistical significance tests, you are learning the probability of getting these results (given the null hypothesis is true), but what you really want to know is what the probability is that the null hypothesis is true (given these results). Although these events sound similar, their probabilities are different. To illustrate that events that sound similar can have quite different probabilities, compare the probability of winning a state lottery grand prize given you bought a lottery ticket to the probability that you bought a lottery ticket given you won the state lottery. The first probability is less than 1 in a million; the second is 100%.

5.7.4 Trusting Labels Too Much: Not Questioning Construct Validity

In addition to questioning the relationship between manipulated and measured variables, you should question the labels that the researchers who conducted the study attached to those variables. For example, suppose that the researchers claim to have manipulated the construct "television violence" and claim to have measured the construct "aggression." They could be wrong on both counts.

The researchers' manipulation would not have *construct validity* if the violent program was more exciting and arousing than the nonviolent program. In that case, a higher level of aggression in the violent-television group may be due to that group's higher levels of excitement and arousal rather than to having seen violence. To determine whether arousal is a *confounding variable*—a variable that is unintentionally manipulated along with the independent variable—you would need to carefully compare the treatment and the no-treatment manipulations to see whether the nonviolent film's excitement level matches the violent film's excitement level (e.g., by seeing whether both films had the same effect on participants' heart rates).

The researchers' measure would not have construct validity if it did not accurately measure aggression. For example, suppose their aggression measure consisted of giving children inkblots to look at and then counting the number of times the children thought that the inkblots looked like aggressive animals. In that case, you should question their measure's construct validity on at least three grounds: (a) their measure does not match up with definitions of aggression, (b) their measure does not correlate with valid measures of aggression, and (c) researchers might bias the results by, for example, counting "cat" as an aggressive animal when it was mentioned by a child who saw the violent film but not counting it as an aggressive animal when it was mentioned by a child who saw the nonviolent film.

In many studies, you should be concerned about the potential for *researcher bias:* the researcher behaving in a way (e.g., being more patient, friendly, or encouraging to participants receiving a certain treatment) that might make participants behave in a way that would favor the researcher's hypothesis. Research has shown researcher bias to be quite subtle and to occur despite the researcher's best intentions (Rosenthal, 1966).

In many studies, you may also need to decide whether the results may be due to *participant bias:* participants' guessing the hypothesis and altering their behavior either to favor or to refute the hypothesis. Participant bias is often a problem in research that asks participants to fill out a scale or to answer a question. In such research, it is easy for participants to give a researcher the answers they think the researcher wants to hear.

Researcher bias and participant bias are often serious threats to research in clinical psychology. For example, suppose that people suffering from depression are randomly assigned either to take a particular treatment (e.g., a new drug or a new therapy) or to take a control treatment (a capsule containing an inert substance or an ineffective therapy). If the researcher knows which people are receiving the treatment and which are receiving the control, the researcher might behave more cheerily toward those receiving the treatment than to those receiving the control—and that cheeriness might improve the treatment group's mood. In such a case, the study's construct validity would be ruined by researcher bias. Similarly, if the participants know whether they have received the treatment, those receiving the treatment might cheer up because they expect the treatment to work, whereas those receiving the control might despair. In that case, participant bias would poison the study's construct validity.

One popular way to deal with both participant and researcher biases has been to run *double-blind* (also called *double-masked*) studies, in which both the participants and the researchers interacting with the participants are kept ignorant of (are blind to) which group is which. For example, in a drug study, the primary investigator might have assigned a code to each bottle of pills. The participants and the research assistants who interacted with the participants would know the pill's code number (e.g., X3987), but would not know whether the pill contained the drug or just a placebo (e.g., a sugar pill).

5.7.5 Not Questioning Generalizations

In addition to questioning the study's construct validity, you should question the study's *external validity:* the degree to which the results of the study can be generalized to different settings and different participants. One clue to the extent to which the results can be generalized will come from the Participants section. If the participants constitute a large, representative sample (e.g., a large random sample) of a broad population, you can be more confident that the results will generalize to people beyond the participants of that particular study than if the participants were not a representative sample of that population (e.g., participants were volunteers from one introductory psychology class). Note, however, that if only two of the participants in a representative sample were Asian Americans, you have little evidence that the results generalize to Asian Americans.

In evaluating generalizations, be cautious, but not cynical; you should neither unquestionably accept them nor unquestionably reject them. Be cautious by realizing that any generalization beyond the evidence may be wrong: The only way to be sure that the results generalize to a particular group or setting is to repeat the study with that particular group or setting. However, do not be so cynical that you completely reject any generalization that goes beyond the immediate study.

It is often reasonable to make tentative generalizations. For example, given that almost all research results obtained in a laboratory setting also hold in field settings, it is usually reasonable to generalize from the laboratory to the field.

Similarly, given that most relationships found with one group also can be found with a different group, generalizing the results to a group that was not adequately sampled may be reasonable. To reject such a generalization, you should do more than say that no generalization is possible because the particular group has not been sampled. Instead, you should have a reasonable explanation of how differences between that particular group and the group studied would prevent the results from applying to that particular group.

5.8 Critical Thinking Checklist

- ☐ My arguments were logical.
  - — I identified my premises and, when possible, cited evidence to make the case that they were true.
  - — I made sure that my conclusion followed logically from my premises.
  - — I avoided appeals to emotion, faith, and authority.
- ☐ I dealt fairly with opposing positions.
  - — I did not engage in ad hominem attacks on proponents of opposing positions.
  - — I did not attack a straw man version of the opposing position.
  - — I did not ignore evidence that appeared to support an opposing position: I either showed how that evidence, when properly interpreted, was consistent with my claims, or I qualified my claims to be consistent with that evidence.
- ☐ I considered alternative explanations for findings.
  - — I did not interpret correlational evidence as proving causality.
  - — I appreciated the difference between failing to find a relationship and proving that a relationship does not exist. Thus, I did not interpret null results as proof of the null hypothesis.
  - — I questioned whether the measures and manipulations really reflected the labels that the researcher gave them.
  - — I considered explanations, other than the ones provided by the authors, for the obtained results.
  - — I was careful when accepting generalizations from a study, especially when there was reason to believe that the sample was biased.

5.9 Summary

1. You have two challenges in making a solid argument. First, you need to make the case that your premises (the facts and assumptions that support your conclusion) are correct. Second, you have to make sure that your conclusion follows logically from your premises.
2. In deductive arguments, premises are couched in absolute terms (e.g., "all," "every," "always") or in unambiguous comparisons (e.g., "A is bigger than B.").

In deductive arguments, if the premises are true and the reasoning is valid, the conclusion must be true. You might use a deductive argument to show that a hypothesis follows from a theory. In that case, your argument might follow this form:

a. According to Theory X, increasing A will increase B.
b. This study will increase A.
c. According to Theory X, this study will increase B.

3. In inductive arguments, at least one of the premises is couched in relative terms (e.g., "few," "some," "most"). Often, inductive reasoning involves making a generalization from what has been observed. Such generalizations are likely to be false if the observations are not based on a representative sample. Even when the generalization is based on a representative sample, the general rule could be wrong because (a) samples are not perfect, (b) things change, and (c) another, more accurate rule may also fit your data.
4. Avoid appeals to emotion or authority.
5. Confront—rather than ignore—evidence that contradicts your argument.
6. Avoid unfair tactics, such as ad hominem arguments (5.6.1) or straw man arguments (5.6.3).
7. Avoid three common errors in reasoning from evidence: (a) inferring a cause-effect relationship from a correlational study, (b) uncritically generalizing the results from a study that used a biased sample, and (c) uncritically accepting the labels that a researcher gives to the measures and manipulations.
8. Recognize that although you cannot safely infer causation from a correlational study, you can reasonably infer causation from a properly conducted experiment (for more, see 5.7.1).
9. Recognize that null results are inconclusive (for more, see 5.7.2).
10. Recognize that statistically significant results are not necessarily large or important (for more, see 5.7.3).
11. Assess a study's construct validity. Did the researcher (a) use commonly accepted measures and manipulations and (b) take steps, such as using "blind" procedures, to decrease both participant bias and researcher bias?
12. Be cautious about generalizing. Although there is always some risk in generalizing the results of a study, you can be more confident that the results apply to a larger group if the study looked at a large random sample of participants from that larger group.

CHAPTER 6

Writing the Wrongs: How to Avoid Gruesome Grammar, Putrid Punctuation, and Saggy Style

Writing a paper is like driving passengers to a destination. In addition to knowing where you are going, you should know enough about the

1. components of a car (parts of speech), what they are called, and how they work together (basic grammar) to get in and start the car;
2. controls (punctuation) to keep the car going, to steer, and to brake;
3. rules of the road (usage) so that you drive on the correct side of the road and respect other road users; and
4. passengers' preferences and the car's handling characteristics (style) to drive with care, and, possibly, with flair.

If you spend a little time studying this chapter, you will be able to understand most of the *Publication Manual's* suggestions about writing, as well as the suggestions that your professor or writing center may make about your paper. If you spend a moderate amount of time studying this chapter, you will be able to write competently. If you spend a great deal of time studying this chapter and practicing what it preaches, you will be able to express your ideas effectively and with style.

6.1 Elements of Grammar

The first step toward being able to understand grammatical rules is to be able to determine whether a word is being used as a noun, a pronoun, a verb, an article, an adjective, an adverb, a preposition, a conjunction, or a relative pronoun. To help you distinguish between these nine different *parts of speech*, we will analyze a sentence written by McDougall (1914):

> The department of psychology that is of primary importance for the social sciences is that which deals with the springs of human action. (pp. 2–3)

6.1.1 Nouns

Nouns are names: person names, place names, object names, and concept names (e.g., "freedom"). Here is McDougall's sentence with the nouns printed in bold italics:

> The ***department*** of ***psychology*** that is of primary ***importance*** for the social ***sciences*** is that which deals with the ***springs*** of human ***action***.

Nouns have a property called *number*, meaning they can be *singular* or *plural*. Singular nouns refer to just one of the named thing (e.g., "department"); plural nouns refer to two or more of the named thing (e.g., "departments"). Most plurals are formed simply by adding *s* to the end of a singular noun (e.g., "cats"). However, not all plurals are formed so simply. Many nouns having singulars ending in *x* (e.g., "appendix," "fox") have plurals ending in *es* ("appendixes," "foxes"). Nouns derived from Latin may have singulars ending in *um* or *us* (e.g., "datum," "stimulus") and plurals ending in *a* and *i* respectively ("data," "stimuli"). Nouns derived from Greek may have singulars ending with *on* or *is* (e.g., "criterion," "phenomenon," "analysis," "hypothesis") and plurals ending with *a* and *es* respectively ("criteria," "phenomena," "analyses," "hypotheses"). Thus, some words ending with *s* are singular (e.g., "stimulus," "syllabus"), and some words ending in a vowel are plural (e.g., "stimuli," "syllabi," "criteria," "data," "phenomena"). To use the correct plural form of irregular nouns, you must memorize the plural form. Start by memorizing the six most misused plurals listed in Table 6.1. Then, when proofing your paper, consult Appendix B to check for other tricky plurals.

Be alert not only to nouns that have unusual plural forms but also to nouns that are singular even though they refer to more than one person. For example, "everybody," "everyone," and "anyone" are all singular. Similarly, *collective nouns*, nouns that stand for groups (e.g., "team," "university," "family"), are treated as singular—if you are treating the group as a single unit. Thus, you should write, "The family was interviewed together."

Sometimes, students have trouble deciding whether a fraction (e.g., one in three) or a percentage (e.g., 33%) is singular or plural. If you are referring to one unit, as in the case of "one in three" (the unit being a third) or 1% (the unit being a percent), use the singular. If, on the other hand, you are referring to more than one unit, as in the case of "33%" or "two in three," use the plural.

Sometimes, students have trouble deciding what to do when a singular noun shares a verb with another noun. However, you will not have that problem if you follow two rules. First, when "and" joins two singular nouns, treat the nouns as plural (e.g., "Smith

Table 6.1
Six Tricky Plurals

Singular	Plural	Examples
criterion	criteria	One criterion of good writing is correct use of plural words. There are several other criteria, including correct punctuation and grammar.
phenomenon	phenomena	One learning phenomenon is spontaneous recovery. There are three other important learning phenomena.
datum	data	A datum for each individual was the time taken for his or her first correct response. These data were analyzed using *t* tests.
medium	media ("Mediums" refers to psychics.)	The most influential medium is television. Other media such as magazines, newspapers, and radio cannot combine moving images and sound.
stimulus	stimuli	Each stimulus was displayed in a circular field. The six stimuli were presented in a random order.
hypothesis	hypotheses	Hypothesis 1 was supported, but the other hypotheses were not.

and Brown provide a useful definition"). Second, when "or" or "nor" joins two nouns, use the form required by the noun closer to the verb (e.g., "Either they or *I am* correct," "Neither I nor *they* are correct").

The final problem students have with nouns is with capitalizing *proper nouns:* names of particular people, events, organizations, languages, buildings, countries, and groups traditionally recognized for sharing a national, racial, ethic, or religious heritage. Remember to capitalize all proper nouns (e.g., "Jones," "Pennsylvania," "Asian Americans").

6.1.2 Personal and Impersonal Pronouns

Pronouns are words that substitute for nouns. *Personal pronouns* stand for people (e.g., "her," "him"). *Impersonal pronouns* stand for things (e.g., "it," "this," "that," "these," "those," "either," "neither"). Here is McDougall's sentence with its impersonal pronoun printed in bold italics:

> The department of psychology that is of primary importance for the social sciences is ***that*** which deals with the springs of human action.

The boldfaced and italicized "that" stands for "the department of psychology."

Personal pronouns have three *persons: first person* (referring to the person[s] speaking [e.g., "I," "me"]), *second person* (referring to the person[s] being spoken to [e.g., "you"]), and *third person* (referring to the person[s] being spoken about [e.g., "she," "he," "him," or "her"]).

In your papers, the focus is on the ideas—not on you. Consequently, you should limit your use of first person pronouns such as "I." In formal papers, you are not to speak directly to the reader, so you should not use "you" or any other second person pronouns. Consequently, although personal pronouns have three persons, most of the personal pronouns you use in your paper will be third person pronouns. Third person pronouns—as well as first and second person pronouns—have three *cases: subjective, objective*, and *possessive.*

Subjective means the pronoun is the *subject* (the focus) of the sentence (e.g., "*I* calculated"). Subjective pronouns, also known as *nominative* pronouns, usually come before the verb. Common nominative pronouns are "I," "we," "they," "she," and "he." "Who" is also a nominative pronoun: If you can replace the "who" in your sentence with "he" or some other nominative pronoun, you have correctly chosen between "who" and "whom."

Objective means the pronoun is the *object* acted upon in the sentence (e.g., "The idea [subject] surprised [verb] *me* [object]"). The pronoun following the verb is almost always an objective pronoun.[1] "Me," "us," "them," "her," and "him" are objective pronouns. "Whom" is also an objective pronoun: If you can replace the "whom" in your sentence with "him," or some other objective pronoun, you have correctly chosen between "who" and "whom."

Possessive means the pronoun owns (possesses) something (e.g., "*Our* argument is"). Note that whereas the possessive form of a noun has an apostrophe (e.g., Mark's), possessive pronouns, even "its," "whose," "ours," "hers," "his," and "theirs," do not have apostrophes.[2]

Like nouns, pronouns have number. Table 6.2 shows all the possible combinations of person, case, and number for most of the personal pronouns. In formal writing, pronouns must agree in number and gender with the nouns they represent:

✗ The technique is best for disciplining the *child* because *they* learn the consequences of their actions [unclear because *child* is singular, but *they* and *their* are plural].

✓ The technique is best for disciplining *children* because *they* learn the consequences of *their* actions [clearer because the noun and its pronouns are both plural].

Reading your paper aloud will not be enough to make sure that your nouns agree with your pronouns. Instead, you will have to take at least two additional steps. First, use your word processor's grammar checker to find some of the disagreements. Second, use your word processor's "find" command to search for "their" and check to make sure that each "their" refers to a plural noun.

When you use the indefinite pronouns "neither" and "either," keep three things in mind. First, realize that both "neither" and "either" are singular (e.g., "Either is a problem"). Second, realize that "neither" and "either" can be used only when you are referring to two things. If you have three items, use "or" instead of "either" (e.g., "the answer could be A, B, or C") and use "not . . . or" instead of "neither" (e.g., "the

---

[1]The pronoun following a verb will be an objective pronoun except when the verb is "was," "is," "are," "were," or some other form of the verb "to be." In such cases, you would use a subjective pronoun rather than an objective pronoun. Thus, you would write, "It was she" rather than "It was her."

[2]Just as you would never use an apostrophe with "his" (the possessive form of "he"), you should never use an apostrophe with hers—or any other possessive pronoun.

Table 6.2
Subjective, Objective, and Possessive Cases of Personal Pronouns by Person and Number

Person	Subjective (Nominative)	Objective	Possessive
Singular			
First	I	me	my, mine
Second	you	you	your, yours
Third	he, she	him, her	his, her, hers
	who	whom	whose
Plural			
First	we	us	our, ours
Second	you	you	your, yours
Third	they	them	their, theirs
	who	whom	whose

answer could not be A, B, or C"). Third, appreciate the intimate relationship between "neither" and "nor." Specifically, you can use the conjunction "nor" in only two situations: (a) after "neither" or (b) to continue negation started in one clause into the next clause.

- ✗ There were *neither* colloquialisms, contractions, foreign words, *nor* proper nouns in the list [wrong because *neither* was used to cover more than two things].
- ✓ There were no colloquialisms, contractions, foreign words, or proper nouns in the list.
- ✗ Neither Smith (1967) or [wrong because *nor* must be used after *neither*] Jones (1973) explained the phenomenon.
- ✓ Neither Smith (1967) nor Jones (1973) explained the phenomenon.
- ✗ Theory Y does not explain paranoia *nor* [*nor* is wrong because it neither follows *neither* nor continues negation started in a previous clause] catatonia, or [*or* is wrong because *or* suggests that the theory does deal with mania] deal with mania.
- ✓ Theory Y does not explain paranoia or catatonia, nor deal with mania [*nor* continues the negation started in the first clause into the last clause].

6.1.3 Verbs

Verbs are words that represent actions; they are the "doers" of the sentence. Here is McDougall's sentence with the verbs italicized (the main verb has been printed in bold italics):

> The department of psychology that ***is*** of primary importance for the social sciences ***is*** that which ***deals*** with the springs of human action.

Verbs have a property called *tense.* Tense refers to when the action of a verb happened. *Future* tense means the action is going to happen. To form the future tense, put the word "will" before the verb (e.g., "will analyze"). *Present* tense means the action is happening now. *Past* tense means the action happened some time ago. To form the past tense of regular verbs, put "-ed" on the end of the verb (e.g., "analyzed"). *Present perfect tense* means that the event happened in the past at some unknown time and is continuing to occur. To form the present perfect tense, put "have" before the past tense form of your verb (e.g., "have analyzed"). (To learn more about using the right tense, see 2.10.)

In addition to tenses, verbs also have moods. One mood is the *subjunctive* mood, used to describe something that did not happen, will not happen, or is very unlikely to happen (APA, 2010). If you use the subjunctive mood in a sentence, you will use the verb "were," and you will probably begin your sentence with the word "if" (e.g., "If the nonsense syllable experiment were to cause a participant distress,").

Unless a verb is in the subjunctive mood, it must be singular if its subject is singular and must plural if its subject is plural. If you are using a regular verb in the present tense, finding the verb form that *agrees* with the subject will usually be easy because *regular* verbs have only two forms for the present tense. One form, with an "s" at the end (e.g., "agrees"), covers the third person singular ("he agrees," "she agrees"). The other form, without an "s" at the end, covers the other cases ("I agree," "you agree," "we agree," "they agree"). Meeting the requirement of subject-verb agreement is more difficult with *irregular* verbs, that is, verbs having more than two forms (e.g., the verb "to be" has "I am," "you/we/they are," and "he/she is").

Verbs also have a property called *voice.* There are two voices: *active* and *passive.* In the active voice, the subject acts on the object (e.g., "Smith [subject] discovered [active verb] the phenomenon [object]."). In the passive voice, the subject is acted on by the object (e.g., "The phenomenon [subject] was discovered [passive verb] by Smith [object]."). The active voice is more direct and less wordy. Usually, you should use the active rather than the passive voice. (For more about voice, see 1.3.2.)

Two "almost-verbs" that writers sometimes mistake for verbs are the *infinitive* and the *present participle.* An infinitive always has the word "to" in front of it (e.g., "to be," "to deal"). A present participle is usually produced by adding "-ing" on the end of the verb's infinitive form (e.g., "being," "dealing"). Neither infinitives nor present participles can function as verbs. Consequently, as you can see from the following examples, trying to use these almost-verbs as verbs will cause you to write incomplete sentences.

✗ To be immoral. [not a sentence] What does it mean? . . . This theory dealing with motivation. [not a sentence]

✓ Defining immoral behavior is difficult . . . This theory deals with motivation.

6.1.4 Articles

Articles come before nouns. There are only three: one *definite* article, "the," and two *indefinite* articles, "a" and "an."

- Use definite articles to (a) refer to a noun you mentioned earlier (e.g., "*The* concept I mentioned earlier") or (b) to indicate that you are referring to one particular noun (e.g., "*The* most important concept for my argument"—there can be only one concept that is most important).
- Use an indefinite article to indicate that you are not referring to one specific, unique individual entity but instead are referring to one among many possible nouns (e.g., "I saw a dog"). Thus, if you write, "An important concept for my argument," you are implying that there are other important concepts relating to your argument.
- "An" is usually used for the indefinite article if the word that follows it begins with a vowel sound (e.g., "an apple"); otherwise, "a" is used (e.g., "a bed"). However, there are exceptions to this ("use 'an' before words starting with vowels and 'a' before words starting with consonants") rule. For example, "a" is sometimes used before words beginning with "u" (e.g., "a university"), and "an" is sometimes used before words beginning with "h" (e.g., "an historical event"). You can detect most of the exceptions by reading your sentence aloud: If you have incorrectly applied the rule to an exception (e.g., "an unicorn"), your sentence will probably sound incorrect.

6.1.5 Adjectives

Adjectives are words that describe nouns and pronouns. Here is McDougall's sentence with the adjectives printed in bold italics:

> The department of psychology that is of ***primary*** importance for the ***social*** sciences is that which deals with the springs of ***human*** action.

There are two serious—and avoidable—problems that students have with adjectives. First, students often use too many adjectives because they think that using adjectives will make their writing more powerful. They are wrong. Powerful writing comes from using nouns and verbs that help readers see what the writer is thinking or what someone is doing (e.g., "I came; I saw; I conquered.").

Second, students sometimes use adjectives to label people in ways that are offensive. For example, students may use adjectives such as "elderly" or "retarded" in such a way that the individuals being referred to are not seen as individuals, but rather as members of a group possessing only that one characteristic. In the most extreme cases of focusing on one characteristic to the exclusion of every other characteristic, some students err by using an adjective as a noun (e.g., "the elderly," "the depressed"). Do not make that mistake (for more about using inclusive language, see 1.3.4).

6.1.6 Adverbs

Adverbs are words that modify verbs or adjectives. Adverbs are usually formed from an adjective with "-ly" tacked on the end (e.g., "correctly," "effectively," "largely"). We have changed the first part of McDougall's sentence to include an adverb (the word "primarily"):

> The department of psychology that ***primarily*** deals with the springs of human action . . .

Take care when placing the adverb "only" in a sentence. Usually, that adverb should come after its verb and right before the word you want to modify:

✗ The participant only pressed one button [The participant did nothing else except press one button: The participant did not look at the stimuli, think, or breathe].

✓ The participant pressed only one button.

Be cautious when using adverbs to modify verbs. Sometimes, you can omit the adverb without losing anything (e.g., "analyze" is no less descriptive than "closely analyze"). Sometimes, rather than looking for an adverb to modify the verb, you should look for a better verb (e.g., instead of adding "closely" to "look at," replace "look at" with "inspect," "examine," or "analyze"). If you must use a word to modify a verb, use the "-ly" adverb form of that word rather than the adjective form (e.g., use "closely" rather than "close"), and place the adverb near its verb.

Sometimes, rather than use an adverb to modify a verb, you might use an adverb as a transition word. For example, you might use words such as "consequently," "similarly," or "conversely" at the beginning of a sentence to point out the relationship between that sentence and the previous sentence. Even as transition words, however, adverbs can get you in trouble because you may try to make the adverb to do a verb's job. Thus, the editors of the *Publication Manual* discourage the use of either "importantly" or "interestingly" because writers often use these words to mean "I find it important that" or "I find it interesting that." Similarly, the editors also point out that it is wrong to use "hopefully" (which means to do something, such as smile or pray, in a hopeful way) to mean "it is hoped." (Note that if one could use "hopefully" to mean "I hope so," one would also be able to use "hopelessly" to mean "I hope not.") Most students would be better off if they never used the word "hopefully."[3]

6.1.7 Prepositions

Prepositions are words, such as "among," "between," "beyond," "during," and "with," that can describe where something is, when something occurred, or how one or more nouns or pronouns are related to other words. Some prepositions could be used to describe a cat's location relative to a box (e.g., "in," "on," "near," "behind," "under," "above," "into," and "off"). Many prepositions are short (e.g., "at," "by," "of," "for," and "to"). Here is McDougall's original sentence with the prepositions printed in bold italics:

> The department ***of*** psychology that is ***of*** primary importance ***for*** the social sciences is that which deals ***with*** the springs ***of*** human action.

---

[3]To see how to have Microsoft® Word automatically eliminate that word from your paper, visit our website.

Whenever you put a personal pronoun after a preposition, make sure that pronoun is not a subjective pronoun such as "I," "she," "he," "we," "they," or "who." Instead, make sure that pronoun is an objective pronoun such as "me," "her," "him," "us," "them," or "whom" (e.g., "to *him*," "between *her* and *me*," "give it to *them*").

Whenever you see the preposition "of" in a sentence, see if you can shorten and strengthen that sentence by using one of the following two strategies. First, if you have a possessive prepositional phrase (e.g., "results *of the study*," "origin *of the effect*"), you can eliminate the "of the" part of the phrase by adding *apostrophe "s"* (*'s*) to the phrase's key noun (i.e., "study's results," "effect's origin"). Second, if you have a phrase, such as "presentation of," in which "of" follows a noun ending in "tion," you may be able to eliminate the "of" by replacing the noun that ends in "tion" with a verb (e.g., changing "the apparatus for the *presentation of* stimuli" to "*the apparatus presented the stimuli*").

See if you can shorten prepositional phrases that (a) begin with the preposition "with" and (b) describe a noun. Often, you will want to replace such phrases with an adjective. Using an adjective is more concise and more powerful than using a prepositional phrase. Thus, writing "the *bloody* knife" puts more emphasis on your description of the knife than writing "the knife *with blood on it*"—a prepositional phrase that emphasizes the noun "knife" but makes your description of the knife (its bloodiness) seem like an afterthought. Sometimes, however, you may wish to emphasize the noun rather than the words modifying the noun. For example, use prepositional phrases when describing people who have disabilities (e.g., "a person with a disability" rather than "a disabled person") so that the focus is on the person rather than on a label (APA, 2010).

Realize that you may mistakenly use the preposition "between" when you should use the preposition "among"—and vice versa. Always use "between" to distinguish two things; usually use "among" to distinguish more than two (e.g., "Our choice is between Theory X and Theory Y"; "Our choice is among Theory X, Theory Y, and Theory Z"). If, however, you are talking about differences, use "between" (e.g., " The differences between Theory X, Theory Y, and Theory Z are subtle.").

6.1.8 Conjunctions

Conjunctions are words that connect other words, phrases, or clauses. The conjunctions you are most familiar with are coordinating conjunctions such as "and," "but," and "or." However, there are many other conjunctions. To illustrate some of the different types of conjunctions, suppose you had two short sentences that you wanted to connect (e.g., "They talked. I walked."). You could connect the sentences using a comma and a coordinating conjunction such as "and" (e.g., "They talked, and I walked."). However, you could also connect the sentences by using either a conjunctive adverb or a subordinating conjunction.

If you use a conjunctive adverb such as "however," "nevertheless," or "moreover" to connect the two sentences, you have two choices. First, you could add the conjunctive adverb to the second sentence (e.g., "They ran. However, I walked."). Second, you could combine the two sentences into one (e.g., "They ran; however, I walked."). Note that in both cases, the comma comes *after* the conjunctive adverb.

If you use a subordinating conjunction such as "although," "if," "while," or "when" to connect the two sentences, you must combine the two sentences into one (e.g., "When they talked, I walked.") because you no longer have two independent sentences. If you put a subordinating conjunction in front of a simple sentence (e.g., "Although they ran"), you no longer have a complete sentence. Instead, you have a sentence fragment. Thus, if you begin a sentence with a subordinating conjunction (e.g., "although," "after," "before," "even," "if," "unless," "when"), use a comma to connect the first part of your sentence to an independent clause (e.g., "Although they ran, I walked").

If you use the subordinate conjunctions "while" or "since," use them only when referring to time (e.g., "While the experimenter waited, the participant continued with the task"; "Since Freud's seminal works, the idea of the unconscious has gained greater acceptance"). If you are not referring to when events occurred, replace "while" with "although," "despite," or "whereas" and replace "since" with "because" (e.g., "Despite keeping the experimenter waiting, the participant continued with the task"; "The idea of the unconscious has gained greater acceptance because of Freud's seminal works").

6.1.9 Relative Pronouns

Relative pronouns such as "that," "which," "who," "whom," and "whose" introduce text that describes a noun. For example, consider the following sentence: "The man *who* is my professor is standing at the door." In that sentence, "who" is a relative pronoun because "who" introduces the words "is my professor" that describe the noun "man." Here is McDougall's original sentence with the relative pronouns printed in bold italics:

> The department of psychology ***that*** is of primary importance for the social sciences is that ***which*** deals with the springs of human action.

In the next section, we address the three most common questions students have about relative pronouns.

1. "*Should I use 'who' or 'that'?* " Although "that" can be used to refer to humans, skilled writers use "who," "whom," and "whose" to refer to humans (e.g., "It was Piaget *who* first showed . . ."; "Freud is the one to *whom* Jung was referring . . ."; "Watson, *whose* ideas shaped the attitudes of a generation of mothers, asserted . . ."). Reserve "that" for referring to animals and objects (e.g., "The animals *that* were in the experimental group . . ."; "The realization *that* changed our approach . . .").
2. "*Should I use 'who' or 'whom'?* " The key is to realize that "who"—like "he," "she," and "we"—is a nominative pronoun, whereas "whom,"—like "him," "her," and "us"—is an objective pronoun (see Table 6.2). Therefore, if you can use "he" and "him" correctly, you can use "who" and "whom" correctly: If you replace "who" with "he" (e.g., "he first showed") and your sentence sounds right, use "who"; if the sentence sounds better using him ("to him"), use "whom."
3. "*Should I use 'which' or 'that'?* " Usually, you should use "that" rather than "which." Use "which" instead of "that" in only two situations. First, use "which" when you are introducing a parenthetical (nonessential, nonrestrictive) clause, that is, a clause that could be left out of the sentence without changing the

sentence's meaning. You can spot such nonrestrictive clauses because they are set off from the rest of the sentence by commas (e.g., "This idea, *which* has been promoted on several previous occasions, is again becoming popular."). Second, use "which" if you would otherwise have to write "that that" (e.g., in our example passage, McDougall wrote, "department . . . is that which" rather than writing, "department . . . is that that").

6.1.10 Phrases

After the individual word, the next major unit in writing is the phrase. A *phrase* contains two or more words that are next to each other and function as a single unit. Because phrases function as a single unit, they can sometimes be replaced by a single word. For example, the phrase "due to the fact that" could be replaced with "because" and the phrase "very happy" could be replaced with "ecstatic." Here is McDougall's sentence with the phrases labeled:

> The department [noun phrase] of psychology [prepositional adjectival phrase] that is [verb phrase] of primary importance [prepositional noun phrase] for the social sciences [prepositional noun phrase] is that [verb phrase] which deals [verb phrase] with the springs [prepositional noun phrase] of human action [prepositional adjectival phrase].

6.1.11 Clauses

After the phrase, the next major unit in writing is the clause. A *clause* contains a subject and a verb. An *independent* clause contains a complete thought and so could stand as a sentence. Note that the first part of the last sentence, "An independent clause contains a complete thought," is an independent clause. A *dependent clause*, although it also has a subject and a verb, does not contain a complete thought, and therefore could not stand as a sentence:

> The department of psychology (*that is of primary importance for the social sciences*) [dependent clause 1] is that (*which deals with the springs of human action*) [dependent clause 2].

6.1.12 Sentences

The next major unit in writing is the sentence. A *sentence* contains a subject and a verb; expresses a complete thought; begins with a capital letter; and ends with a period, a question mark, or an exclamation point. The average sentence should contain about 17 words.

In informal writing, the shortest sentences may contain only a single word: a verb. In such sentences, the subject is implicit (e.g., [You] "Eat."). In formal writing, the subject of a sentence should be explicit (e.g., "*You* should eat."). Furthermore, in formal writing, if the sentence also contains an object (a recipient of the verb's action), the object should be explicit (e.g., "You should eat *all the prunes.*").

When editing your sentences, try to make sure that you have not committed either of the two most serious errors in sentence construction: (a) writing a sentence that is incomplete (a "fragment") or (b) writing a sentence that is too long. The first error, writing an incomplete sentence, rather than a complete sentence, usually occurs when a student does the following:

- leaves out a verb;
- employs an "almost-verb" (e.g., "to deal" or "dealing") rather than a verb (e.g., "deals"); and
- turns what would have been an independent sentence (e.g., "I walked.") into a subordinate clause by putting a subordinating conjunction (see 6.1.8) such as "although" or "while" in front of it (e.g., "Although I walked.").

The second error, writing a sentence that is too long, leads to sentences that exceed not only the reader's patience but also the reader's short-term memory capacity. Often, such long sentences also lead the writer to make at least one of the following three errors.

First, because there are more nouns, more pronouns, and more verbs, the writer has a greater chance of losing track of whether a particular noun, verb, or pronoun is singular or plural. As a result, the writer is more likely to make (a) more subject-verb agreement errors (e.g., "data . . . is") and (b) more pronoun-noun agreement errors (e.g., "data . . . it").

Second, because there are more words in the sentence, the writer has a greater chance of putting a pronoun too far from its noun and a modifier too far from what it should modify. If your teacher does not know to which noun the pronoun refers, your teacher may circle the pronoun and write "vague referent"; if your teacher does not know what a modifier is supposed to be modifying, your teacher may circle the modifier and write "misplaced modifier."

Third, because there are more clauses, there is greater potential for making errors in joining clauses. For example, the writer may leave out a comma needed to link a dependent clause to an independent clause. Alternatively, the writer may make the mistake of creating a *run-on sentence* (see 6.3.4) by (a) trying to join two related independent clauses with only a comma or (b) trying to join two unrelated independent clauses with only a comma and a conjunction (e.g., "The theory has won wide acceptance, and I will consider methodological errors").

6.1.13 Paragraphs

After the sentence, the next major unit in writing is the paragraph. A *paragraph* expresses one major idea. It must consist of at least two sentences. Although some of your paragraphs may consist of only two sentences, most should be longer: Your average paragraph should consist of about 100 words. If a few of your paragraphs are well under 100 words, do not be concerned. If, on the other hand, any of your paragraphs are well over 100 words (130 words or more), be concerned.[4] Put another way, your paragraphs should usually be shorter than half of a page and should never be longer than one double-spaced page. (To learn more about writing paragraphs, see 6.4.2.)

6.2 Punctuation

6.2.1 End Marks (Periods, Question Marks, Exclamation Points)

In formal writing, you will almost never ask questions, and you will never make exclamations. Therefore, you will almost never use a question mark to end a sentence, and you will never use an exclamation point to end a sentence. Instead, you will probably end each sentence with a period. When you use a period to end a sentence, that period will be the last character of that sentence, except in two cases:

- if the last word of the sentence is in quotation marks, in which case the quotation mark ends the sentence; or
- if the entire sentence is in parentheses, in which case the right parenthesis ends the sentence.

6.2.2 Commas

Use a comma in the following situations:

- after transition words such as "however," "consequently," and "furthermore";
- after transition phrases such as "on the other hand," "for example," "consistent with this explanation";
- to separate items in lists of three or more, including authors' names (e.g., Jones, Smith, and Taylor);
- to set off parenthetical phrases (e.g., "This idea, which Freud originated, has had enormous influence");
- to connect a dependent clause that starts a sentence (such clauses often start with "although," "as," "after," "if," or "when") to the independent clause that follows it (e.g., "Although rewriting is hard work, it should be done."); and
- before conjunctions such as "and," "but," "for," "nor," "or," "so," and "yet" (e.g., "The participant made a response, and the computer recorded that response.")—when those conjunctions connect two independent clauses.

However, do not use a comma before a conjunction such as "and," "but," or "or" when the conjunction (a) connects the second element to the first element of a two-item list (e.g., "Jones and Smith") or (b) connects a second verb to the subject of the sentence (e.g., "The first researcher greeted the participants and handed out the test booklets").

[4]The word count feature of your word processor can tell you how many words are in a paragraph.

6.2.3 Semicolons

Use semicolons in three situations. First, use a semicolon to separate two or more lists of words. In such cases, the semicolon lets readers know when one list stops and another begins.

> Here is an example list of related terms: conditioned response, unconditioned response, conditioned stimulus, and unconditioned stimulus; milligram, gram, and kilogram; and intelligence quotient, chronological age, and mental age.

Second, use a semicolon to connect closely related, independent clauses without using a coordinating conjunction such as "and." For example, you should write

> Theory A is popular; theory B is not popular.

Note that if you make the mistake of using a comma instead of a semicolon to connect two independent clauses, you will make a run-on sentence (see 6.3.4).

Third, use a semicolon to connect highly related independent clauses with linking words such as "consequently," "furthermore," "however," "moreover," "therefore," "nevertheless," "indeed," and "thus" (e.g., "I think; therefore, I am."). Note that you must put a semicolon *before* the linking word and a comma *after* the linking word (e.g., "; therefore,"). One way to check whether you have put the semicolon in the right place is to replace the semicolon with a period: If you now have two sentences that make sense (and the second sentence starts with the linking word), you have put the semicolon in the right place.

6.2.4 Colons

Use a colon either to introduce a list of items (e.g., "There were four conditions: control, auditory, visual, and olfactory") or to emphasize the final element of a sentence (e.g., "Skinner devoted his life to one concept: operant conditioning"). In either case, you can use a colon only if the clause coming before the colon is an independent clause. That is, if you replace the colon with a period, that period should mark the end of a complete sentence. If the words in front of the period would not make a sentence, you should not use a colon. Thus, you should never write, "Three reasons are:" or "This experiment will:"—indeed, you should almost never put a colon right after a verb.

6.2.5 Apostrophes

In informal writing, an apostrophe may signal that some letters have been omitted from a word to form a *contraction* (e.g., "wasn't" is a contraction of "was" and "not," "o" being the omitted letter). In formal writing, however, you cannot use contractions. In formal writing, you can use apostrophes for only one purpose: to signify a possessive (e.g., "the experiment's design").

To form the possessive of a singular noun, add *apostrophe* "*s*" (e.g., "the theory*'s* assumptions," "the stimulus's duration," "Jones's paper"). To form the possessive of a plural noun ending in s, add only an apostrophe (e.g., "these theories' assumptions," "The Joneses' [i.e., Fred and Myrtle's] contribution"). To form the possessive of a plural noun ending in anything other than *s*, add *apostrophe* "*s*" (e.g., "children's toys," "the stimuli's origin").

Note that apostrophes are not a part of any of the possessive pronouns: *my*, *mine*, *his*, *her*, *hers*, *yours*, *ours*, *theirs*, *whose*, and *its*. In other words, "it's" is not the possessive form of "it" but rather the contraction for "it is." Because you should not use contractions in formal papers, you should never write "it's" in a formal paper.

In conclusion, the big problem students have with apostrophes is that students use them too much. Use apostrophes only to indicate possession—and even then, do not use apostrophes with pronouns. Do not use apostrophes to indicate plurals—even with dates (e.g., write "1950s," not "1950's"). Do not use contractions (e.g., "don't") in your papers—and especially do not use the contractions "it's," "they're," "who's," and "ain't."

6.2.6 Parentheses

Use parentheses to enclose parenthetical material unnecessary for the meaning of the sentence. Parentheses signal to the reader that the enclosed material could be ignored. Each time you use parentheses, ask yourself if the material is vital to the meaning of the sentence. If the material is vital, build it into the sentence. If it is not vital, consider omitting it because parenthetical asides may distract the reader from your main point. In short, except for citations, you should probably avoid using parentheses.

6.2.7 Dashes

Use *em dashes*—like these—to enclose parenthetical material or short definitions (Silvia, 2007). You can make em dashes—given that name because they are the width of a capital letter "M"—with your word processor.[5] As is the case for material set off by parentheses, material set off by an em dash is often material that should be edited or deleted.

6.2.8 Hyphens

Use hyphens only in words that could otherwise be misinterpreted (e.g., "I re-sent your letter" could be interpreted differently from "I resent your letter"). Thus, you may have to use hyphens in some compound words (e.g., if you are describing a man, "woman chasing man" might be misinterpreted but "woman-chasing man" would not be). You are especially likely to need hyphens with compound words in which the first word is a number (e.g., "The 3-year-olds" has a different meaning from "The 3 year-olds" and "the 10-item lists" has a different meaning from "the 10 item lists").

Do not use hyphens for common phrases (e.g., day care center) except for phrases that start with "self" (e.g., "self-esteem," "self-report"). Do not use hyphens at the end of a line (turn off your word processor's hyphenation feature).

[5]If you type two hyphens, your word processor may automatically create an em dash for you. If not, choose "Symbol . . ." under the "Insert" menu, then choose "Special Characters," and then choose "Em Dash." Alternatively, if you have a Windows® machine, hold down the following three keys at the same time: the "Alt" key, the "Ctrl" key, and the minus sign key that is on the number pad; if you have a Macintosh®, hold down the following three keys at the same time: the "Shift" key, the option key, and the hyphen key.

6.2.9 Quotation Marks

When to use quotation marks. There are only two reasons to surround words with quotation marks: a good one and a bad one. The good reason is to signal the reader that those words are a brief quotation (see 4.8.1). The bad reason is to signal the reader that you are using the selected word or words in a different way from how the word or words are normally used.

> Participants waited in an anteroom with two other "participants" [appropriate only if you had previously explained that these two people were actually confederates of the experimenter].

Keep the latter usage to a minimum. For example, you should not write anything like the following:

(✗) The computer "knew" which alternative the participant had chosen.

If you had written the previous sentence, you would be saying to the reader, "I want you to understand the word 'knew' in a way other than you would normally understand it because I did not bother to find the right word. I hope you can figure out what I meant to say." Rather than telling readers to figure out your unconventional meanings of words, you should find the right words:

(✓) The computer recorded which alternative the participant had chosen.

How to use punctuation with quotation marks. Students often make mistakes punctuating material in quotation marks. Fortunately, you can avoid most of these mistakes by following one rule: Put commas and periods inside quotation marks but put colons and semicolons outside of quotation marks.

Usually, the only time you will have a question mark near quotation marks is when the person quoted is asking a question. In those cases, put the question mark inside the quotation marks (e.g., She said, "What is the rule?").

6.3 Usage

6.3.1 Know What You Mean

Make sure you know the meaning of all words you use. Be careful when using a thesaurus to find synonyms. Check the dictionary definition of any synonym to ensure that it does not have a different meaning from the one you intend.

Sometimes, students see a similarity between two words and end up using the wrong member of that pair. For example, students often use "effects" when they should use "affects"—and vice versa. To be sure that you are using the right member of these "problem pairs," consult Table 6.3. By consulting Table 6.3, you will avoid common errors such as writing "my analysis infers" (writers may imply, but readers infer) and "stress effects memory," and instead write, "my analysis implies" and "stress affects memory."

Also, be careful about words and phrases that sound identical. Don't use "their" when you mean "there," "to" when you mean "too," or "would of" when you mean "would have."

Table 6.3
Problem Pairs

Problem Pair	Part of Speech	Meaning	Example
affect	noun	emotion	The client had depressed *affect*.
affect	verb	influence	Learning the prior list *affected* recall of the test words.
affect	verb	pretend	The client *affected* a cheerful mood.
effect	noun	result	The *effect* of diffusion of responsibility was to delay helping.
effect	verb	bring about	The therapist *effected* a quick recovery in her client.
alternate	verb	change back and forth from one to another	The experimenter *alternated* the order in which the stimuli were presented.
alternative	noun	one of two or more possibilities	Choose the correct *alternative*.
alternative	adj	allowing a choice between two or more possibilities	They wanted an *alternative* candidate.
amount	noun	how much (refers to an uncountable quantity)	The dependent variable was *amount* of stress.
number	noun	how many (refers to a countable quantity)	The dependent variable was *number* of errors.
casual	adj	informal	We will be playing outside, so wear *casual* clothes.
causal	adj	relating to the causes of an effect	They found a *causal* relationship between smoking and cancer.
complement	verb	to go well with something else	Rather than competing with each other, the two theories may *complement* one another.
compliment	verb	praise	She was liked because she was skilled at *complimenting* others.
continually	adv	recurring often	The writer was *continually* interrupted by the telephone.
continuously	adv	without interruption	The intensity of the tone was reduced *continuously* until the participant could no longer hear the tone.
dependent variable	noun	a measure of the participant's behavior	The *dependent variable* was the participant's score on the measure.

(continued)

Table 6.3
Problem Pairs—continued

Problem Pair	Part of Speech	Meaning	Example
independent variable	noun	the factor that is manipulated in a study	The *independent variable* was the noise level.
disinterested	adj	impartial, fair, unbiased	Smith, coming from neither side of the controversy, is a *disinterested* judge.
uninterested	adj	without interest, unconcerned	The participant, having just eaten, was *uninterested* in eating more.
experiment	noun	a type of study, usually involving random assignment, that allows researchers to make cause-effect statements	In this *experiment*, participants were randomly assigned to one of three groups.
study	noun	any type of research, including nonexperimental studies, such as survey research	In this *study*, we asked participants about their views.
farther	adj	more distant	Observers judged the distance of the *farther* of the landmarks.
farther	adv	to a more distant point	Maze-bright rats progressed *farther* in the maze than maze-dull rats.
further	adj	additional	With *further* research, the phenomenon might be explained.
further	adv	more	Jones developed the theory *further.*
fewer	adj	fewer in terms of how many (refers to a countable quantity)	Participants made *fewer* errors.
less	adj	less in terms of how much (refers to an uncountable quality)	Participants seemed *less* anxious.
fortuitous	adj	occurring by chance	The meeting between the mail carrier and the sharp-toothed dog was *fortuitous.*
fortunate	adj	lucky	We are *fortunate* to be living in the information age.
gender	noun	masculine vs. feminine	*Gender* refers to the psychological characteristics associated with being a man (e.g., aggressive) or a woman (e.g., supportive) in a given culture.

Table 6.3
Problem Pairs—continued

Problem Pair	Part of Speech	Meaning	Example
sex	noun	boys and men vs. girls and women	*Sex* refers to the biological characteristics of being a man (i.e., having XY chromosomes) or a woman (i.e., having XX chromosomes).
imply	verb	suggest	The author *implied* that the previous research was not methodologically sound.
infer	verb	generalize from evidence	From my analysis of the literature, I *inferred* that much of the previous research was not methodologically sound.
insignificant	adj	unimportant	The effect, although statistically significant, was small and *insignificant.*
nonsignificant	adj	not statistically significant	The *nonsignificant* results may have been due to the study's lack of power.
literally	adv	exactly as written	The patient *literally* threw stones inside a glass house (use *literally* only when readers might otherwise think you were writing figuratively).
figuratively	adv	involving a figure of speech	The comedian *figuratively* died during his act (use *figuratively* only when readers might otherwise think you were not using a figure of speech, e.g., if they might otherwise think that the comedian actually died).
method	noun	procedure, technique	I used Donders's subtraction *method.*
methodology	noun	system, or study, of methods	In one class, we studied the *methodology* of single-case designs.
principal	adj	main, first	The *principal* effect of caffeine is stimulation.
principal	noun	director of a school	The *principal* of the school resigned.
principle	noun	law, tenet, rule	Psychologists should understand the *principles* of reinforcement.
reliable	adj	consistent, replicable	Participants' scores on the retest were similar to their original test scores, suggesting that the test is *reliable.*

(continued)

Table 6.3
Problem Pairs—continued

Problem Pair	Part of Speech	Meaning	Example
valid	adj	accurate	Participants' scores on the test predicted their behavior in a real life situation, suggesting that the test is *valid.*
significant	adj	unlikely to be due to chance	The effect, although small, was statistically *significant.*
substantial	adj	large	The difference between carrying 100 pounds and 200 pounds is *substantial.*
use	noun	purpose	One *use of* debriefing is to learn how participants viewed the study.
usage	noun	the manner of using	Word *usage* is discussed in this chapter.

Note. adj = adjective, adv = adverb.

6.3.2 Let the Reader Know What You Are Comparing

Relational words, (e.g., "different [from]," "similar [to]," "bigger [than]," "oldest [of]," "irrelevant [to]") compare or contrast two things. The main problem students have in using relational words is that, in trying to be brief, students may not make it clear which two things are being related. For example, a student wrote, "*The participants liked the experiment better than the experimenter.*" The student's sentence is ambiguous because the reader cannot know whether (a) participants liked the experiment more than they liked the experimenter or (b) participants liked the experiment more than the experimenter liked the experiment. Note that completing the comparison results in an unambiguous sentence: "The participants liked the experiment more than they liked the experimenter."

6.3.3 Use Comparatives and Superlatives Correctly

Comparatives. A *comparative* is an adjective or adverb used to compare two things. It is usually formed either by adding "-er" to an adjective (e.g., "strong" becomes "stronger") or by placing the word *more* before an adverb (e.g., "strongly" becomes "more strongly"), and then adding "than" (e.g., "The mean of group A is *larger than* the mean of group B"; "Participants in the X condition pressed the button *more* rapidly *than* participants in the Y condition").

Less versus fewer. If you can say how much of a quality (e.g., affection) there is but not how many there are, use "less" (e.g., "less affection"); if you can count how many there are, use "fewer" (e.g., "fewer items"). The word after "less" must always be singular; the word after "fewer" must always be plural.

✗ Theory A has more applications and less problems than Theory B. [Because there can be more than one problem, you should not use "less" with "problems."]

✓ Theory A has more applications and fewer problems than Theory B.

Different From, Not Different Than. Realize that "different" is not a comparative: It does not state that one thing has more of a quality than another thing. For example, whereas one thing can be "bigger than," "smaller than," louder than," or "quieter than" something else, it cannot be "different than" something else. Therefore, follow "different" with "from" (e.g.,"A is different *from* B.")

Superlatives. Use a *superlative*, rather than a comparative, when you are comparing more than two things. Usually, a superlative is formed by adding "est" to an adjective (e.g., "Of the three groups, participants in A scored the *fewest* hits") or by placing the word "most" before an adverb (e.g., "Of participants in all four conditions, those in B pressed the button *most* rapidly"). Do not use superlatives when you are comparing two things.

6.3.4 Divide or Reconnect Run-On Sentences

There are at least two types of *run-on sentences*. The first occurs when two independent clauses that are—or seem to be—unrelated are fused into one sentence (e.g., "There are problems with classical theories, and Smith proposed a new theory"). Defuse such sentences either by splitting them into two (e.g., "There are problems with classical theories. Smith proposes a new theory.") or by making the connection between them clearer (e.g., There are problems with classical theories, so Smith proposed a new one.").

The second type of run-on sentence, often called a *comma splice*, occurs when two (or more) independent clauses are joined by only a comma. You have three options for fixing comma spliced sentences: (a) replace the comma with a period, (b) replace the comma with a semicolon, or (c) add a conjunction (e.g., "and") after the comma.

✗ The choice among the classical theories is complicated, there are problems with all of them and Smith proposes a new theory that I will discuss.

✓ The choice among the classical theories is complicated; there are problems with all of them. Smith proposes a new theory that I will discuss.

6.3.5 Help Readers Get "It" (and Other Pronouns) by Specifying Nonspecific Referents

All sentences you write should be clear. These cause problems. We hope you recoiled in horror at the second sentence of this paragraph. You should be wondering what we mean by "These" (a *nonspecific referent*). One possibility is that "these" refers to "All sentences," the subject of the first sentence. However, we were referring to "nonspecific referents," the last part of the heading.

Take two steps to avoid problems with nonspecific referents. First, be sure that each of your sentences stands independently of the previous paragraph, heading, or title. Thus, if, as in our example of a problem sentence ("*These* cause problems."), you had a pronoun that referred to a noun in a heading, replace that pronoun with the heading's noun ("*Nonspecific referents* cause problems."). Second, any time you use a pronoun, ensure that the reader knows which noun that pronoun represents.

One way to see whether a pronoun ("a pointing word") could mislead or confuse a reader is to draw an arrow from the potentially ambiguous pointing word (e.g., "this," "that," "which," "they," "it," "those") back to the word or idea to which it refers. If the arrow passes other words that could also fit, you have a problem. Solutions to the problem include the following:

- replacing the ambiguous pronoun with the noun to which the pronoun referred (e.g., change "it is" to "cognitive dissonance theory is");
- distinguishing the targeted noun from other nearby nouns by making it the only plural (or only singular) noun near your plural (or singular) pronoun (e.g., change "There were several potential causes of these effects. They include" to "There were several potential causes of this effect. They include");
- using "who" to refer to humans rather than using "that" (e.g., change "the participants that were most influenced" to "the participants who were most influenced"); and
- adding a word or a descriptive phrase after words such as "this" so that the reader knows what "this" refers to (e.g., replace "this is" with "this psychoanalytic idea is").

6.3.6 Attribute Humanity Only to Humans

Only humans do such things as point out, argue, or suggest. Do not attribute human abilities to theories, concepts, data, or other nonhuman entities. To attribute human abilities to nonhuman entities is to commit the error of *anthropomorphism*. Next, we show you some examples of anthropomorphism, followed by solutions:

✗ Smith's (2009) theory suggests an alternative explanation.

✓ Smith (2009) suggested an alternative explanation.

✗ This concept prefers a different perspective.

✓ Holders of this concept prefer a different perspective.

✗ The data speak to my hypothesis.

✓ Figure 1 shows that the data are consistent with my hypothesis.

✗ The results emphasize the connection between temperature and aggression.

✓ The results indicate that there is a relationship between temperature and aggression.

6.4 Writing With Style

6.4.1 Accentuate the Positive

Your English teachers probably taught you not to use a double negative (e.g., "Do not not turn on the light") because a positively worded statement (e.g., "Turn on the light") is easier to understand. What your English teachers might not have taught you is that a positively worded statement is also easier to understand than a single negative, as you can see from studying the following pair of examples:

(✗) To create a good test, do not use negatively worded questions.

(✔) To create a good test, use positively worded questions.

6.4.2 Point the Way Within and Between Paragraphs

Every paragraph you write should contain a *topic sentence:* a sentence that expresses the paragraph's main idea. If your paragraph does not have a topic sentence, you may be able to generate one for it by either summarizing the paragraph or referring to your outline. If you cannot generate a topic sentence for a paragraph, that paragraph probably either (a) does not have any worthy ideas or (b) has too many worthy ideas. If it does not have any worthy ideas, delete it; if it has too many worthy ideas, break it into several paragraphs.

Usually, you will use the paragraph's topic sentence to tell the reader what point you are going to make in the paragraph [e.g., "Smith and Jones (2003) identified three problems with previous research"], and so you will make it the first sentence of the paragraph. After presenting this paragraph preview, you would spend the rest of the paragraph developing, defending, or explaining the topic sentence.

Occasionally, you will use the topic sentence to tell the reader what point you made in the paragraph (e.g., "Therefore, previous research is flawed in at least three ways" or "Consequently, I hypothesize that . . ."), and so you will make it the last sentence of the paragraph. In that case, you would start the paragraph with evidence supporting a position and hope that the reader will come to your conclusion before the reader actually reads the topic sentence stating your conclusion.

The paragraph's topic sentence, regardless of where it is, helps readers navigate within that paragraph. However, not only must you help the reader get through each paragraph, but you must also help the reader get to the next one. In short, you must ensure that each paragraph stands independently of others, yet flows logically and gracefully from the one before it and the one after it.

To ensure that each paragraph stands independently, check any of your paragraphs that begin with the words "This," "These," or "Those" (such pronouns are known as *nonspecific referents;* see 6.3.5). The problem with using nonspecific referents is that such words are meaningless on their own. As a result, using one of these words to start a paragraph makes that paragraph depend on the previous paragraph for its meaning. Therefore, do not use "this" or a similar word in your paragraph's first sentence as shorthand for a concept, idea, study, or criticism stated in a previous paragraph. Instead, restate the concept, idea, study, or criticism.

Starting a new paragraph by restating an idea from the previous paragraph not only helps the new paragraph stand independently, but it also helps readers see connections between adjoining paragraphs. To give the reader even more help, you may, occasionally, put connecting words or connecting phrases such as "In addition to," "Next," "Consequently," or "Although" in front of your restatement. However, be selective in your use of connecting words: If most of your paragraphs start with connecting words, it will hurt the flow of your paper.

Often, the smoothest way to ensure that paragraphs flow is to use the concluding sentence of the previous paragraph to set up the next one. Concluding sentences that accomplish flow look like the following.

> Researchers could use three tactics to overcome these methodological problems. [The next paragraph would begin with a sentence about the first tactic.]

> These ranges must be limited, however, when adaptation phenomena are considered. [The next paragraph would begin with a description of an adaptation phenomenon.]

6.4.3 Use Parallel Construction

You can improve both the flow and the clarity of ideas within a paragraph by using *parallel construction:* expressing related ideas by repeating the same or similar words or patterns of words. As you can see from the following examples, having parallel structure within a sentence can make the sentence shorter, smoother, and clearer.

✗ The participant began each trial with a button press, using the keyboard to give a response, and the trial finished when the participant pressed another button.

✓ The participant used key presses to start a trial, to give a response, and to end a trial.

✗ The results showed no significant differences in the area of anxiety, or regarding depression; psychoses also did not differ.

✓ The results showed no significant differences in anxiety, depression, or psychosis.

Having two or more sentences share a parallel structure helps the reader see the relationships between the ideas expressed in those sentences (Silvia, 2007). For example, if you use parallel structure when describing two different experimental conditions, the reader can easily see how the two conditions are similar and how the two conditions differ (Silvia, 2007). Note that parallel structure works especially well when you link two related sentences with a semicolon (Silvia, 2007).

✗ The digit group read a set of 12 digits at 1 digit per s. In contrast, participants in the letter condition were exposed, at a rate of 1 letter every second, to a 12-item letter list.

✓ The digit group read a set of 12 digits at 1 digit per s; the letter group read a set of 12 letters at 1 digit per s.

6.4.4 Use a Consistent, Formal Tone

To keep a formal tone, avoid jokes, and do not let the clichés and colloquialisms you use in casual conversation sneak into your paper. In addition, use metaphors sparingly, and carry through any you do use.

(✗) When all is said and done [cliché 1], the moral of the story [cliché 2] is that the bottom line [cliché 3] of my study is that children trained with the X technique were literally [cliché 4] out of hand [colloquialism 1], so the results are up the creek [colloquialism 2] . . . When the results were analyzed with a finer-toothed [metaphor 1] statistical test, the hypothesis still lay bleeding on the ground [metaphor 2].

(✗) In conclusion, my study showed that children trained with the X technique misbehaved so badly there were no significant results . . . When the results were analyzed with a finer-toothed statistical test, the only new results combed out were statistical dandruff. [Although the author did not mix two different metaphors, the author used a metaphor that is too informal for scientific writing.]

(✓) In conclusion, the unruliness of children trained with the X technique obscured any significant results . . . When the results were analyzed with a higher-powered test, no new meaningful findings emerged.

6.4.5 Use Small Words and Short Sentences

Obsolescent prolixities are to be eschewed. Note that if you replaced the previous sentence's unfamiliar words with familiar ones and if you changed the previous sentence's voice from passive to active (for more information about voice, see 6.1.3), your new sentence would be the following useful tip: "Avoid words that might be unfamiliar to your reader."

In addition to using simple, short, familiar words, try to keep most of your sentences shorter than 20 words. A good test of a sentence's length is to read it aloud, taking a breath only when you find a period. If you are running out of breath and a period still has not come into sight, the sentence is too long. The solution is to break long sentences into a number of shorter sentences. On the other hand, avoid going to the opposite extreme of using only short sentences; using too many short sentences will make you repeat yourself unnecessarily, will make it hard for you to show the connections between your ideas, and will make your paper sound like a children's book.

6.4.6 Be Precise

Your writing will be more powerful if you replace vague adjectives and imprecise adverbs with numbers. Thus, instead of writing "*numerous* times," be precise by writing "17 times." Similarly, instead of writing phrases like "a *relatively large* number of participants" and "a *fairly big* effect," be precise by writing "25 participants" and "a 55% increase."

6.4.7 Be Concise

Another problem with using adjectives and adverbs is that such words are often unnecessary. Consequently, adjectives and adverbs can weaken your sentences by making your sentences wordy. Remember, shorter is often more powerful. Thus, rather than writing "a *disastrous* event," save words—and gain power—by writing "a disaster."

In addition to cutting adjectives and adverbs that dilute your prose, you should cut unnecessary paragraphs, sentences, phrases, and expressions.

- Eliminate paragraphs dealing with material not directly relevant to your paper.
- Replace pairs of sentences that restate one another (i.e., sentences beginning explicitly or implicitly with phrases such as "In other words" or "To put it another way") with the better of the two.
- Replace passive sentences (e.g., "The unconscious *was emphasized by* Freud") with active sentences (e.g., "Freud *emphasized* the unconscious").
- Replace nouns trying to do a verb's job (e.g., "We did *a modification of*") with verbs (e.g., "We *modified*").
- *Replace phrases (e.g.,* "The theory applied *in the context* [phrase 1] *of sensory processes* [phrase 2]") with single words (e.g., "The theory applied to *sensation*").
- Replace prepositional phrases referring to time (e.g., "at the present time") with single words (e.g., "now").
- Replace prepositional phrases for "about" (e.g., "in relation to") with "about."
- Replace wordy expressions (e.g., "despite the fact that") with single words (e.g., "although").
- Replace redundant pairs of words (e.g., "actual fact") with their essential elements (e.g., "fact"). To see examples of redundant pairs and other multiple word expressions that you should replace with single words, see Table 6.4.

6.4.8 Be Cautious

The good writer obeys all the writing rules—even those that most readers would not mind seeing violated. The good writer realizes that obeying all the rules will not offend anyone, whereas disobeying the rules may offend someone. To make reading an agreeable experience for all readers, the good writer tries to obey even those writing rules that most readers ignore, such as not ending sentences with prepositions and not splitting infinitives.

Do not end any sentence with a preposition. For example, do not write a sentence like the following: "This is an impertinence which I will not put up with." Winston Churchill is reputed to have objected to the rule of not ending sentences with prepositions by saying, "This is an impertinence up with which I will not put." Although Churchill's sentence sounds stilted, realize that his sentence can be rewritten in a way that honors the rule, yet sounds natural: "I will not put up with such impertinence."

Keep infinitives intact. Writers *split infinitives* when they put something, usually an adverb, between the *to* and the *verb* part of an infinitive. A famous phrase from the television series "Star Trek" is an example of a split infinitive (and sexist language): "to

Table 6.4
Wordy Expressions to Remove From Your Writing

Replace This	With This
Prepositional phrases about relationships	
in terms of	in, on, about
vis-à-vis	in, on, about
with respect to	in, on, about
in relation to	about
Prepositional phrases about time	
at the present time	now
at this point in time	now
in the process of	now
at that particular time	then
in the near future	soon
Other wordy expressions	
be of the opinion	believe
despite the fact that	although
in spite of the fact that	although
owing to the fact that	because
the reason is because	because
Double trouble: Redundant pairs	
actual fact	fact
close proximity	close
completely unanimous	unanimous
consensus of opinion	consensus
final conclusion	conclusion
future planning	planning
must necessarily	must
new innovation	innovation
reason why	reason
true fact	true
very unique	unique
Triple threats	
consensus of opinion	consensus
the fact that	that
whether or not	whether
in many cases	often

boldly go where no man has gone before." You could rewrite the phrase to rejoin the infinitive (and to remove the sexist language): "to go boldly into new frontiers."

6.5 Your Own Style

To resume the analogy we made at the start of this chapter, writers ignorant of grammar and punctuation are like drivers who, although they know the way to their destinations, fail to arrive because they drove on flat tires, ran out of gasoline, or crashed into poles. Writers ignorant of good usage are like drivers who reach their destinations, but only after running over curbs, grinding the gears, and losing their passengers. Writers ignorant of style are like drivers who reach their destinations, but who make some wrong turns and who circle some blocks many times. Skilled drivers have their own styles: Some drive slowly, admiring the view along the way; others drive fast, showing flair and verve. As you master the skills of driving your words, you can develop your own style. Remember, however, that the point is to arrive at your destination with your passengers still on board.

6.6 Checklists

6.6.1 Parts of Speech

- ☐ I put pronouns close to their respective nouns.
- ☐ I made sure that pronouns agreed with their nouns. That is, I do not have a plural pronoun (e.g., "they") referring to a singular noun (e.g., "child").
- ☐ I usually followed the pronoun "this" with a word or phrase that made it clear what the referent was for "this."
- ☐ When referring to humans, I used the pronoun "who" instead of the pronouns "that" or "which."
- ☐ The subjects of my sentences agree with the verbs of my sentences. That is, I do not have a plural noun (e.g., "data") with a singular verb (e.g., "is").
- ☐ I made sure I knew what the subject of the sentence was, even if that meant shortening or simplifying that sentence.
- ☐ I remembered that if I had two nouns as subjects and they were joined by the conjunction "and," I used the plural form of the verb. However, if the nouns were joined by the conjunction "or," the noun closest to the verb determined whether I used the singular or plural form of the verb.
- ☐ I checked Appendix B of this book to make sure that the subject of the sentence was in the form (singular or plural) that I intended—unless I was sure I knew what the singular and plural forms were (e.g., "dog," "dogs").

- ☐ If I referred to either (a) a specific event that occurred in the past or (b) a certain study (including the results of my own study), I used the past tense (e.g., "the study found").
- ☐ If I referred to something that started at some time in the past but continues to the present, I used the present perfect (e.g., "studies have found").
- ☐ I usually used the active voice instead of the passive voice.
- ☐ When possible, I eliminated adverbs.
- ☐ If I needed an adverb to modify a verb, I made sure that I used the proper "-ly" ending for adverbs rather than using the shorter, adjective form. For example, I wrote that participants "worked quickly" rather than "worked quick."
- ☐ If I used an adverb, I put it right after the verb it was modifying.

6.6.2 Punctuation

- ☐ I used commas at places where I would pause if I were reading my paper aloud—unless another punctuation mark was more appropriate.
- ☐ I used commas between a dependent clause (such clauses often start with "although," "as," "if," or "when") that starts a sentence and the independent clause that follows it (e.g., "When he fell, he did not cry").
- ☐ I used commas before a conjunction such as "and" that joined two independent clauses.
- ☐ I used commas between all lists of three or more items—unless the items contained commas.
- ☐ I used semicolons to separate list items when those list items contained commas.
- ☐ I used semicolons to join two independent clauses without a conjunction.
- ☐ I did not overuse apostrophes, quotation marks, parentheses, or hyphens.
- ☐ I do not have any contractions in my paper, and I have not used apostrophes with the pronoun "its" or with years (e.g., I wrote "1990s" rather than "1990's.").
- ☐ I used hyphens only when the meaning of a sentence would be unclear without them. For example, I did not use hyphens merely to make my right margins even.
- ☐ I used quotation marks sparingly. I used them only with quotations that were shorter than 40 words or with words that were being used in an unconventional way. Furthermore, I rarely used quotations and I rarely used words in an unconventional way.
- ☐ I put commas and periods inside quotation marks.

6.6.3 Style

- ☐ I outlined my paper.
- ☐ I made sure that all my paragraphs had topic sentences—and I made sure that those topic sentences referred to entries in my outline.
- ☐ I used subheadings.
- ☐ I built bridges between paragraphs by using transition words or repeating key phrases and ideas.
- ☐ I did not use one-sentence paragraphs.
- ☐ I did not use contractions.
- ☐ I did not use the word "you" to refer to the reader.
- ☐ I did not use exclamation points.

6.7 Summary

1. The main parts of speech are nouns, pronouns, verbs, articles, adjectives, adverbs, prepositions, conjunctions, and relative pronouns.
2. Use adjectives sparingly.
3. Use adverbs sparingly.
4. When you use a pronoun, make sure that the reader can easily tell to which noun it refers.
5. If a plural noun has a pronoun, its pronoun must also be plural; if a singular noun has a pronoun, its pronoun must also be singular.
6. If a subject is plural, its verb must also be plural; if a subject is singular, its verb must also be singular.
7. Most of your sentences should have fewer than 20 words, and most of your paragraphs should be less than half a page long.
8. Usually, a period will end your sentence. However, if the last word of your sentence is in quotation marks, the period will be inside the quotation marks.
9. Use apostrophes only to indicate possession (e.g., the participant's score). Do not use apostrophes for contractions (e.g., write "it is" rather than "it's," write "they are" rather than "they're") or to indicate the plural form (e.g., write "1950s" rather than "1950's").
10. An independent clause can stand alone as a sentence. An independent clause must have a verb and must contain a complete thought.

11. If you are using a coordinating conjunction such as "or," "and," or "but" to join two independent clauses, put a comma before the conjunction.
12. If you are combining two independent clauses without a coordinating conjunction, combine them with either a semicolon or a colon.
13. Do not use a colon unless the words in front of the colon could stand alone as a sentence.
14. Do not overuse parentheses, hyphens, quotation marks, question marks, and dashes.
15. Often, people will use one word (e.g., "affect") when they should use another (e.g., "effect"). If you consult our "Problem Pairs" table (Table 6.3), you will be less likely to make that kind of mistake. Be especially careful not to use "since" when you mean "because" or "while" when you mean "although."
16. All paragraphs should have topic sentences.
17. Obey conventional rules of writing. For example, do not use contractions; do not split infinitives; do not start sentences with the coordinating conjunctions "and," "but," "so," or "or"; and do not end sentences with prepositions.
18. Try to use the active voice.
19. Try to use parallel structure.
20. Eliminate unnecessary words.

CHAPTER

7

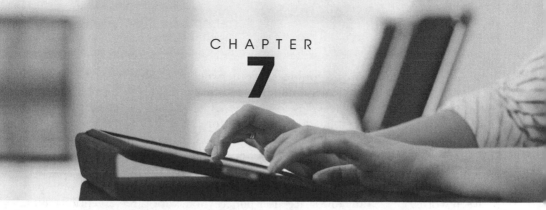

Preparing the Final Draft

7.1 Presentation: Appearance Matters

Even professors who do not specifically award points for how well papers conform to APA format tend to give higher grades to papers that adhere to it than to papers that do not. If your paper is correctly formatted, your professor will be under the impression that it was written by someone who is conscientious and competent—and will tend to evaluate the paper's content accordingly. If, on the other hand, your paper fails to meet even basic formatting requirements, your professor will be under the impression that it was written by someone who is careless and incompetent—and will tend to evaluate the paper's content accordingly. In this chapter, we show you how to turn in a paper that will make a good first impression and how to avoid the mistakes that make some students' papers "dead on arrival."

7.1.1 Paper, Margins, Spacing, and Spaces

Paper. Some professors may require only that you turn in your paper electronically. If your professor requires you to turn in a printed paper, use letter-sized (8.5 × 11 in. [22 × 28 cm]), 20-lb, white, 100% cotton bond. At the very least, use sturdy, white, letter-sized printer paper (i.e., do not use flimsy paper, colored paper, or copier paper). Print on only one side of each sheet.

Margins. Leave 1-in. (2.54 cm) margins at the top, left, and right. Leave at least a 1-in. (2.54 cm) margin at the bottom.

Spacing between lines. Double-space between each line of text. The only place you can leave more than a double-spaced line is on the title page—and you can only do that in two places: (a) to put the title well below the running head and (b) to put the centered heading "Author Note" well below the centered line containing your school's name. The only place you can single space is in a table—and then only in places in your table where single-spacing looks better than double-spacing.

Spaces between words and punctuation. Within each line, leave only one space between words. Leave only one space after punctuation, with three exceptions. First, do not leave any spaces after either hyphens or dashes. Second, do not leave any spaces after periods that are part of an abbreviation ("e.g.," "n.d.," "p.m."). Third, if possible, add an extra space after the period at the end of each sentence so that sentences are separated two spaces.[1]

7.1.2 Word Processor Settings: Making Your Word Processor Help You

By default, your word processor will tend to put the right number of spaces—one—between words and after most punctuation. However, if you are like us, you may accidentally add unnecessary spaces. To find those extra spaces, use your word processor's grammar checker.[2]

To have your word-processing software do even more of the formatting work for you, go to its "Format" menu and make the following selections:

- Under the "Font" submenu, select 12-point Times New Roman.
- Under the "Paragraph" submenu, click on the "Indents and Spacing tab," then select double-spacing.
- Under the "Paragraph" submenu, click on the "Lines and Page breaks" tab, then select the "Don't hyphenate" box.

Next, go to the "Tools" menu, then to its "Autocorrect options" submenu, and, when you get to the "Autoformat as you type" tab,[3] choose the following options:

- Under "Replace as you type," select the "Straight quotes with smart quotes" option so that your quotation marks and apostrophes look typeset rather than typewritten ("Jolley's examples" instead of "Jolley's examples").

---

[1]Your professor may not care about this aspect of APA style. If you want to see how your computer can help you have two spaces between sentences, see the Chapter 7 section of www.writingforpsychology.com.

[2]In MS Word, you can access the grammar checker by pressing the "F7" key. Another way to find and remove unnecessary spaces is to use the "find and replace" command: Put two spaces in the "find" box and one space in the "replace" box.

[3]If you do not find the "Autoformat as you type" tab, see our website.

- Select the "hyphens (-) with dash (–)" box.
- Deselect the "Internet and network paths with hyperlinks" links box so that URLs are not underlined.

7.1.3 Fonts

If you use the word-processor settings described previously, your text will be in "regular" (plain—not italicized, not boldfaced, not underlined), black, 12-point font. The only time to override these settings is when you need to italicize some text (to know when you need to italicize, see 7.2.4) or to set some headings in boldface. Never print in a color other than black, never use a font other than 12-point, never underline, and never use capital letters to emphasize words (e.g., do not write, "THIS IS IMPORTANT").

7.2 APA Format

Your psychology professor will probably require you to format your paper using APA copy style.[4] This is the format emphasized in the *Publication Manual* and used by authors who are submitting their work for publication. Thus, you will prepare your paper the same way an author would submit a manuscript to a journal.

7.2.1 Page Headers and the Title Page

Page headers, page numbers, and copy style. In papers submitted for publication, the page header for the title page consists of two parts. The left side consists of "Running head:" followed by, in all capital letters, the RUNNING HEAD—a two- to six-word phrase that includes your paper's topic or key variables. The running head has a 50-character limit—and both spaces and punctuation count against that limit. The right side consists of the page number. The title page is always page 1. So, if your running head was "DESCRIPTOR ORDER ON LIKING," the top of your title page would look like this:

Running head: DESCRIPTOR ORDER ON LIKING 1

The header will be the same for all other pages except that the header on other pages will omit the phrase "Running head:" (e.g., it might start "DESCRIPTOR ORDER ON LIKING") and will have different page numbers.

We suggest you format your headers by going to page 2 of your document and then putting the running head and the page number in the word processor's "header" area. (To put text in the header area, choose "View header and footer" from the "View" menu, then type your text into the "header" box.) Then, click on the "page

[4] If your professor wants you to write your paper in the APA final-form style, visit our website for instructions on how to format your paper in that style.

set up" button, click on the layout tab, select the "different first page" box, scroll to the header box for the first page, and type "Running head:" followed by your running head. Then, type "1" in the right corner. That way, your word processor will automatically put the header and the correct page number on all your pages. (If you need help getting your word processor to put the running head and page number into the header area or getting your word processor to put a different header on the title page, see the instructions on our website.)

7.2.2 Paragraphs

The first line of most paragraphs should be indented five characters. To accomplish this, press the tab key once. However, there are three exceptions to this indentation rule. Specifically, do not indent the first line of (a) the Abstract, (b) the figure captions, and (c) the table notes.

7.2.3 Headings

The *Publication Manual* provides five levels of headings. You, however, will probably not use more than three levels. The following examples illustrate the three levels of headings that you are most likely to use.[5]

To announce a major section of your paper (e.g., "Method"), your heading should be

A Centered, Capitalized (and Usually Boldfaced) First-Level Heading

Do not boldface the heading for "Author Note," Abstract," "References," or the title of your paper. Otherwise, boldface first-level headings. For example, in a research report, boldface the "Method," "Results," and "Discussion" headings.

One double-spaced line below this heading, start your text with a new paragraph. Unless your heading is "Abstract" or "References," start that paragraph as you start almost all paragraphs—by indenting five spaces.

To signal that you split a major section into two or more subsections, make each of those subheadings

A Flush-Left, Capitalized, Boldfaced, Second-Level Heading

Start the text after a second-level heading the same way you would start the text after a first-level heading: Go down one double-spaced line below the heading, indent five spaces, and then start a new paragraph.

If you split a subsection into parts, make each of those subheadings

An indented, boldfaced, third-level paragraph heading ending with a period. Begin your text immediately after the heading, as we have done here.

---

[5]If you have conducted two or more studies and are writing up those studies in a single research report, you will need more headings than we describe here. To see how to format your headings for a multi-study paper, visit our website.

In a short term paper (fewer than 2,000 words), the first-level heading is probably the only one you need. You use it to break your paper into its major sections: title page, Abstract, main text (its heading is the term paper's title), and References. In a lab report, you use the first level to head the major sections: title page, Abstract, Introduction (its heading is not "Introduction" but rather the report's title), Method, Results, Discussion, References, and Appendixes. Note, however, that only **Method**, **Results**, and **Discussion** will be boldfaced.

For term papers and essays longer than 2,000 words, you may wish to use a first-level heading to indicate the beginning of the Conclusion, and you probably need to use second-level headings to divide the body of your argument into subsections. To see how these headings can follow from your outline, look at the sample term paper (2.10) and its outline (Box 2.1).

For research reports, you may use subheadings to subdivide the Introduction, Results, and Discussion sections. For example, in the Introduction, you might have one second-level heading to introduce relevant theory, one to introduce relevant past research, and one to introduce the purpose of your study. In the Results section, you might use one second-level heading (e.g., **Accuracy**) to introduce findings for first dependent measure and another (e.g., **Reaction Times**) to introduce findings for your second measure. You might also use second-level headings such as **Limitations** and **Implications** to subdivide your **Discussion** section.

Although you may use the second level to divide your Introduction, **Results**, or **Discussion** sections, you must use the second level to divide the **Method** section into subsections. Those subsections will almost certainly include both a **Participants** (or, if you studied individuals incapable of giving informed consent, a **Subjects**) subsection and a **Procedure** subsection, but may include additional subsections, such as a **Design** subsection, a **Materials** (or **Apparatus**) subsection, and a **Measures** subsection.

If you need to divide a second-level subsection such as **Measures**, use third-level headings. For example, if, under the **Measures** subsection of your **Method** section, you had five separate measures, you could divide your second-level **Measures** subsection into five third-level subsections so that each measure had its own heading.

7.2.4 Italics

In your papers, never underline. Use boldface only for certain headings (see 7.2.3). Other than boldfacing some headings, the only style you will use other than plain is italics—and you must use italics sparingly. Italicize only the following seven types of items:

1. Italicize book titles, journal titles, and journal volume numbers. Do not italicize article titles or journal issue numbers.
2. Italicize normal letters of the alphabet when used as an abbreviation for a statistical term (e.g., *F*, *M*, *p*, and *t*). Do not italicize Greek letters (e.g., "μ") even when used as an abbreviation for a statistical term.
3. Italicize normal words that serve as labels (labels for the end-points of a rating scale such as "*strongly agree*," labels for experimental conditions

[e.g., "*shock*" and "*no shock*" conditions], or labels for a study's task, device, or procedure).

4. Italicize words or letters that serve as examples (e.g., "Participants were shown words related to forgetting such as *Alzheimer's* and *absent-minded* for 2 seconds, and then the words were covered up with a row of *X*s.").
5. Italicize scientific names of species (e.g., *Homo sapiens*).
6. Italicize technical terms—but only the first time they are used (e.g., "These stimuli are known as *reversible figures*.").
7. Italicize foreign words that would be unfamiliar to English speakers (e.g., *estados*). Do not italicize foreign terms that English speakers commonly use or could find in an English dictionary, such as "taco," "et al.," "i.e.," "e.g.," and "a priori."

To understand how to use italics, study the examples and explanations in the following paragraph.

> The experimenter asked participants in the *hold* and *no hold* conditions [italicize your labels for the experimental conditions] to press the *yes* button [italicize your labels for devices, such as buttons] when they heard words containing the *phoneme* [italicize first use of a technical term] */a/* (such as *forgot* and *potty*) [italicize linguistic examples]. After the button press, participants rated the subjective strength of the phoneme [technical terms such as "phoneme" are italicized only the first time they are used] on a scale from *weak* (1) to *strong* (5) [italicize rating scale anchors such as "weak" and "strong"]. One participant complained that the task induced feelings of déjà vu [although "déjà vu" is a foreign phrase, it is in plain text because it is also an English phrase]. The correlation between reaction time and strength rating was $r = -.40$ [italicize *r* because it is a normal letter of the alphabet being used as an abbreviation for a statistical term].

7.2.5 Abbreviations

As a general rule, do not use abbreviations in the main text of your paper. As Roediger (2007) commands, "Write in words, not in code" (p. 20). However, this general rule has four exceptions.

First, you can use well-accepted abbreviations such as IQ and ESP. Such abbreviations are so common that they are more like words than like code.

Second, you should abbreviate units of measurement, such as minutes, meters, and milligrams. Thus, you should write "min" instead of "minute" and "m" instead of "meter" (see 3.6.8). Note that, unlike most abbreviations, you do not add "s" to make abbreviations for units of measurement plural. Thus, you would write "5 min"–not "5 mins."

Third, within parentheses, you must abbreviate certain words and terms. For example, within parentheses, you must use "e.g.," instead of "for example," "i.e.," instead of "that is," "cf." instead of "compare," and "et al." instead of "and others." Furthermore, within parentheses, to separate two authors' names, you must use an ampersand ("&") instead of the word "and." (For a complete list of the terms you must abbreviate when they are within parentheses, see Table 7.1.)

Table 7.1
Abbreviations Used in Parentheses

Abbreviation	Literally	Translation	Usage
&	and per se and	and	Before the last author's name
c.	circa	about	Before a citation date if the date is uncertain
cf.	confere	compare	Before a source that provides a counter-example; often used as the opposite of "e.g."
e.g.	exempli gratia	for example	Before an incomplete list of examples that support a point; do not confuse with "i.e."
et al.	et alii	and others	For secondary authors' names after first complete citation (see 4.5.3)
etc.	et cetera	and so forth	Rare in scientific writing; avoid
i.e.	id est	that is	Before a complete list or synonymous phrase; use instead of "in other words"
ibid.	ibidem	in the same	Rare in APA style; avoid by repeating the citation reference
n.b.	nota bene	note well (take careful note)	Rare in APA style
op. cit.	opere citato	in the reference	Rare in APA style; avoid by repeating the citation already quoted
p.	page	page	In a citation, to note the page from which a quotation was taken; in a reference, to note the page of a newspaper article
pp.	pages	pages	In a reference, to note the pages in a book where a chapter begins and ends (e.g., "pp. 70–103")
viz.	videlicet	namely	Rare in APA style
vs.	versus	against	To compare different conditions or explanations
–	to	to	As in "pp. 22–33"

Fourth, you can use an abbreviation for a term after you have properly introduced that abbreviation. To introduce an abbreviation, first write the unabbreviated term, then—in parentheses and in all capital letters—write its abbreviation. For example, you might write, "Many psychologists belong to the American Psychological Association (APA)." After that introduction, you would write "APA" instead of "American Psychological Association."

Note that, like all other abbreviations consisting of all capital letters, the abbreviations you introduce should be free of periods. Thus, abbreviate "American Psychological Association" as "APA"—not as "A.P.A." Similarly, abbreviate "reaction time" as "RT"—not as "R.T."

If the abbreviation you introduce is singular, but you want to make it plural, simply add "s" (e.g., "RTs"). Just as adding "s" will give you the plural form of most abbreviations, adding apostrophe "s" ('s) will usually give you the possessive form of the abbreviation (e.g., "APA's membership figures").

If you want to avoid making some common abbreviation errors, say the spelled-out version as you write the abbreviation. For example, you will say "a reaction time" and know to write "a RT" rather than "an RT" because you would never say "an reaction time." Similarly, you will say "revolutions per minute" and know to write RPM rather than RPMs because you would not say "revolutions per minutes."

Saying the spelled-out version also helps you punctuate standard abbreviations. For instance, if you say, "compare" as you write "cf." and "for example," as you write "e.g.," you will put a comma after "e.g." but not after "cf." To review the rules for using, punctuating, and pluralizing abbreviations, study the following paragraph.

> To test the hypothesis that reaction time (RT) **[introduce a lesser known abbreviation by preceding it with the unabbreviated term]** is related to IQ **[well-known abbreviation for "intelligence quotient"]**, Garcia (2000) administered the WAIS **[well-known abbreviation]** to 200 students and measured their RTs **[add "s" just as you would to pluralize a regular word]** to light onset. Mean RT was 205 ms **[abbreviate standard units; see 3.6.8]** (cf. **[well-known abbreviation, commonly used within parentheses]** Woodworth & **[within parentheses, use "&" instead of "and"]** Schlosberg, 1954), and the correlation with IQ was .40. The correlation between RT and IQ may be due to a third variable. For example, **[abbreviate "for example" as "e.g." only within parentheses]** those with high motivation could have tried hard on both the IQ test and on the RT task.

7.2.6 Numbers

When should you spell out a number ("nine"), and when should you express it in digits ("9")? If the number is bigger than nine, you should almost always use digits—unless the number begins a sentence (e.g., although you would write "Participants were 10 . . . ," you would write, "Ten participants were . . .").

If, on the other hand, the number is a whole number between zero and nine, you should—as a general rule—spell out the number. Unfortunately, however, there are many exceptions to this general rule.[6] For example, the following whole numbers between zero and nine must be expressed in digits:

---

[6]Therefore, if you want to ensure that you have not written out a number below 10 that you should have expressed in digits, you need to study pages 111–113 of the *Publication Manual.*

- Numbers in the manuscript's Abstract. Thus, in your Abstract, you would have to write "3 observers" rather than "three observers."
- Numbers that relate to the number of participants, to amounts of money, or to time. Thus, in your Method section, you might write, "Participants were 6 women," "Participants were paid $6," and "Participants were retested 6 weeks later."
- Numbers that immediately precede another spelled-out number. Thus, in the Results section, you should write "3 two-way interactions" rather than "three two-way interactions."
- Numbers that relate to measurements (e.g., "5 cm"), scores, or statistics. Thus, almost all the numbers in your Results section will be expressed in digits.

If, instead of dealing with whole numbers, you are dealing with numbers between zero and one, you will use digits to express those numbers. The specific way you express those numbers, however, depends on whether you are dealing with percentages or decimals.

Percentages. With percentages, follow the digit with a percent sign (e.g., "3%").

Decimals.

- Usually, do not use more than two decimal places. However, if you have a probability value and you believe it is important to use three decimal places, you may (e.g., you can report that $p = .036$ and that $p < .001$).
- If the decimal refers to a probability value, a correlation coefficient, or any other index in which scores cannot be greater than 1.0, do not put a zero in front of the decimal point (e.g., write "$p = .04$," not "$p = 0.04$"; write "$r = .10$," not "$r = 0.10$"). If the decimal refers to a score or a measure in which scores can be greater than 1.0, put a zero in front of the decimal point (e.g., write "0.5 cm," not ".5 cm").

The examples and explanations in the next paragraph will help you understand the rules about how to express numbers.

> Twenty [never use digits at the beginning of a sentence] participants completed three [number less than 10 and not a measurement] tests consisting of 15 [number greater than nine] subscales each. The mean score on the first test was 3.45 [two decimal places for a fraction], $SD = 0.45$ [zero in front of the decimal point for a fraction], but the mode was 5 [use numeral because it is based on measurements; do not use decimal point because the mode could only be a whole number] items correct. The correlation between test A and B was $r(19) = .47, p < .001$ [correlation coefficients and probability values never have zeroes before the decimal point].

7.2.7 Tables and Figures

In term papers, avoid using tables and figures. You should be able to communicate the important points of experiments and theories without resorting to figures or tables. In reports, you may use tables or figures (to see how to use tables, see 3.6.5; to see how to use figures, see 3.6.7).

7.3 Conclusions

If you have followed the instructions in this chapter, your paper should look professional. To make sure that you have not overlooked any important formatting details, use the following checklists.

7.4 Format Checklists

7.4.1 General Appearance Checklist

- ☐ I followed any specific requirements that my professor imposed. For example, if my professor said that unstapled papers would not be accepted, I stapled my paper. Similarly, if my professor required a cover page, I had one.
- ☐ If my professor required a printed copy of my paper, I printed my paper on one side of sturdy, white, 8.5 × 11 in. (22 × 28 cm) printer paper using a printer that produced clear, dark, black print.
- ☐ I set my word processor to the following options: 12-point type, Times New Roman font, and 1-in. (2.54-cm) margins.
- ☐ I double-spaced everything.
- ☐ I started every paragraph by indenting five spaces with only two exceptions: I did not indent the Abstract, and I did not indent notes at the bottom of tables.
- ☐ I did not hyphenate words at the end of a line.
- ☐ I did not use underlining or any other typographical tricks.
- ☐ I italicized letters that served as abbreviations for statistical terms (e.g., "*p*" as the abbreviation for probability value).

7.4.2 Headings and Headers Checklist

- ☐ I used all capital letters to write the running head on the top left corner of each page. In addition, I put the page number on the top right corner. For the title page header, I introduced the running head with the phrase "Running head:."
- ☐ I centered all my first-level headings (e.g., Abstract, Conclusion, References). I capitalized only the first letters of words of those headings.
- ☐ I boldfaced and centered the headings **Method, Results**, and **Discussion**.

- ☐ I boldfaced all my second-level headings (major subheadings, e.g., **Participants**, **Procedure**, **Overview of Study Design**) and put them flush against the left margin (I did not indent them). I capitalized only the first letters of important words of those subheadings.

7.4.3 Numbers Checklist

- ☐ I tried not to start a sentence with a number. If I started a sentence with a number, I spelled out that number.
- ☐ When I wrote a number in my Abstract, I never started a sentence with it, and I always expressed it in digits.
- ☐ When I wrote a number greater than nine, I expressed it in digits (unless I started a sentence with it).
- ☐ When I wrote a number less than 10, I spelled it out unless it was being compared to a number greater than 10 or it represented a unit of measurement (e.g., "3 cm"), a fraction (e.g., "3/4"), a percentage (e.g., "6%"), a score (e.g., "the mean was 4"), a point on a scale (e.g., "a 7-point scale"), the number of participants (e.g., "3 participants"), or a statistical result (e.g., "all *F*s <1").
- ☐ I did not put a zero before the decimal point for any correlation coefficients or probability values.
- ☐ I put a zero before the decimal point for fractions (e.g., "0.1 cm").
- ☐ I rounded numbers to two (or fewer) decimal places unless going to three decimal places would help the reader.

7.4.4 Citations and References Checklist

- ☐ I used the citation checklist (4.11.2).
- ☐ I used the reference list checklist (4.11.4).

7.4.5 Abbreviations Checklist

- ☐ Within parentheses, I used abbreviations such as "&" and "e.g."
- ☐ When I used units of measurement, I abbreviated those units, did not use a period in those abbreviations (except that I abbreviated "inches" as "in."), and did not add "s" to express their plural forms (e.g., I wrote "5 min" instead of "5 min." or "5 mins").
- ☐ When I used abbreviations (a) for terms other than units of measurement and (b) outside of parentheses, I used either common abbreviations (e.g., "IQ") or abbreviations that I had introduced earlier (see 7.2.5). I put these abbreviations in all capital letters, and I punctuated them like words (e.g., I formed the plural form by adding *s*, I formed the possessive by adding *'s*, and I did not separate the letters with periods.).

7.4.6 Title Page Checklist

- ☐ I have a separate title page.
- ☐ In the top left corner, I have "Running head:" followed by the RUNNING HEAD—a two- to six-word description of my topic.
- ☐ My running head is in all capital letters and is fewer than 51 characters (including spaces) long.
- ☐ In the top right corner, I have the page number: "1."
- ☐ My paper's title starts near the middle of the page.
- ☐ I centered the title and capitalized the first letters of each *major word* [7] in the title.
- ☐ My title is short and to the point.
- ☐ My name (if I go by my first name, I typed my first name, middle initial, and last name; if I go by my middle name, I typed my first initial, middle name, and last name) is one double-spaced line below the title, centered, and not accompanied by the word "by."
- ☐ My school's name is one double-spaced line below my name and centered.
- ☐ My Author Note starts several lines below my name with "Author Note" as its centered heading. For more on the Author Note, see 2.3.3.

7.5 Summary

1. Double-space your paper and leave 1-in. margins on all sides.
2. The running head—a two- to six-word phrase, typed in all capital letters, that summarizes the title of the article—should appear on the top left corner of each page. The page number should appear on the top right corner. On the title page the running head is introduced by the phrase: "Running head:" followed by the running head. On all other pages, the running head simply starts on the top left corner.
3. Use first-level headings to divide your paper into major sections (e.g., Abstract, References). Use second-level headings to divide major sections into subsections (e.g., to divide the **Method** section into **Participants** and **Procedure** subsections).

[7] *Major words* include all words that have more than three letters as well as all nouns, pronouns, verbs, adjectives, and adverbs. Thus, if a word has fewer than four letters and is an article (e.g., "a," "an," "the"), a preposition (e.g., "in," "on," "of"), or a conjunction (e.g., "and"), it is not a major word.

If you need to subdivide a second-level subsection, use third-level headings (to see how to format headings, refer to 7.2.3).

4. For short term papers (under eight pages), you may not need to divide the main text of your paper. Thus, you may only need three first-level headings: Abstract, the title of your paper (to announce the beginning of the main text of your paper), and References. For term papers and essays longer than eight pages, you may need to divide the main text into subsections.
5. If a number starts a sentence, spell out the number. If a number does not start a sentence and is greater than nine, use digits to express that number.
6. Follow any special instructions that your professor gives you.
7. Type your paper using dark, black, 12-point type, and Times New Roman font. Print it on one side of white printer paper.

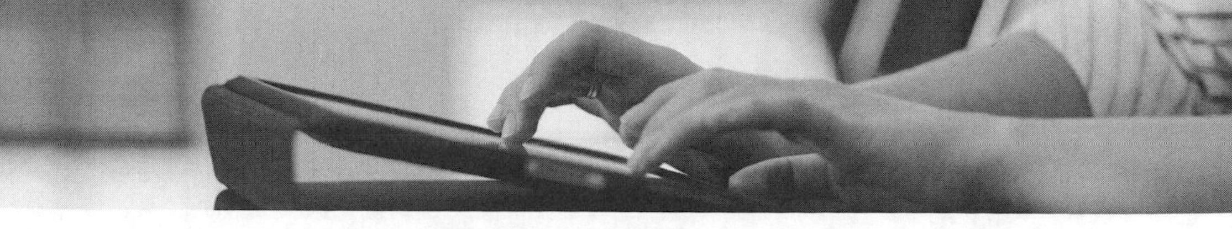

References

American Psychological Association. (1974). *Publication manual of the American Psychological Association* (2nd ed.). Washington, DC: Author.

American Psychological Association. (2002). Ethical principles of psychologists and code of conduct. *American Psychologist, 57*, 1060–1073. doi.10.1037/0003-066X.57.12.1060

American Psychological Association. (2010). *Publication manual of the American Psychological Association* (6th ed.). Washington, DC: Author.

Barkas, J. L. (1985). *How to write like a professional.* New York, NY: Arco.

Bem, D. J. (1987). Writing the empirical journal article. In M. P. Zanna & J. M. Darley (Eds.), *The compleat academic: A practical guide for the beginning social scientist* (pp. 171–201). New York, NY: Random House.

Clarion University of Pennsylvania. (n.d.). *Plagiarism* [Brochure]. Clarion, PA: Author.

Cohen, J. (1990). Things I have learned (so far). *American Psychologist, 45*, 1304–1312.

Cohen, J. (1994). The earth is round ($p < .05$). *American Psychologist, 49*, 997–1003.

Cooper, H. (2011). *Reporting research in psychology: How to meet journal article reporting standards.* Washington, DC: American Psychological Association.

Goldsberry, S. T. (2005). *The writer's book of wisdom: 101 rules for mastering your craft.* Cincinnati, OH: Writer's Digest Books.

Hahn, P. R. (2005). *The only writing book you'll ever need: A complete resource for perfecting any type of writing.* Avon, MA: Adams Media.

Hart, J. (2006). *A writer's coach: The complete guide to writing strategies that work.* New York, NY: Anchor Books.

Howard, V. A., & Barton, J. H. (1986). *Thinking on paper.* New York, NY: William Morrow.

Kahneman, D. (2011). *Thinking, fast and slow.* New York, NY: Farrar, Straus and Giroux.

Keith-Spiegel, P., Wittig, A. F., Perkins, D. V., Balogh, D. W., & Whitely, B. E., Jr. (1993). *The ethics of teaching: A casebook.* Muncie, IN: Ball State University.

King, S. (2000). *On writing: A memoir of a craft.* New York, NY: Scribner.

Kuehn, S. A. (1989). *Prospectus handbook for Comm 352.* Unpublished manuscript.

Lipson, C. (2006). *Cite right: A quick guide to citation styles.* Chicago, IL: University of Chicago Press.

McDougall, W. (1914). *An introduction to social psychology* (8th ed.). London, England: Methuen.

Meyer, H. E., & Meyer, J. M. (1993). *How to write: Communicating ideas and information* (Rev. ed.). New York, NY: Barnes & Noble Books.

O'Shea, R. P. (2002). *Writing for psychology* (4th ed.). Melbourne, Australia: Thomson.

O'Shea, R. P., Moss, S. A., & McKenzie, W. A. (2007). *Writing for psychology* (5th ed.). Melbourne, Australia: Thomson.

Roediger, H. L., III. (2007, June/July). Twelve tips for authors. *American Psychological Sciences Observer,* p. 20.

Rosenthal, R. (1966). *Experimenter effects in behavioral research.* New York, NY: Appleton-Century-Crofts.

Silvia, P. (2007). *How to write a lot.* Washington, DC: American Psychological Association.

VanderBos, G. R. (2007). *APA dictionary of psychology.* Washington, DC: American Psychological Association.

Wegner, D. M. (2007, January). *Ten (previously) unwritten rules of psychological writing.* Paper presented at the meeting of the Society for Personality and Social Psychology, Memphis, TN.

Whyte, J. (2005). *Crimes against logic.* New York, NY: McGraw-Hill.

Zechmeister, E. B., & Johnson, J. E. (1992). *Critical thinking: A functional approach.* Pacific Grove, CA: Brooks/Cole.

APPENDIX A

APA Copy Style Versus APA Final-Form Style

Some of you are reading this appendix because your teacher is requiring you to use APA final-form style instead of APA copy style. Your teacher probably has excellent reasons for requiring final-form style. The bad news is that, despite the wisdom of your teacher's decision, most descriptions of APA style focus on copy style. The good news is that, although final-form style is different from copy style, final-form style gives you more freedom than if you had been required to use copy style.

Some of you are reading this appendix even though your teacher is requiring you to use APA copy style. Your problem is that you want to use a published work as a model, but you realize that there are differences between acceptable format for published work and acceptable format for manuscript. Table A1 will help you see what you can model and what you should not. As you can see, you should not model a published article's single spacing, hyphenation at the end of lines, title page, placement of tables, and placement of figures.

Table A1
APA Copy Versus Final-Form Style

Question	Answer If Using APA Copy Style	Answer If Using APA Final-Form Style
What is on the title page? (Note that the title page is different from the cover page.[1])	The page header—the phrase "Running head:" followed by the running head (a short description of the paper's topic) and the page number ("1")—is on the top of the page. Below that are the title, the author's name, the author's affiliation, and the Author Note (for more information, see 3.2).	The page header—the title—is at the top of the page. Below that are the author's name, author's affiliation, Abstract, and the start of the Introduction. The Author Note may also appear on the page as an unnumbered footnote. Centered, at the bottom of the page (the page footer), is the page number ("1").

(continued)

[1]Although neither APA style requires a cover page, some professors may. Often, the cover page includes information that would not be on the title page, such as student identification number, course number, section number, date, and word count.

Table A1
APA Copy Versus Final-Form Style—continued

Question	Answer If Using APA Copy Style	Answer If Using APA Final-Form Style
What is on the title page in this format that is never on the title page in the other format?	"Running head:" followed by the running head	Abstract
What is on the top and bottom of each page? (Where do you put page numbers and headers?)	Near the top, left corner of each page, put the running head; near the top, right corner, put the page number.	Put a centered header on the top of every page. For the title page, the header will be your title; for all the even-numbered pages, the header will be your last name; for all the other pages, the header will be the running head. The running head is a short description of your paper's topic (to learn about the running head, see 3.2.1). Center the page number on the bottom of the title page; place it on the top left corner of each even-numbered page; and, for all other pages, place it on the top, right corner.
Must I always double space between lines?	Yes—except that you can quadruple space between sections on the title page, and you can single space in tables.	No—in fact, most of the paper will be single spaced.
Can you use hyphens and your computer's "justify right margin" feature to keep your right margin even?	No, the right margin is ragged (uneven), and you cannot use hyphens at the end of lines.	Yes, you can have a justified right margin, and you can use hyphens to keep the right margin even.
What sections begin on a new page?	Abstract, Introduction, References, the Appendix, each table, and each figure.	None.
Can I place a table on the same page that I refer to it?	No, you must place tables near or at the end of your paper (after the References and Appendix, but before the Figures).	Yes, you can put the table on the same page as the corresponding text. If it will not fit there, you can put it on the next page.
Can I place a figure on the same page that I refer to it?	No, you must place figures at the very end of your paper.	Yes, you can put the figure on the same page as the corresponding text. If it will not fit there, you can put it on the next page.

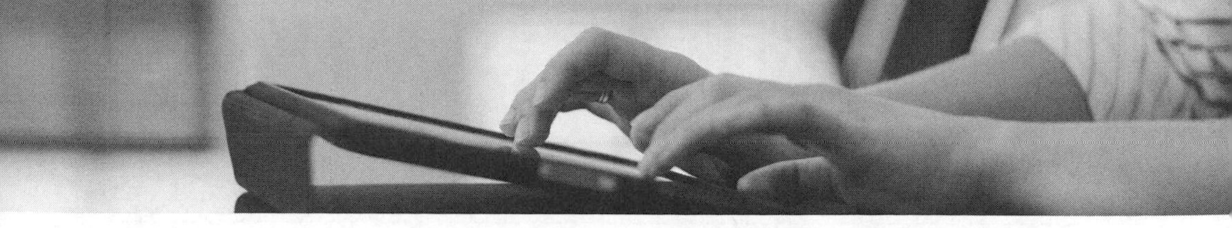

APPENDIX B

Problem Plurals

Singular	Preferred Plural	One Brief Definition
alumna	alumnae	female graduate
alumnus	alumni	graduate
analysis	analyses	a study of
apparatus	apparatus	equipment
appendix	appendixes	supplementary material
axis	axes	straight line
bacterium	bacteria	germ
cannula	cannulas	tube used to administer drugs and other chemicals into the body
carcinoma	carcinomas	malignant tumor
chiasm	chiasms	crossing point
continuum	continua	continuous whole
corpus	corpora	body
corpus callosum	corpora callosa	nerve fiber tract joining brain hemispheres
crisis	crises	emergency
criterion	criteria	standard
curriculum	curricula	course
curriculum vitae	curricula vitae	academic résumé
datum	data	information
degree of freedom	degrees of freedom	statistical term
die	dice	dotted cube
emphasis	emphases	importance
erratum	errata	error
focus	foci	central point
formula	formulas	equation
fovea	foveae	retinal area
ganglion	ganglia	group of nerve cells

Singular	Preferred Plural	One Brief Definition
genus	genera	group of species
hypothesis	hypotheses	conjecture
index	indexes	guide
kudos	kudos	acclaim
lacuna	lacunae	gap
locus	loci	place
manipulandum	manipulanda	stimulus object
matrix	matrices	array
medium	media	type of mass communication
millennium	millennia	1,000 years
minutia	minutiae	trivial detail
nexus	nexuses	connection, link
nucleus	nuclei	center
octopus	octopuses	eight-armed mollusk
opus	opera	work
parenthesis	parentheses	rounded bracket
phenomenon	phenomena	occurrence, fact
phylum	phyla	taxonomic division
prospectus	prospectuses	summary
quantum	quanta	indivisible amount
radius	radii	distance from center to edge
referendum	referendums	electoral question
retina	retinas	part of eye
schema	schemas	outline, model
scotoma	scotomata	hole in visual field
sequel	sequelae	bad outcome of a disease
soma	somata	body
spectrum	spectra	range
stratum	strata	layer
stimulus	stimuli	something sensed that may trigger a response
sum of squares	sums of squares	the result of calculating the difference between each score and the mean, squaring those differences, and then totaling up those squared terms

Singular	Preferred Plural	One Brief Definition
syllabus	syllabi	outline
synthesis	syntheses	combination
thalamus	thalami	brain region
thesis	theses	dissertation
vertex	vertices	point
virus	viruses	germ

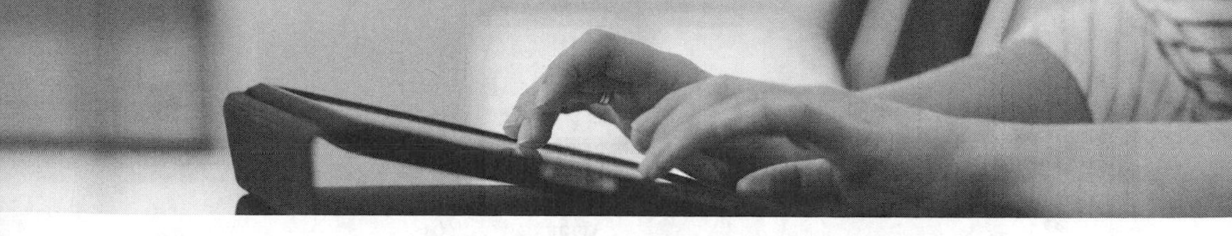

INDEX

D

E

I

J

Y

Z